Excuse Me ...
Your Rejection is
Showing

Noel and Phyl Gibson

Sovereign World

PO Box 777
Tonbridge
Kent TN11 9XT
England

ISBN 1 85240 110 9

Other available publications by Noel C. Gibson

'The Fisherman's Basket'
A text-book of evangelism both outdoors and indoors.

'Konfused'
A teenage tract published by the American Tract Company.

'20 Minutes to Decide'
An evangelistic tract.

By Noel and Phyl Gibson

'Evicting Demonic Intruders and Breaking Bondages'
A deliverance manual for adults.

'Deliver our Children from the Evil One'
A guide to deliverance and protection for children.

Typeset by CRB (Drayton) Typesetting Services, Drayton, Norwich.
Printed by Richard Clay Ltd., Bungay, Suffolk, England.

Acknowledgements

The author thanks special friends who have so generously and significantly contributed to the publication of this book. Their assistance has been most valuable.

... the manuscript review and commendation from four close professional friends
It is often said that if you want a job to be done efficiently, and quickly, ask a busy person to do it. Because the Lord brought their names to mind, their love for Jesus Christ, and their desire to see rejection sufferers set free, each one willingly gave time they could ill afford, and have given valuable advice and a generous commendation. I owe each one my very sincere thanks.

• *Jon Allan* is a Sydney medical practitioner who, with his wife Ruth (a registered nurse), served the Lord for four years as medical missionaries with the Africa Inland Mission in Uganda and Kenya. They are actively engaged in counselling, both privately, and in the Church of Christ they attend. They have three children.

• *Laurence Banks*, a graduate in theology, trained at Moore Theological College, Sydney, and was ordained in Canberra in 1966. He later served the Australian Government in management training and consultancy. He also pioneered and directed YWAM's counsellor training programmes, and community service. With his wife, Freda, Laurence is much in demand for conducting training seminars in all areas of human relationships throughout Australia and overseas.

● *Vivienne Riches* lives in Sydney with her husband Rodger, and their two children. Vivienne is a Spirit-filled psychologist who has worked for a large Government department in both assessment and counselling, and in private practice. Currently, she is a Research Fellow, Unit of Rehabilitation Studies, School of Education, Macquarie University, Sydney. Vivienne's advice has been deeply appreciated in determining the final form of the book's contents.

● *Principal Emeritus Stewart R. Dinnen MA, MBE, FRGS.* Words are inadequate containers for warmth of feeling when used to express appreciation to Stewart Dinnen for two reasons. Firstly, this is the fourth book manuscript he has cheerfully read and played a major part in editing in the past eight years, despite his schedule being always ready to burst at the seams. He has been constantly on the move, lecturing, teaching, advising, writing, and reading others' manuscripts while continuing to administer the international office of the Worldwide Evangelisation Crusade. After living in London, England for five years as General Secretary to WEC Int'l, Stewart and his wife Marie have now returned to live in Tasmania, while continuing to act as advisors to the international leaders of the mission, and maintaining a busy schedule of travelling, and Bible teaching. Marie's Bible study materials known as WORD WORLDWIDE, are used extensively in many countries.

It was Stewart Dinnen who actually put a writer's pen in the author's hand during times of teaching evangelism at 'Worldview', WEC's Australian Missionary Training College. So another book will be a fitting punishment, or reward! Having taken full theological training for the Presbyterian ministry (but declining ordination), I am sure I gave him 'theological indigestion' at times with some biblical exegesis, but he has always been gracious, and tolerant. I am more than grateful for his generous assistance in making the book concise, more readable, and biblically accurate. No one could have been more qualified academically, spiritually, or practically having been the principal of WEC's Glasgow College for 8 years, and the Tasmanian College for 18 years.

Secondly, it seemed so right to invite Stewart Dinnen to write the foreword for this final book of the trilogy on the subject of how Jesus Christ provides freedom from the oppressions of the evil one. Over the years he has spontaneously, generously, and faithfully helped me. As a friend, he has been, and is the very best. I appreciate his scintillating sense of humour, frankness, encouragement, and the generous commendation of his foreword. I honour him, and praise God for his dedication to serve the King of Kings, and his fellow servants. And so, Stewart, even if inadequately, I express my deepest gratitude to you.

... the use of the New International Version in biblical references
The author wishes to express gratitude to the New York International Bible Society, for biblical quotations from The Holy Bible, New International Version, copyright 1973, 1978, 1984, New York International Bible Society.

Dedication

With joyfulness, I dedicate this book to Phyl, my precious partner of over 45 years. She has immeasurably blessed me by her dedication, patience, and support, and by her frank but always loving evaluation of my lifestyle and writings. Above all, she has blessed me by her beautiful love, faithful intercession, and partnership as we have ministered to the needs of many precious lives.

Without rejection, she helped me overcome mine; without selfishness, she has always been an example of Christ's selflessness; and without compromise, she has always made me feel second in her life's priorities. By mutual agreement, Jesus Christ has been made Lord, and honoured as such as the first priority of our marriage and ministry.

Noel C. Gibson

Contents

Contents

Preface

The author praises God for the alleviation of much human suffering through the highly skilled services of psychologists, doctors, and social workers.

Without having any of their professional qualifications, the author has examined the causes and treatment of behavioural problems from a biblical perspective, and has experienced God's power releasing, and remaking human lives.

It has also been a privilege to have worked together with members of the three professions named, and to have seen the many-faceted wisdom of God being expressed in such cooperation.

The spiritual therapist is totally dependent on the revelation and wisdom of the divine teacher as he deals with people who have very complex symptoms of problem behaviour. Without his understanding, authority, and power, lives cannot be released from demonic spirits, healed, and revitalised to the glory of Jesus Christ.

This book has also been written from an insider's perspective. The author was controlled by rejection for very many more years than he has been free, and so the basics of the contents have been personally experienced.

Although my beloved wife Phyl has not made written contributions to this book as she did in the first two volumes of this series, because of the unity God has given us, her part in advice and review of this manuscript has been as important as ever.

Noel Gibson

Foreword

'How do you know so much about me?' This sentence immediately captured my attention when I read this book. They were the words of someone seeking help from the Gibsons. After just a few probing questions, Noel had been able to describe many of the symptoms of this person's condition, even though she had not yet mentioned them.

This is just one of the many instances that reveal the vast knowledge and understanding of rejection which the Lord has enabled the Gibsons to acquire.

In their earlier years they had an **adding** ministry in evangelism and as a result hundreds found the Saviour. But now the capacity to investigate and identify rejection and liberate individuals from its entrapment, plus the ability to train others for such work, have resulted in a **multiplying** ministry that is being felt around the nation and overseas.

There is no doubt that the analysis of rejection, the teaching on deliverance, and the graphic accounts in the case histories, together comprise a definitive treatment of this subject.

For me personally, the chapters on its root causes, outworkings, and methods of releasing rejection sufferers were a total revelation. How I wish I had had this book on my desk thirty years ago! I am sure my capacity to counsel young people preparing for missionary service would have been far more insightful and effective.

I just thank God that Noel – in spite of three major heart attacks – has been willing for the arduous task of compiling and arranging the material that has gone into this tremendously instructive manual.

My advice to the reader is: don't attempt to rush through this book. Take it in small doses! Allow the significance of each chapter to penetrate your understanding. Ponder the case histories. And take careful note of the very crucial advice about follow-up and true discipleship.

Of recent years many have been encouraged by the Gibsons' writings and seminars to move into a ministry of deliverance. Perhaps this book will be a signpost for you. Don't be afraid of such a ministry. Rely on the Holy Spirit (whose personality, authority and guidance are so beautifully described by the author) and the Lord will use you for HIS glory and the release of many rejection sufferers.

Stewart R. Dinnen
Youngtown, Tasmania
November 1990

Chapter 1

Nobody Wants to Experience Rejection, But Most of Us Have Either Had It, or Still Suffer From It

This book has been written to expose rejection as one of Satan's most insidious forms of oppression, and to offer some well-tested Biblical principles for spiritual release and wholeness.

As much as some may desire a clear definition of rejection to begin with, it is really not possible to summarise a whole book in a few sentences. In any case, how does one adequately define a deeply personal experience which may commence at any age, be due to a great variety of causes, and last so long, with vastly different results? Complex personality problems defy simple definitions.

Rejection undermines, breaks, or prevents normal and harmonious relationships between family members, marriage partners, fellow workers and social contacts. A most serious consequence is that it may keep a sinner from coming to God for salvation, or a Christian from reaching his or her full potential with God, and for him.

As we sift through Biblical evidence, and case histories, with the revelation of the Holy Spirit each reader will be able to identify past or present experiences of rejection. This will be more helpful than any technical definition. We will commence with the background stories of two adults who recently asked for spiritual help.

The little boy was born into a family where rejection was a fact of life. His father worked so hard on a farm that he was seldom seen for six months of the year. His school teachers made him feel socially inferior, and he grew up feeling worthless, and a failure. When he was eleven years old, his parents were divorced and he became a loner. From five years of age he dreamed of sexually molesting smaller children, and did so once, when he was fourteen. From his late teenage years he rode with a motor cycle gang getting involved in alcohol, drugs, violence, group sex, and some witchcraft. He became depressed, suicidal, full of fears, and wished he was dead. Then the miracle happened. He was saved, and some real changes took place. But the cause and effects of rejection remained, along with some of the lust, and the voices he heard in his mind seemed almost audible. Then a second miracle happened, but more of that later.

For the little girl, deep rejection was her constant companion. Her father was a passive man, and she was convinced he hated her. Her mother was manipulative, and neither parent spent time with her. She grew up lonely, unhappy, insecure, and convinced she was a failure. She became proud, independent, rebellious, and unforgiving, just like a number of the women in her family background. She was extremely fearful, depressed, and tried to commit suicide. (A number of her family had ended their own lives.)

As an adult she followed Indian gurus, practised yoga and meditation, together with a range of witchcraft activities. Her adult sexual life was a total disaster, leaving her feeling guilty and very much alone. Then the miracle happened and she was saved. But the matted root system of rejection remained untouched. Her intellectual faculties had been highly trained, but emotionally she was in a deplorable condition and believed she was a failure. Then the second miracle happened.

Within the last six months, Phyl and I have had the joy of seeing Jesus Christ perform the second miracle on that little boy (now in his thirties), and the little girl (now in her forties). Both of them were freed from the basic causes of their rejection and the sense of failure which had dominated their lives to that point. They are now free to live as they have always wanted to do, and to glorify Jesus Christ as well.

In one way rejection may be compared to a mosquito bite. Occasionally we see the aerial blood-tanker alight and prepare to commence drilling operations. Our reaction is usually swift, and if we happen to be fast enough only a mosquito's smudge will mark the spot. Some potential rejection-producing circumstances are like that. If recognised in time, they can be avoided. But a lot depends on the potential victim's spiritual condition and state of alertness. When Jesus Christ is Lord of an intended victim's life, victory is assured.

But there are occasions when a mosquito is almost completely loaded before the tell-tale itchiness draws the victim's attention to the winged bloodsucker's activities. What normally follows is the sound of flesh striking flesh; the remains of the mosquito and its red cargo are smeared over a whitish raised lump on the drilling site. Although the raiding party has been appropriately disposed of, the physical disturbance will be evident for some time and may need some medical attention. Similarly, once rejection has really got under a person's skin, symptoms of inner distress may appear, and continue to be evident for some time. Just as some people who are allergic to mosquito bites scratch a little too vigorously and cause the area to become inflamed or infected, so some respond to rejection. The effects last a long time.

Finally, there are those who neither see nor hear their attackers, but afterwards discover they have been 'got at'. Deprived of revenge on the culprit, all the victims can do is to try to ameliorate their inflamed spots. Similarly, some individuals do not realise that they have been hurt until some time afterwards. Because they have begun to feel bad about themselves, it takes time to pin down the source of rejection. But unlike the mosquito bites, those who suffer rejection do not know how to treat themselves, and the symptoms don't go away automatically. They may even get worse. And the 'rejection mosquito' lives on to strike again.

Probably every reader has had one or more of these rejection experiences, and has either refused to accept them or dealt with them on the spot. Some may have become victims without realising what was happening. Regrettably most people fall into the last grouping. Let us examine this more carefully.

Category 1. Stop rejection before it stops you

How many times have you heard a person reply to the question 'How are you?' with these words, 'Not so bad under the circumstances'. The obvious answer is, 'What is a Christian doing living

under the circumstances?' The born again, Spirit-controlled believer has all he or she needs to maintain a victorious attitude all the time. It was God, not Moses who really led his people out of Egypt into their pre-selected land through one victory after another. When the Israelites looked at what faced them, they were defeated every time. When they trusted God they were always delivered.

Regrettably, many believers who claim to be Spirit-filled turn to their pastor, counsellor, family members or friends for counsel and solace when facing problems, rather than seeking guidance from the Comforter himself (John 14:16, 17). If we claim to be Spirit-filled, then we should show it in daily living (Galatians 5:16). We should be led by the Spirit (Galatians 5:18), display the character of the Spirit (Galatians 5:22, 23), and keep in step with our divine guide (Galatians 5:25).

For much of my Christian life, and even as the servant of the Lord, I presumed I was Spirit-filled because I had passed through the approved experiential 'turnstile'. But my reactions to people and situations were often self-defensive, even authority-orientated, and the fruit of the Spirit was undersized and scarce. It was not until I allowed Jesus to be Lord of my whole life that I was able to recognise rejection and deal with it as a none-too-subtle attack of the enemy.

Category 2. Counteract the effects of rejection on the spot

Everyone knows the cliché 'It takes two to tango.' As soon as we realise that a person or a circumstance is working against us, we should terminate the infective process. This may have commenced with what someone said, a hurtful attitude, devious or direct attempts to manipulate, some offensive act, or even an outburst of our own feelings of failure or defeat. As soon as the alarm bells sound, the fuse should be pulled so that damage is controlled.

It is important that the 'rejection tango' be terminated immediately, rather than just smiling blandly and pretending that all is well while the inner hurt increases. To turn one's back and silently walk away from the person or situation does not mean that an otherwise good relationship will be broken, or a marriage wrecked. Fear of the other person's reaction is not nearly as important as swatting that 'mosquito', thus preventing further damage. It may take courage and determination to do this, but the Holy Spirit will help. (I know, from personal experience.)

Category 3. I really do feel rejected, but I can't remember when it started

We have probably all enjoyed an outdoor barbeque, then suffered for hours afterwards from the stinging lumps which have appeared on our arms and legs. We know where we were bitten, but not when.

Quite often I am asked, 'Can you tell me what is wrong with me?' After asking a few probing questions, it soon becomes obvious that the basic problem is rejection. When a number of well-known symptoms are named, the eyes usually light up, and we are asked, 'How do you know so much about me?' Believe me there is nothing extraordinary about that. Phyl and I have prayed for countless thousands of rejection sufferers, and the symptoms (to be listed in the next chapter) should be obvious to any discerning person.

Unlike mosquito bites, rejection may lie dormant for years, and not emerge as a problem until further rejection causes a sudden outbreak of symptoms. Illustrations:

- A woman in her mid-thirties whom we shall call 'Ann' told us that her father died when she was 6 years old. Her mother used to rubbish her father in front of her, accusing him of being a gambler and a womaniser. She said her mother 'spoiled her rotten', and she grew up demanding her own way, manipulating others to get it. At 13, 'Ann' became sexually active, although the act repulsed her. When she reached 18, she commenced drinking. After the first time she was intoxicated, she woke up in bed, remembering nothing. Later she had an abortion. She then became sexually puritanical, but couldn't resist drugs and occultism. It was not until she was married that her rejection and associated problems surfaced and crippled her ability to cope with life. 'My personality stinks' she told me.

  I wish every reader could see the radiant wife and mother that 'Ann' has now become, and could enjoy the harmony of her family home. No one would ever again doubt that Jesus Christ

19

does deliver sufferers from the root causes of their rejection and associated problems, and gives inner healing and wholeness.

- 'Harley' came for deliverance while in his mid-forties. As a child he was a PK (Preacher's Kid). His father did not receive a salary from the church he pastored, but survived on gifts of food from parishioners. 'Harley' wore second-hand patched clothes much to his embarrassment, particularly when the school kids recognised their own cast-offs, and joked about them. 'Harley's' childhood poverty caused him a lot of shame, and through constantly feeling threatened by his peers, was very insecure.

  Marriage did nothing but increase his problem. To build up his business, 'Harley' spent more and more time away from home; meanwhile, unknown to him, his wife spent more and more time with a male neighbour whom she eventually married after divorcing 'Harley'. But apparently that did not extinguish the fire of his love for his ex-wife, because he married and divorced her three times. Finally, she entered a mental hospital and left 'Harley' alone with his rejection. He wondered whether he could ever trust a woman again. But Cupid did reload his bow, and another prospective partner came on the scene. After many long counselling sessions, 'Harley' finally remarried.

  Things went well for seven years until he discovered that his new wife was addicted to prescription drugs which she was obtaining by devious means. He felt deceived and rejected all over again.

  By the time 'Harley' came to see Phyl and me, he was overloaded with rejection symptoms which extended from his marriages and childhood. And just like 'Ann', the Lord set 'Harley' free, and re-established him, restored his self image, and renewed his zeal in living the Christian life.

- 'Christine's' rejection began as a child, and at 19 years of age she rushed headlong into marriage, looking for security. Her mother's marriage had been resented by her grandparents, and mutual resentment had become so strong between her parents, that Christine's mother often publicly humiliated her father, threatening to leave him and take 'Christine' with her. Here is her story.

'My mother brought us up to fear men, in order to protect us from sin; the major sin in her mind was to have sex. My mother wasn't a Christian, and constantly threatened to take us to an institution for bad kids when we misbehaved. At times her anger was uncontrollable. Once, she hit me across the face with a dog-chain for no apparent reason.

'My sister never wanted me. From early childhood until I was 16, she constantly hurt me physically when my parents were not looking. Because I wanted her love, I never told them.

'When I was 16 I fell in love, but because of my parent's opposition, I had to lie and cheat to be able to see my man for the next few years until I married him. My husband dominated my thinking and behaviour. I was forced to submit to sexually depraving acts which, he said, were "expressions of love".

'I longed to know God's love, but only felt rejected, worthless, and suicidal after seven and a half years of this treatment. Then I met a married man who was nice to me. We had sex together, and I divorced my husband. I had tremendous guilt over my adultery, but I was so hungry for love I couldn't let go. I didn't want him to leave his family, and he promised he wouldn't. So to get love and attention, I slept around.'

'Christine' had only been a Christian for eight months when she came for counselling, at 30 years of age. Burdened by accumulated rejection, self-hatred, insecurity, guilt, and convinced she was a permanent failure, she was full of fears, and bound by self-condemnation. She was also a worrier, full of unbelief, and blamed God for all the misery of the past. But Jesus Christ delivered her from the causes and effects of her rejection, and established her in the pathway of discipleship.

Before we leave the 'mosquito-rejection' analogy, it needs to be remembered that the female of the anopheles variety is also capable of depositing a malaria parasite in its victim's bloodstream. Its new host or hostess may be unaware of its presence for quite some time until some physical trauma causes fever and other symptoms to develop. The parasite is most difficult to destroy, and malarial symptoms may periodically re-appear during the lifetime of the sufferer.

Rejection follows a similar pattern. It may be unrecognised when received, and its symptoms may not develop until some emotional trauma triggers it. Rejection is also most difficult to eradicate, and may continue to manifest itself throughout a lifetime. A friend in the medical profession recently told me that a 78 year old woman had sought counselling because of rejection and guilt she had carried for sixty years because of sexual experiences as a teenager. She had not had the courage to tell anyone because she feared the disclosure would cause further rejection. Finally, the emotional pressure became so intolerable that she forced herself to ask for help.

Chapter 2

A Review of Some of the Root Causes of Rejection

Some basic factors in rejection suffered by children, teenagers, and adults have been covered in the two previous books in this series, *Evicting Demonic Intruders and Breaking Bondages* and *Deliver Our Children From The Evil One*.

So that we may understand this subject more fully, the important features of rejection previously outlined need to be re-emphasised. Some will also be expanded in later chapters.

1. Rejection is the masterpiece of Satanic oppression

When Satan caused Adam and Eve to sin, he presented temptation in a most attractive wrapper. He certainly made no reference to the heartache of rejection which he knew would follow the acceptance of his package deal. After all, he is the 'father' of lies and deception (John 8:44).

Rejection, whether active or passive, real or imaginary, robs Jesus Christ of his rightful position as Lord in the lives of his children, and keeps believers from experiencing the vitality and quality of life he alone gives.

2. Rejection is the greatest undiagnosed, therefore the most untreated, malady within the Body of Christ today

Almost all the people released from demonic oppression during our ministry in Australasia, Asia, Europe and Hawaii, have suffered from rejection. In the majority of cases it was the primary cause of their problems, and with the others, rejection developed as a complication from other events which will be outlined in a later chapter.

Because of the many different ways in which rejection expresses itself, some counsellors do not recognise the root-cause of many of their counsellee's problems. This means that their advice is usually insufficient to bring total release to the rejection sufferer.

3. Rejection may commence at any time between the womb and the tomb

(a) Pre-natal rejection

● Babies can suffer rejection while still in the womb. Perhaps the parents did not want a family, or already had a large family. Maybe they feared the arrival of the little one would overtax accommodation or financial resources. Babies born to single women, who have become pregnant through adultery, incest, rape, or whose mothers were alcoholic or drug dependent, will also show rejection symptoms from birth onwards.

● When prospective parents have bad relationships, or experience a traumatic event during pregnancy such as an accident, or the death of a family member or a close friend, rejection usually begins in the unborn child. When no other physical problem is diagnosed, babies who cry continuously, have paddy tantrums, refuse the breast, or a mother's comfort, are usually expressing their rejection feelings.

(b) Rejection caused by the manner of birth

Rejection can come from protracted labour, a prolonged pregnancy, the shock of fast delivery, and by caesarian or instrumental births. Babies born to women who were unaware of their pregnancy until the time of delivery, or whose health has deteriorated during pregnancy will also show rejection symptoms.

(c) Some causes of rejection in early babyhood

One of the earliest post-delivery causes may be the lack of emotional bonding between baby and mother, particularly when illness prevents them from being together. Children who are placed in a humidicrib or are hospitalised because of sickness will suffer rejection despite expert medical attention. Other causes include a

24

mother's insecurity in coping with motherhood, inadequate care and attention, or physical abuse. Other factors are:

- Parental disappointment in a baby's sex.
- Adoption.
- Medical disorders causing feeding problems.
- Hereditary rejection in parents will automatically show up in a baby. The baby's mother and father often compound the situation because of their insecurity and inability to express love.

(d) Some causes of rejection from early childhood onwards

- Physical disabilities which limit children's learning ability, or prevent them from being active in sports. They feel inferior to others, and reject themselves.
- A spoilt or pampered child (often an only child) will very often show symptoms of rejection.
- A child who is criticised, over disciplined, victimised, ignored, or is treated as a favourite, will also experience rejection.
- When parents persistently confront one another in front of their children, they create a feeling of rejection and insecurity. Even talk of separation or divorce can have a devastating effect on children. It often leads to them blaming themselves for having caused their parents' problems.
- When children of one ethnic background are brought up in an entirely different culture, rejection can occur.
- Children who suffer from speech impediments caused by birth defects, or who even lisp badly will feel rejected if they are mimicked, or scorned.
- Parents who only speak to one another through the children will make them feel rejected.
- Being sent to a boarding school will cause deep rejection in a child who is insecure, over sensitive, or who is forced to attend against his or her will. Being bullied, unfairly treated, or sexually harassed at boarding school will also cause rejection.
- A stern, legalistic, or over disciplinary father will make his children feel rejected.

- Fathers who are weak-willed, apathetic, or dominated by their wives will cause rejection.

- Parents who have to give more care and attention to one child because of sickness or injury may inadvertently cause other family members to feel rejected if they do not accept the reason for the special care. Even imagined favouritism can commence the rejection process.

- Sometimes a parent will say something derogatory to a child in the heat of the moment, and afterwards regret it, and say so. But the damage has been done. Some of the worst are: 'I hate you'; 'I never wanted you in the first place'; 'You're nothing but a bird-brain'; 'I would gladly give you away but no one would have you'; etc. Lifetime resentments sometimes commence through remarks such as these. Fortunately the rejection process can be halted by the offending parent sincerely apologising to the child, explaining the frustrations which caused the remarks, and asking for forgiveness.

- The 'middle-child syndrome' frequently causes rejection. Sometimes a child born into a family will ask his or her parents if he or she has been adopted. Many adults have been released from this form of rejection.

- Physical, mental, verbal or sexual abuse by parents, friends, teachers, or other school students.

- Alcoholism in one or both parents.

- Failure to be trusted, or forgiven for wrongdoings.

- Pressure or bribes to make a child lift his or her academic level.

- School expulsion, or being 'sent to Coventry' by a child's peer group.

- Embarrassment caused by parent's religious beliefs, or odd behaviour.

- A father showing more attention to, or favouring a child's friend more than his own children.

- A fire or earthquake which damages or destroys a family home.

- The conviction or jailing of a close family member.

- A sudden fall in family living standards caused by the unemployment, redundancy, or bankruptcy of the family bread-winner.

- Financial meanness without just cause. (Children can resort to lying or stealing as a rejection cover-up with their peers.)
- Long periods of loneliness because of their parents' disinterest, social activities, or protracted hours of work.
- Absence of the parents from their children's extra curricular or school activities, particularly sports or social events.

Causes not listed in previous publications:

- Poverty in the family home.
  One adult being counselled by us had been one of seven children, all sharing one towel with their parents. During winter, they all had to put hessian sacks on their beds for extra warmth. The children grew up feeling 'second class'.
- Immigration language difficulties.
  When families of non-English speaking people migrate to English-speaking countries, the children absorb the shock waves of cultural adjustment much more quickly than the adults. They master the language much more quickly, and often have to interpret for their parents. Consequently, they sometimes have to make family decisions which are traditionally made only by parents. This sometimes unsettles the family, causing both parents and children to feel rejected.
- Sickness.
  Children who are constantly sick usually drop below their class achievement level because they cannot attend school. They will soon feel inferior, reject themselves, and fear being rejected by others.
- An overload of home responsibilities.
  When a mother becomes constantly sick, bedridden, suffers from mental illness, works full time, or is just lazy, the eldest child often becomes so overloaded with household duties that there is little or no time left for relaxation or play. Children usually cope physically but can suffer rejection and age emotionally.
- Dominant parents cause rejection.
  Children who are never allowed to express an opinion without interruption, or are constantly put down, corrected, or lectured, will quickly experience rejection and feel insecure and worthless.

- Problems caused by child-minders.
  Some adult counsellees have confessed to bizarre treatment of children in their care. One person physically hurt children in order to make them cry so that they would be able to comfort them. Others have confessed to sexual interference with their charges, or have forced children to do indecent acts.

- The probems of intellectualism.
  Some highly intellectual or academic parents find it almost impossible to communicate effectively, or show practical love. So their children feel starved of affection, and rejected.

- Other communication problems.
  There are people who just cannot communicate. Marriages break up because of it, and children are made to feel of no value. This is very often hereditary, and children who grow up in this atmosphere and who later become parents themselves, will treat their own children in the same way, thinking it quite normal.

- Severe or cruel punishment.
  When the method, severity, or duration of any punishment far exceeds what a child considers to be fair. Rejection will result. Examples include severe whipping, being tied to a bed or chair to be beaten, or being locked in a cupboard. The latter punishment will always cause a child to become fearful, especially of confined spaces.

(e) School life may be a rejection 'breeding ground'

- Life-lasting rejection may commence if a child is called by a deprecating nickname because of some obvious physical defect or personal mannerism. Examples include 'hoppy', 'four eyes', 'buck teeth', or 'lithspy'. Some nicknames stick for life and have to be tolerated, but are deeply resented.

- Rejection can follow the injustice of not being believed when telling the truth. Teachers sometimes hand out punishments based on uninformed judgements, with the innocent often suffering for the guilty. Injustice always causes rejection and resentment, and often lasts into adulthood.

- Teachers are of course no different from ourselves. We all have personality likes and dislikes. But when a teacher continually picks on one child without reasonable cause, makes him or her the subject of ridicule, sarcasm, or prescribes menial duties, the teacher (sometimes supported by the rest of the class), may do some point scoring, but the child usually withdraws hurt, and feels rejected.

- When the academic record of a child's older brother or sister is used against a younger less-gifted family member, the child will feel inferior, lose confidence, and be convinced that he or she is a failure. Then rejection takes over.

- Children of workaholic parents often feel neglected, therefore rejected.

- Younger children are easily hurt by fickle changes in their friends' attitudes. Words such as 'I don't want to be your friend anymore', 'I don't like you now', or even an exclusive playground huddle are as rejecting as a public announcement.

- A teacher's failure to detect a hearing or eyesight problem (sometimes not even known to parents), may cause a child to become seriously disadvantaged, and wrongly accused of inattention, or stupidity. Unless remedied, this treatment will cause rejection.

- Over-sensitive children who cannot understand the subject matter being taught, usually slip further and further behind the class average. If rejection is the original cause of the problem, it will certainly grow worse, and if not, it will be sure to develop.

- Feelings of shame or embarrassment over one's sex. Parents who openly speak of the boy or girl they had hoped for, but did not get, will cause deep rejection to the child they did receive. Some parents will even dress a child as if he or she were the opposite sex, just to satisfy their fantasy.

(f) Further factors causing rejection from teenage years, through to adulthood

- Guilt over an unwanted pregnancy which has caused family hurt or embarrassment.

- A bad sexual experience.

- Abortions, whether planned or forced. Resentment and bitterness to the person(s) responsible often follow.

- Inability to cope with menopause (or the mid-life crisis for men).

- Embarrassment over some undesirable physical feature. Examples include being extremely short, having a long nose, large ears (of the 'will he walk or fly?' variety), protruding teeth, unsightly birth marks, being grossly overweight, and for the ladies, the lack of, or over-endowment of breast size.

- An inability to find permanent relief from mental, emotional, or physical problems after having exhausted all forms of counselling and professional help.

- Rejection in love, or a broken engagement.

- Becoming bed ridden, or dependency upon the help of others to remain mobile.

- Being put under pressure unexpectedly, or being faced with a situation beyond one's ability to cope. Illustrations include: a sudden double workload, employment demands beyond a person's training or experience, and a sudden influx in family size because of a crisis among relatives.

- Redundancy, particularly in later years, or unemployment for a long period, despite constant attempts to obtain work.

- Being isolated and treated with contempt by family, friends, or work mates (sent to Coventry).

- Financial disasters such as bankruptcy, a stock market crash, a business failure, or being cheated by financial manipulators.

- An over fertile imagination, and self-pity.

- Self-condemnation after a moral failure.

- A feeling of uselessness in retirement.

(g) Some special factors within married life

- When a husband has had a moral lapse, and a wife becomes uncertain as to whether the affair has ended, or whether he will be faithful to her in the future, rejection comes. The moral failure of a wife has the same effect on the husband.

- The inability of either, or both partners, to communicate effectively. While love is primarily a commitment, unless it is shown by actions and effective communication, either or both partners will feel rejected because their basic needs are not being met. I have often said to Phyl, 'You are my pal, and I don't need a friend because I have you.' Of course I am not friendless, but Phyl is 'numero uno'.

A Review of Some of the Root Causes of Rejection

Married life is a true test of effective communications. Either, or both parties may be good conversationalists with friends, but when alone, there can be a wall of silence.

- Sometimes lethargy caused by an enervating climate may cause a mother to feel guilty about not being physically able to meet her family's needs.

- When a husband is financially mean, wives always feel rejected. Meanness may be manipulative, and is always hurtful because it is a personal attitude which has nothing to do with money supply.

- When one parent obviously takes sides with a child against the other parent, the child will experience rejection. It can easily happen with an only child.

- When a wife refuses to have sexual relations with her husband for capricious or malicious reasons, a husband will feel rejected. One woman became so angry with her father that she punished her husband by refusing to have sex, and literally tossing poor quality meals across the table at him. He was a gracious, but a very rejected man.

- When one partner develops Alzheimer's disease, companionship becomes non-existent, and the caring person suffers rejection.

Other causes:

- Death, divorce, or separation.
- The unfaithfulness of a partner.
- Mental, physical or sexual cruelty.
- The inability to bear children, particularly after exhaustive medical tests.
- Poverty because of the drinking or gambling habits of one party.
- A husband dies, and the widow finds he was intestate (left no will).

Please don't think that this is by any means an exhaustive list. These are some of the more obvious causes of rejection we have found in people who have asked for help. Just ask any social or welfare worker, pastor, counsellor, doctor, psychologist, or psychiatrist and you will find that the list is endless.

Check point

Maybe you, the reader, are feeling terrible after having read this chapter. You are thinking, 'I know I have had so many of these rejections, it makes me feel depressed!' Some painful memories may have been revived which you have tried to forget, but have never really dealt with.

There is good news to come. After we have more fully examined this rejection monster, and shown it to be a satanic device which Christ has totally conquered and exposed, you will find that the freedom and wholeness he offers can be yours. So with that promise, please read on ...

Chapter 3

These Are Some of the Symptoms

Just as the causes of rejection are varied, so are the effects it produces. Although the 'fallout' is so widespread and diverse, three special groupings are clearly discernible. Firstly, how the sufferer outwardly responds to the impact and significance of having received rejection. Secondly, the emotional shockwaves on the inner personality. Thirdly, the self-defensive measures normally taken to offset, and/or prevent, any repetition of rejection damage.

In *Evicting Demonic Intruders and Breaking Bondages*, major causes of rejection were illustrated as the roots of a tree with three main branches, each bearing specific fruit. Some lifetime circumstances causing rejection were summarised in the last chapter, together with some extra causes in keeping with the more definitive study of the subject. This schematic diagram may be seen in later chapters, when various means of deliverance are examined.

Having looked at rejection's root system we now focus attention on the symptoms related to the following three categories shown as branches growing from the trunk of rejection.

Preliminary note: The number of symptoms that rejection sufferers may manifest will vary from person to person. The cause, severity, and numbers of times a person has been rejected, together with the way in which each person reacts and deals with the problem will, to a large extent, determine whether the resultant 'fruit' is plentiful or scanty.

1. Aggressive reactions

- Refusing comfort.
  Both children and adults usually refuse to allow anyone to touch

or comfort them immediately after a rejection-producing incident. Children will usually shut themselves in their room (sometimes slamming the door) and either refuse to come out, or allow
anyone to go in. Adults often follow the same pattern, but usually
more aggressively. Some even jump into their crs and drive off,
just to be alone. In that disturbed emotional state their driving is
often dangerous, and sometimes the cause of accidents. Hurt
emotions are always more difficult to handle than physical ones.

- Rejection of others.
Rejected people need space and time to vent their feelings. So
don't be surprised if the signal is – 'Everyone out – I want to be
alone!' If the victim is initially aggressive, it is often because there
has been insufficient time to think calmly and rationally, and to
bring the emotional turmoil under control.

- Signs of emotional hardness or harshness.
Hurt feelings are a natural reaction when the exposed nerves of
self-esteem are roughly handled. The automatic reaction is often
the firing of that most offensive weapon – the tongue. It is usually
our first line of defence. In the heat of emotional hurts, everyone
or anyone including loved ones, can become a target. The aim is
often indiscriminate.

- Scepticism, doubt, and unbelief.
When a person becomes rejected, trust in family, friends, and
people in general, usually goes into reverse gear, because the one
experiencing rejection loses faith in people's motives and
becomes suspicious of everyone. Street kids periodically react
like this because they fear people are going to take advantage of
them. An American negro on a sidewalk with whom I once
shared the Gospel, suddenly screamed out 'He's going to knife
me!', just because I had reached for my wallet to show him my
identification.

- Aggressive attitudes.
Some people use aggression to parry potential or actual rebuffs.
That sort of individual imagines that aggressiveness is the logical
way to prevent another dose of rejection. Verbal or physical
aggression is an expression of anger, caused by a victim's belief
that he or she has been denied their basic rights to love, acceptance, or approval. Like a diver in muddy water, a disturbed mind
cannot see issues clearly.

- Thoughts or acts of revenge.
  Victims of rejection may become so resentful that they plan, or carry out acts of revenge aimed at causing guilt, or remorse, to those who have rejected them. This may range from 'sending them to Coventry', to attempts to commit suicide.

- Swearing, foul language.
  (Some hen-pecked husbands may use fowl language.) Swearing vents explosive inner pressures, particularly when it has not been a regular habit. It is usually over in a flash, but when a Christian has an outburst, what follows is a fall-out of guilt. It is surprising how many rejected believers of both sexes confess to using blasphemies and obscenities in private, when under pressure.

- Argumentativeness.
  The emotional turmoil stirred up by rejection is a very unreliable basis for rational discussion. Argumentativeness is often self-defensiveness without logic. When a rejection sufferer strongly disagrees with someone, verbal aggression can turn a healthy discussion into a reprisal exercise in which point-scoring, rather than agreement, becomes the goal.

- Stubbornness, defiance.
  We have probably all read about the boy whose mother forced him to sit down against his will, and who defiantly said, 'I may be sitting down on the outside, but I'm still standing up on the inside.'
  Rejection always brings out the worst in an affected person, and it is no wonder that some protest is made to all and sundry, particularly to the person who is the obvious cause.

- Rebellion, fighting.
  This cannot be called 'unarmed' combat as sometimes arms, legs, and any weapon at hand is used to fight off rejection. Probably most readers have at some time either received, or given such treatment. In what is often inappropriately called 'adulthood', kitchen items may become projectiles, such as 'flying saucers'.
  Some bury their emotions but tend the grave continuously. Others with a short tolerance-fuse quickly become physically aggressive every time they feel rejected. This has caused many a fight in hotels or clubs, the beating up of wives or husbands, gang

warfare, and even murders. Alcohol fuels it just as wind sometimes fans the embers of a fire into a forest blaze. The aggressor
gets the blame every time, not the rejection which caused it.

2. Self-rejection symptoms

As bruises, fractures, and bleeding indicate physical injury, so do
behavioural symptoms reveal the presence of the rejection 'disease'.

- Low self-image. Flowers and fruit are easily damaged by rough
  handling, and rejection causes the crushed personality to crash-
  dive. The reasoning behind it goes something like this: 'If so and
  so whom I thought loved me, or whom I respected, did or said
  that to me, then they obviously don't think as much of me as I
  thought they did. Then I must be of no real value!' The more that
  attitude remains, the deeper the self-rejection becomes.

  We live in the days of sure-fire remedies for every problem. So,
  sure enough the New Age Movement offers the very latest self-
  image recovery programmes such as spiritual wet or dry
  rebirthing, transcendental meditation, or fire-walking ego boost-
  ing. There are also 'channelling', crystals, humanistic sermons
  and many other devices for lifting self-images in 'five easy
  lessons'. Because their work-kits ignore Jesus Christ, users are
  drawn into greater deception and rejection. If anyone receives a
  bee sting, the embedded sting itself needs to be removed before
  treatment can begin. Jesus Christ alone can remove stinging
  rejection roots, and perfect the healing process.

- Inferiorities, insecurity, and inadequacy naturally flow on from
  the low self-image of the crushed ego. From the depths of low
  self-evaluation, the three symptoms automatically appear, and
  get worse each time the victim compares himself or herself with
  others. Before long, they become personality features as firmly
  set as concrete. Denials, disguises, and cover up techniques are as
  effective on the inner feelings as a cork is at keeping a ship from
  sinking.

- Sadness, grief, and sorrow are outward manifestations of a
  wounded or crushed spirit. The degree of reaction will be determined firstly by the amount of hurt received, and secondly, by the
  amount of self-pity in which the individual indulges.

- Self-accusation and self-condemnation. As strange as it may seem, many people accuse themselves of having caused their own rejection. They constantly put themselves down, and will reject personal commendation, no matter how genuine it is. Some will even punish themselves for being the way they are.

- Inability, or refusal to communicate. Shock may cause the first, stubbornness the second. Regarded at times as 'being in a huff', it may quickly become a permanent condition unless remedied. When some of our grandsons were at the 'ankle-biter' stage, one of our daughters would sometimes tell us that 'so-and-so' was 'packing-a-sad' (sulking, and not talking). Occasionally it was a 'dark-sad'.

- Fears of all kinds. The fear of other people's opinions must rank high on the list of rejection symptoms. And so is fear of rejection, fear of inability to cope, fear of inadequacy, and fear of failure. Children or adults who were self-confident before being rejected, afterwards become unsure of themselves, then begin to fear many things which had never worried them before. Fear of the dark is a certainty with children.

- Anxiety, worry, or depression. This is the musty basement beneath the ground floor of rejection. If these problems are hereditary (from a family background), rejection will certainly increase them. If not, they often commence after rejection, and may become established emotional problems.

- Blocked goals may produce anger. Uncertainty of achieving goals may cause anxiety. Feelings of hopelessness in failing to reach goals may cause depression. These goals may not be major achievements, but everyday needs such as love, acceptance and a sense of self-worth. Negativity, pessimism, hopelessness, and despair are also symptoms of underground emotional living. In the darkness there is no glimmer of hope, no encouraging voice, and no way of finding a way out alone. Regrettably, some squeeze into a sewer man-hole labelled 'suicide' when their calls for help are ignored or not heard. Without hope and faith, many trapped in that oppressive darkness do not know that Jesus Christ has the remedy to their problem because he IS himself, the remedy.

3. Symptoms of the fear of rejection

- Striving, achievement, performance, and competition. This syndrome may commence in childhood by simply giving an apple to the teacher, or taking her flowers. The next attention-getting step may be the making of intense efforts to top the class in exams, or to perform outstandingly such as in the dramatic arts. Other means include constant humour, showing off, or striving for excellence in sports activities. When performance really gets serious, it may become no-holds-barred competition. Adults do the same thing in perhaps a more sophisticated form, but the attempts to please people and get their approval are just as noticeable.

- Independence and isolation. Rejection often triggers the withdrawal syndrome which damages friendships and marriage. This is where the recluse or hermit mentality finds a launching pad.

- The 'look-after-me syndrome'. Self-centredness covers a nasty collection of egocentric attitudes and behaviour such as self-protectiveness, self-indulgence, selfishness, self-justification, self-righteousness, and the particularly odious self-idolatry. 'Me-itis' is a particularly nasty syndrome because it is selfish, and others may not realise that they are being manipulated to keep the 'bless-me' club operating.

- The 'my-rights' attitude. The rejected ego demands to be treated fairly and justly, according to its prescribed standards. It may be expressed verbally, or be obvious by body-language. A psychologist friend describes the syndrome as a one person crusade for 'I' justice.

- Criticism, judgement, envy, jealousy, and covetousness. These five nasty uninvited little characters huddle together in rejected people and exert considerable influence over their host's thinking and speaking. They pollute the sufferer's self-opinion and attitude to others, and in reality cause the rejection symptoms to increase.

- Pride, egotism, haughtiness, and arrogance. This family of professional intruders convince rejection victims that they really do have a lot to be proud of. They even help promote self-advertising publicity campaigns to convince others. They force the gauge of inferiorities and low self-image to rise to an unreasonable level, and cover over the warning of Proverbs 27:2, '*Let another praise you, and not your own mouth; someone else, and not your own lips.'*

- Possessiveness and manipulation. From childhood to old age, in unmarried as well as married rejected victims, the message goes out, 'That's mine, leave it alone.' Just as the Australian bower bird fills its nest with any blue object it can lift, so rejected people comfort themselves with 'possessions'. They will jealously guard what they feel are their rights, even to the amount of time others give them. And they are very versatile in getting more of what they want.

- Emotional immaturity. Childhood, or teenage rejection will retard emotional development while normal physical development is unimpeded. This syndrome will be expanded in a later chapter.

- Perfectionism. While this is often an hereditary problem, it also may commence through rejection. The reasoning is – 'If I put my very best effort into doing what is expected of me, I will please people and that must make them like me.' But whatever is spawned by fear will be unhealthy, and in the end, self-destructive.

- Disturbed sleep patterns. The mind and emotions of rejected people often switch on like an alarm clock out of control. Sleep may be interrupted unexpectedly, even frequently. Unless the rejection is removed, permanent patterns of disturbed sleep may become established.

The evil thing about rejection is that every objectionable symptom outlined so far, and those yet to come, reflect the nature of the enemy of all born again believers. What is even worse, is that the fruit on those three branches become ongoing demonic activities. For deliverance to be effective, those dominating spirits of cause and effect need to be driven out in order to destroy the whole system of rejection's roots, branches, and fruit. Only then will the release and renewal be complete.

Chapter 4

Rejection May Begin Unexpectedly, Stay Indefinitely, and Leave Reluctantly

It is very difficult to describe adequately the extent of this syndrome. Unfortunately, people are not like fruit on a shop shelf. After you have placed your selected items in the tear-off plastic bags and head for the check-out cashier, the fruit left behind never sheds even one drop of tearful juice for having been overlooked, or pinched, squeezed, and then rejected.

We humans are very, very different. Just think back to your childhood days and you will probably recall times when you were told you were a nuisance, troublesome, a burden, or at least, exasperating. Or even worse, you were ignored, unloved, and made to feel unwanted.

Feelings play a very important part in person-to-person relationships from babyhood onwards. And they can be hurt – badly. Is this scene familiar? In a playground two of your friends are choosing teams to play a game. So you stand tall amongst the rest of the kids available to play, and on your chest is an invisible notice board which reads, 'I'm the best – the very best – you can't win without me!' But apparently neither team leader can read so well because they both continually ignore you. Finally there are only two of you left, and the other person gets the final nod, and you end up being drafted. You weren't a choice, only a left-over. Your heart goes 'plunk', as your feelings hit rock bottom. With leaden feet you join the team stuck with you, and with zero self-confidence you confirm why no-one selected you.

Rejection-creating circumstances are a lifetime hazard. The causes listed only emphasise the conscious beginnings of the problem from early childhood onwards. Let's push a little deeper into this maze.

1. Rejection may become a life-sentence

Whether rejection has been experienced for a short time, or long term, it will certainly continue to be a dominant life factor, unless a remedy can be found. However this seldom happens.

One of the first questions Phyl and I ask adult counsellees concerns their childhood relationship with their parents. We often discover the taproots which have produced negative, or harmful 'fruit' even up to sixty or seventy years later. Hurt and angry children usually grow into hurt and angry adults. Some learn to live with their problems, or cover them up, and psychology or psychiatry may assist in attitude adjustments, but only deliverance and inner renewal by the Holy Spirit can bring total release and permanent personality changes. The Holy Spirit reaches areas of the psyche where words and other measures are powerless. No human palliative can reverse the bad habit patterns of a lifetime. Only the love of God can.

The following case histories are from people with whom we have been involved in a deliverance ministry:

● 'Beatrice' was a 45 year-old spinster never wanted by her father. He had been unable to give her mother the love she longed for. 'I tried in my own way to make up for that', she said. 'My mother made me believe that men are just selfish beasts. I have had a few men friends but was terrified when they tried to make love to me, and became hysterical afterwards. I still have patches of uncontrollable bitter crying coming from deep within me.'

As a child, she went to eight different schools and had to board in a children's home. She grew up with inferiorities, low self image, worthlessness, insecurity, and was convinced that she was a failure. Withdrawal, loneliness and unhappiness were natural to her, and the rejection symptoms were still evident, along with some psychosomatic physical problems.

- 'Harry' was 50 years-old. When he was two years of age his mother was admitted to a mental hospital, where she died. His father remarried, and he was brought up by a disciplinarian uncle and aunt who showed him no tenderness or love. 'Harry' became stubborn and rebellious, and withdrew from people, fearing more of the rejection he knew only too well. Even as a married man with a family he loved, he found it very difficult to communicate, or show them the physical love he had been denied in childhood. 'Harry' continued to be very much a loner.

During our counselling session, he gained enough confidence to tell us he had attempted to counteract his feelings of rejection by heavy masturbation, sexual masochism, and the drinking of alcohol. Because rejection had commenced so early in life, it was still an inseparable part of him when he came to see us.

- 'Bert' was 52 years of age when he wrote to us. 'My father left home before I was born, but returned when I was around 8 years old, leaving again periodically after that. He was never close to me, never held me, or told me that he loved me. He was a gambler, a playboy, and wasted a fortune. He was also a perfectionist and treated me with coldness and hardness, just as his own father had treated him. When he died, I did not go to his funeral.

My mother incessantly complained to me about all her problems, particularly those my father caused. She suffered heavily from anxiety, worry, depression, fear of death, and bitterness. My dearest love was my grandmother who brought me up during my first 8 years, but I feared my paternal grandfather who had disapproved of my parent's marriage. Although wealthy, he left nothing in his will for my mother or any of us grandchildren. In fact we lived in relative poverty.

During childhood, I suffered many indignities in our neighbourhood because we had an ethnically different background to everyone else. Both my mother and father told me I'd grow up to be a "bum". A teacher at Junior school called me "Dopey Berty", and once threw a screwdriver at my head. I ducked, and it stuck in a board beside me.'

'Bert' had tried to counteract his rejection with arrogance, intellectualism, and rationalism. His university education and business activities had turned him into an aggressive sceptic. He had also tried to find reality in New Age activities and occultism.

43

It took some time before he was prepared to humble himself sufficiently to ask for ministry. He finally came when he felt God wanted to set him free. He was certainly released from rejection and the rest of his probems, received inner healing, and began his life over again.

2. Rejection may strike unexpectedly

Some rejection sufferers may have lived well-adjusted lives until something happens which changes everything. Examples:

- Artistic rejection. Having done some writing, the writer is well aware of the suspense which follows sending a manuscript to a potential publisher. What an author may genuinely regard as imaginative creation, or even special revelation, a publisher views through 'dollar-sign' spectacles. 'Is this within my publishing guidelines?'; 'What is the likely demand for this book?'; 'Will it be sufficiently profitable to justify the initial outlay?' and so on. Meanwhile the writer waits uncomfortably for good news, which more often than not turns out to be a rejection slip.

  Writer's rejection may cause a variety of reactions ranging from mere disappointment, or frustrations, through to despair or depression. Some keep on trying and finally succeed, while others give up, and remain angry, bitter, and defeated by what they regard as a rebuff, rather than a temporary set-back.

  One imagines that many people with other artistic abilities experience this, such as those whose works are never hung in a prestigious gallery, musicians who just don't quite make band or orchestra acceptance, and poets whose only audience is a fireside family.

- The 'crushed' feeling. This has nothing to do with a large lady leaning over a diminutive man. But it does apply to those who have to suffer the interminable vapourings of insufferable egoists who believe they are never wrong. In marriage this can be so devastating that one party feels that he or she has become a 'non-person'. The husband or wife retreats, falls silent, and doesn't dare offer an opinion. When this happens to a father, the fallout is particularly severe on the children because they lack the security of an authoritative, decision-making male parent. This usually causes them to suffer rejection.

- Debility caused by illness. Some reference has already been made to this, but there are some illnesses which may make a sufferer particularly prone to rejection. A few which come to mind are kidney failure (with dependence on dialysis), some cancerous conditions, heart diseases which severely limit mobility, and AIDS. The necessity of withdrawing from an active life and normal socialising can cause feelings of uselessness, hopelessness, and rejection. Any lifestyle-restricting illness can have the same effect.

- The 'I-can't-stand-you-being-religious' syndrome. A number of people who have come for counselling have had a marriage partner walk out when they became a Christian. One man's wife told him, 'I could cope with adultery, but I can't live with someone who has become religious.' This can make the rejection much worse if the deserted partner is still in love. Children of course suffer badly in the 'fall-out'.

- Rejection may begin in the imaginations. Most of us at one time or another have been seemingly ignored by someone we know well. And we have probably unconsciously done it to others. When no sign of recognition is given, most people will shrug it off, but there will always be the few who will allow the incident to produce rejection and resentment. The first thing you usually know about it is when you are charged with deliberate rudeness. Watery eyes and the piqued look often emphasise the point.

  But what is unintentional is never as bad as when a rejected person deliberately gathers fuel for their rejection syndrome purely from imagination. A member of a congregation confronted her pastor, saying, 'Why do you preach at me, more than anyone else in church, and why do you always point out my problems in your sermons rather than those of others?' It is no wonder that Jesus Christ said he was the good shepherd. In every congregation there are sickly sheep!

3. Rejection does not disappear if ignored, or simply treated with quick-fix advice

Rejection may be compared to lawn grass which constantly needs to be mowed. As long as the roots remain in the soil, the grass will grow. Rejection sufferers likewise will constantly respond to preacher's appeals, do the round of counsellors, 'buttonhole' the pastor on every possible occasion, and spend hours on the telephone 'me-deep' in conversation. No wonder pastors and counsellors find themselves drained by such people. Phyl and I have found that deliverance is the quickest, surest, and really the only way to get rid of rejection's deep root-systems. It sure saves lawn-mowing time! God told Amos:

> *'I destroyed the Amorite before them* (the Israelites) *though he was tall as the cedars and strong as the oaks. I destroyed his fruit above and his roots below.'*   (Amos 2:9, emphasis added)

The body of Christ needs rejection 'root-pullers', not mere diagnosticians.

Chapter 5

Some Self-prescribed Rejection Remedies

Our bodies generally react quickly and automatically when our comfort or safety is threatened, or affected. Pain signals the need for rest when injury occurs, fingers are withdrawn immediately they touch a burning object, and even the blood rushes extra white corpuscles to fight infection wherever it occurs. Our non-physical natures also automatically react when feeling rejected.

It has been said that most people react to bad news such as the diagnosis of a serious illness, in five different ways. Rejection sufferers seem to follow a similar pattern.

Phase 1. The individual becomes silently or visibly angry that such a thing should have happened at all. Children and teenagers may passively rebel by not answering when called, or by failure to do what they were asked or expected to do. Older people sometimes express anger by sullenness, refusal to cooperate, not talking, or by flashing antagonistic looks. Some psychosomatic illnesses come from this phase of rejection, such as a type of arthritis which is caused by buried resentment and anger. Other people consult one medical specialist after another hoping to find someone who will diagnose their imagined serious illness.

Phase 2. The sufferer denies reality, refusing to believe the prognosis, rather like a person who pulls down the blinds, or draws the curtains to convince themselves that the real world outside does not exist. They think: 'This can't be happening to me.' It seems that most of us believe that we are somehow exempt from the misfortunes of others. I certainly felt that way about cardiac problems, until my first heart irregularity was diagnosed.

Phase 3. The person withdraws, and refuses to discuss what is happening. Like the ostrich with its head in the sand, the rejected person hopes this terrible problem will just go away. But it is not easy to keep inner hurts from expressing themselves in some kind of body language. When an outgoing personality suddenly goes silent, or a gregarious person shuns company, the silent message is, 'Can't you see, I want to be alone'.

When feelings of rejection become intolerable, some people withdraw so completely that they become hermits, or live in inaccessible high country visited only by the occasional hiker. Communes have also become popular in the last decade with those who have either rejected 'plastic' society, or who feel rejected by that society. In withdrawal they flock together to live the lifestyle of their ideals, or drug-induced fantasies.

Phase 4. Depression sets in when a rejected person becomes convinced that nothing will ever change. The inevitable then becomes intolerable. The visible effects will of course vary with the intensity of the rejection, or the grief it causes. Depression may follow a fall in a victim's self-confidence and personal security. Emotions overrule logic, and the stress sometimes causes a person to withdraw from the company of others, often with an obvious change of lifestyle. Some form of mental and emotional heaviness often follows the downward spiral to self-rejection and fear of rejection. Only the degree and duration vary.

Phase 5 is the final acceptance of the problem, and the taking of what practical steps are possible to tolerate, or counteract the situation. Some people feel that they are unable to adjust in the same surroundings, so change locations, and build up a circle of new friends.

We humans have the ability to 'bounce back' after times of stress, and this is certainly so with many rejection sufferers. Without giving particular thought to how to counteract the problems, certain behavioural patterns usually emerge which experienced counsellors will recognise as signs of the rejection syndrome. These may be introvertive, extrovertive, passive or aggressive:

1. Turning to false comforts

(a) Alcohol. Many people commence drinking in times of stress, and society lightheartedly refers to it as 'drowning your sorrows'.

Unfortunately, the sorrows usually survive, and the 'drowning' process becomes a habit. Our hotel bars and drinking oases are filled with rejected, dispirited, and lonely people who kill both time and brain cells at the same time. Not many born-again Christians join the daily 'happy hour' stampede in public, but in the privacy of their own homes, who knows how much is consumed? The glass of wine, or two or three, during dinner, and the evening; the relaxing can of beer after a hard day's work (or the exhaustion of thinking about it!); or that special home-made wine fit to fuel an out-of-space rocket. It may be disguised as socialising, but more often it is just escapism, liquid-courage, or an anaesthetic to dull one's reaction to the intolerable. It certainly never solves rejection, it only distorts it.

(b) Sexual gratification. Both males and females may commence self-stimulation and masturbation from childhood onwards as a pleasurable distraction from the hurts and disappointments of rejection. Of course masturbation may also be caused by hereditary lust, sexual interference, the lack of satisfaction in marriage, or by the stimulation of pornography. Whatever prompts the practice, it often leads to other sexual practices and always leaves Christians with deep guilt. The use of sensual self-comfort activities will never cancel out rejection, it only increases self-rejection, by lowering self-respect.

(c) Food. Some men, and many women become compulsive eaters in order to counteract the pain of rejection. Because the women folk usually spend time in the kitchen, 'nibbling' is a constant temptation. Unfortunately, the little extras for comfort sometimes become habit-forming, with disastrous effects on the figure. When the mirror, the outgrown clothes, or the comments of others emphasise the obvious, self-rejection gets worse. Crash diets are not the final answer. Deliverance from the rejection syndrome will not only remove the compelling urge to eat, but will make self-discipline much easier.

(d) Drugs. Rejected people of all ages, particularly teenagers, turn to some form of drug taking to make their rejection more tolerable. Household medicines, prescription remedies, and all forms of hallucinatory drugs may be tried in the hope of relieving emotional pain. Knowledge of the possibilities of addiction is often no deterrent.

49

2. Self-protective measures ('the snail-syndrome')

We all know what the snail does when it senses danger ahead. It infolds its feelers and withdraws into the security of its shell. Emotionally hurt people have a wider range of options available. For example:

- They become 'book-worms', so engrossed in reading that everyone and everything around them are totally ignored.

- They select hobbies which require a lot of time, but no assistance.

- They choose pastimes such as bush-walking, fishing or sailing, which justify prolonged absences. (Please don't confuse them with genuine sports addicts!)

- Some married men have built workshops in their back yards in order to stay away from the family as long as possible.

- Some escapists will become TV addicts.

- Some learn to play the guitar, and spend endless hours by themselves, strumming, and singing mournful dirges.

- Others go for long walks, or drive around aimlessly for hours because they feel restless and want to avoid people.

- A few consistently spend 'justifiably' long hours at work, but in reality are seeking to avoid others.

Some of these activities are obviously right in moderation, but excesses are often symptoms of 'the snail-syndrome'.

3. The 'damaged-emotion' syndrome

In order to assess the mental capacity and aptitude of applicants for certain studies or positions of employment, professional advisers have devised tests which establish each person's intelligence quotient (IQ). Another equally important factor is often overlooked. Unless brain power is balanced by emotional stability, the IQ level may be a faulty indicator of the person's over-all ability. Some intellectuals have difficulty in expressing any type of emotion, while others have problems in controlling their emotions.

It seems that the emotional quotient (EQ) has not always been recognised as being essential to personal assessment. In researching principles of deliverance for rejection sufferers, it has become all too obvious that both sexes suffer varying degrees of emotional and behavioural problems caused by the trauma of rejection. This is why people often categorised as 'intellectuals' sometimes 'go to pieces' when rejected. From our observation it seems that people with a balanced 'IQ' and 'EQ' appear to be more capable of coping with rejection.

This condition often seriously restricts a person's emotional balance and function from childhood onwards, and can cause *emotional reactions which are disproportionate to the age of the individual*.

The physical size and intellectual development of rejected children may be normal, with no obvious emotional problems, but the emotions usually lag behind general growth and development. The symptoms may take time to appear.

Our normal counselling procedure is to ask two questions, the answers to which can indicate a rejection problem. The first is to ask the counsellee what is his or her biological age. The second goes like this, 'How old do you feel *emotionally*?', or 'What is your emotional age?'. The answers are quite often surprising, particularly when mature adults say that they 'feel' and act like a child, or a teenager. Most of us probably have had an occasional immature emotional reaction and have felt embarrassed, or tried to pass it off lightheartedly. But the person with impaired emotions will constantly show immaturity while trying to pretend that nothing is wrong. Some women folk actually will wear clothes normally associated with a younger age-group, or allow their hair to grow long to give the impression that they are not as old as people think.

Occasionally, the emotional age swings in the opposite direction, and people become 'over-mature'. This is particularly so when rejected children live with grandparents, or associate only with adults. Emotional premature-ageing can affect both personality and physique. Some adults have confessed to feeling emotionally twenty or thirty years older than their actual age.

In extreme cases of emotional immaturity,

- some withdraw from their peer age-group and associate with younger people with whom they feel more comfortable.

- others mix with an older age-group. Some of them have sadly confessed to having missed the joys of being a teenager.

But praise God there is good news for readers who may now understand why they have felt emotionally immature. When the Lord releases people from the roots of rejection and from adolescent spirits, normal emotional balance is restored.

4. The striving, competitive syndrome

Another means to counteract rejection is to continuously try to gain the approval of other people. The deflated self-image assumes that everyone (including family and friends) has also downgraded them. This is mainly an imaginative delusion, but it can prompt:

- an intense desire to reach high standards. We have already said that children and teenagers sometimes become competitive in school work. Adults seek approval by the way they dress, carry themselves, academic attainment, their choice of profession, art, social activities, and even by the purchase of expensive cars. Women may also use their cooking skills, ability to decorate, and their attractive gardens to obtain approval. Some people achieve the highest results spurred on by wrong motives. The basic problem of low self-image remains in all of these. This in turn often stimulates even greater efforts for approval.

- perfectionism for approval. This type is neither hereditary, nor a sign of professionalism, but another attention-seeking manoeuvre. Unfortunately, I was caught in this trap before the Lord released me from my roots of rejection. What was worse, I imposed my false standards on my family and work associates, all to boost my own flagging ego! I have repented of that, but too late to undo the damage. I now aim to use my talents and abilities to the maximum for the glory of Jesus Christ, without any bondage to performance.

5. The academic syndrome

Many rejected people, particularly women, bury their rejection under an avalanche of academic studies. Although intellectually gifted, some university students are in reality lonely people with low self-image, seeking self-fulfillment by degrees! Some proceed to doctoral level, or master one discipline after another without ever feeling fulfilled. Only Jesus Christ can satisfy these deep desires.

6. The 'bluff' syndrome

People suffering from rejection are often versatile in masking their true feelings:

- Some become talkative, and try to be the life of every party with an endless supply of humorous stories. No one ever is allowed to outdo them; they always have something in reserve.

- Others attract admiring attention by flamboyant clothes and ostentatious behaviour, wearing hats or 'shades' indoors, day and night, or by constantly cracking their knuckles.

- Occasionally, a rejection sufferer will wear a fixed smile which is meant to signal, 'Everything's OK with me'. It certainly can deceive people, and it is only when the grin remains in adverse circumstances that the masquerade becomes obvious.

7. The 'popularity-at-any-price' syndrome

Sadly, we have had to pray over a number of people who were so desperate for acceptance and affection that they subjected themselves to all kinds of sexual indecencies. This twisted sense of self-worth is boosted by the demand for their particular 'specialty'. Although each one hated what they were doing, they were unable to stop, until Jesus Christ intervened.

8. The 'works-of-mercy' syndrome

Some lonely (usually single) ladies will offer their time and practical skills to local charities, or to international organisations serving the poor and needy in under-developed countries. Many of these are Christian volunteers motivated by a deep concern for those less fortunate than themselves. A few however, hope that by doing 'works of mercy' they will get some sense of fulfillment to compensate for their inner feelings of 'valuelessness'.

All these attempts to counteract the wretchedness of rejection should be viewed in the light of Ezekiel 13:10–12.

> '... *when a flimsy wall is built, they cover it with whitewash,
> therefore tell those who cover it with whitewash that it is going to
> fall. Rain will come in torrents, and I will send hailstones*

hurtling down, and violent winds will burst forth. When the wall collapses, will people not ask you, "Where is the whitewash you covered it with?"'

Rejection cover-up measures are just like whitewash. The only permanent cure is for the dominating demonic forces to be thrown out, and the Holy Spirit allowed to reshape the personality to the glory of Jesus Christ.

9. Rejection may be deeply rooted in our national, ethnic, or cultural ancestry

World history is anything but a pretty picture – wars, revolutions, coups, refugees and displaced persons, famines, poverty, disasters both natural and accidental, crimes, violence, drug and alcohol abuse ... the list seems endless. But the end result is that the earth is full of people suffering rejection.

For this reason, among others, people migrate in search of their personal utopia, most of them being unaware that they are carrying rejection as a lethal, but unrecognised personal possession. It remains active in their children and grandchildren for several generations.

Pastors and counsellors need to remember this when helping migrants and their descendants. Apart from their Aboriginal indigenes, a high percentage of Australians fall into this category, either as migrants or as children of migrants from countries around the world. Even the United Kingdom is made up of four distinctly different ethnic groups, plus a number of others who do not always harmoniously relate to one another.

National, ethnic, and cultural disharmony sometimes becomes acrimonious, and is counter-productive to spiritual unity. Deep spiritual roots of rejection and counter-rejection need to be removed to allow the principles of spiritual fellowship (Gr. *koinonia*) to operate.

The special case of ethnic Chinese rejection
East and West express their emotions very differently. The American film industry has featured, and over-dramatised the Western style of hugging and kissing. But until relatively recently little of it

has featured in countries across Asia, particularly with Chinese people and their ethnic relatives in Japan, Korea, and wherever their descendants have migrated. Even now, only the young people are showing some evidence of change.

The traditional conservatism of Asia is at last beginning to crumble under the influence of films, overseas travel, and students going to universities overseas. However, the older people remain bound to a tradition which still does not allow public expressions of emotion. Many adult Chinese have told us that they never saw their parents display any affection in the home. It is little wonder that children grow up feeling emotionally rejected. To them, love is traditionally expressed by family loyalty, caring for one another, and providing for the needs of children and parents in old age. Maybe the West has a lesson to learn from this!

In *Evicting Demonic Intruders and Breaking Bondages*, I told of hearing the Lord's voice telling me to 'break cultural bondages' when praying with Korean young people. The spontaneous embraces, even tears, which followed this was repeated in Japan, and other Pacific countries whose populations were basically of Chinese origin.

Let me describe the greatest spontaneous display of love overcoming conservative tradition that I have ever seen. It was in Australia's national capital, Canberra. Having first lectured for several days, and ministered deliverance to around 15 Chinese undergraduates and graduates, the concluding session was taken up with sharing practical suggestions as to how personal freedom could be maintained. At the end one student stood up and said, 'We would like to thank you'. I acknowledged this by saying that I was sure that they had appreciated what Jesus Christ had done for them. But the young man remained standing, and replied, 'You don't understand'. I was certainly not prepared for what followed. All the students crowded excitedly around the lectern, and I was hugged and thanked in turn by every young man and woman in the class. Because each one had been freed from their ethnic, hereditary and personal rejection, the Holy Spirit had simply opened a fountain of expression that neither they nor I believed was possible. Since then, whenever I have met any of them, a warm hug has always been part of our mutual greeting.

Around the world there is at present a ground-swell of bitterness and hatred being expressed by peoples of different colour, ideology, religion and lifestyle. Polarisation caused by rejection at any level can be destructive to harmonious relationships, property, and human lives.

We all need to pray for a Holy Ghost revival of international proportions, so that people will be saved, and set free from every attitude and activity which continues to be fuelled by past rejection. Only then will the love of Jesus Christ unify people of every 'tribe, kindred, and nation'.

Chapter 6

Rejection May Lead to Violence – Even Murder

He was a big man and heavily bearded. He slouched in his chair, and looked me over carefully. He was obviously trying to make up his mind as to whether I could handle what he had to share and be able to give some practical help. I don't know whether it was my age, my attitude, his desperation, or the encouragement of the Holy Spirit that finally gave him the confidence to tell his story.

'Because I wasn't the girl my parents expected, I was rejected from birth. My mother gave all her attention to my two year-old brother. My father harassed me and beat me up almost every day, so when I reached nine years of age, I left home.

By the time I was thirteen, I had my own apartment, a motorbike, a forged licence, and was sexually active. By nineteen years of age I was riding with two motor cycle gangs and collecting their debts, mostly with the aid of a gun.

I had a violent temper. I once beat up a man with a billiard cue; he was in intensive care for six and a half months. One day a drunk in a bar greatly annoyed me. I hated sloppy bars and sloppy drunks. Five or six times I asked the barman to get this fellow off my back, or I would. He didn't, so I floored him with one blow to his jaw, then headed home. I showered, changed, and went to a 'posh' club. It wasn't long before the cops came in asking for me. The drunk I had decked had died. I started a fracas with the cops, but I ended in a matchbox sized prison cell, sleeping on a bare steel plate concreted to the floor. I had no clothes, no mattress, no blankets, no sheets, and no pillow. But I did have a toilet – a hole in the floor. After a year my lot improved considerably. I was given a thin horsehair

57

mattress, and a visiting Catholic priest gave me a Bible which I used for a pillow. I read a little of it twice, but thought it must have been written by a clown.

After four years of solitary confinement I was released, and vowed I would kill myself rather than go back to prison again. I was convinced that marriage would help me, even though I had failed at it before. When I was around 22, my parents and relatives forced me to marry a girl who had just given birth to my baby daughter. After six weeks I split – with the baby. I gave her to my parents to look after seeing that they had wanted a girl instead of me.

So, one after another, "I shacked up" with six different women, rejecting each one in turn. Then I met a single mother who attracted me. We drove over the mountains one night, and I married her in the morning. I threatened to cut her down with the machine gun I kept on the lounge coffee table if she ever tried to run out on me. And she knew I meant it.

I didn't know she was a non-practising Christian. The first time I went to church with her, I parked my machine in the lobby, and put my Russian fur cap on the floor under the chain oiler so that nothing would drip on the carpet. As we went inside, there was a shocked silence and the pastor suddenly changed his sermon style to the hell-fire stuff. That got me mad, so I stomped out, got on my bike, fired it up, then roared down the aisle, picked up my bird. I shot out the back door leaving the church filled with exhaust fumes. I hadn't been home very long before the pastor drove up. I jumped on the machine and started the motor, but before I could take off, the pastor had walked over and switched it off. Then he apologised.'

That is a shortened and sanitised version of 'Arnold's' story. God had begun to close in on him. A fine Christian friend of his wife, in her seventies, was the next to influence him. She constantly badgered him to go to church and the madder he got the more she asked him. The climax came one Sunday morning where Mrs. 'O' whipped the sheet off the bed, and demanded that he would promise to go to church that night. In blind rage he roared at her, 'Get out you old broad, or I'll kill you!' Nothing and no-one was going to stop him seeing his Sunday night TV movie. But Mrs 'O' wasn't that easily moved, so she stood her ground and bargained with him: 'If you come to church with me tonight, I will never ask you again'. That clinched it; it was an offer he couldn't refuse. So, accompanied by his wife and God's faithful servant, he sat under the preaching of Mario Marillo. Both the women asked him to respond to the appeal. He refused. So they simply took one arm each, and propelled him down to the front where they asked the pastor to pray for him. During the prayer, 'Arnold' crashed to the floor, out cold. When he came to, he was really puzzled as to what had happened. So puzzled in fact that he voluntarily went to the evening services on the following two Sunday nights looking for answers. On both occasions after being prayed for, he woke up on the carpet surrounded by people, but still no wiser about who or what had caused it. Then the inevitable happened. Shortly afterwards he was born again and his life slowly started to change.

All these things had taken place years before he came to us for counsel and prayer. During the session he sat slumped on a chair, his hands hanging limply by his sides, while all the time growling like a bear. He afterwards told us he remembered nothing. He said, 'I know I came in filled with darkness, and went out filled with light.'

There was no doubting that the deep and continued rejection 'Arnold' had received from birth onwards had formed an explosive force which he vented in aggressiveness, violence, brutality, and bullying.

As he began to grow in Christ, some of these problems came under control, but the emotional fire fuelled by rejection remained, and he had difficulty in establishing meaningful relationships. The old problem of lust started to rear its ugly head again.

Deliverance was not the total answer for this man (or for anyone else with the same problem for that matter), but it is the essential beginning. Discipleship is never a 'flash-in-the-pan' effervescent experience, but a slow, progressive lifestyle development brought about by submission to the principles of godly living and personal discipline. Habits are hard to break, and the counsellee may feel discouraged many times, until he or she learns to be victorious by the power of the indwelling Holy Spirit. When we moved out of personal contact, 'Arnold' was grateful to the Lord for his freedom and healing from the past, and had committed himself to establishing new relationships.

'George' was a man to whom both Phyl and I have ministered. He told us that he was made to leave school when he was 7 years of age so that he could go to work and supplement the family budget. His lack of education was a constant embarrassment as he could only write phonetically. His childhood days were extremely miserable, both parents beating him for the slightest cause.

His deep rejection had two other outlets. Firstly, he withdrew from people-contact as much as possible; when a teenager he bought an old truck and a number of hunting rifles, and spent as much time as possible up in the mountains firing at targets.

Secondly, his anti-social feelings were released in violence. He and some relatives, armed with baseball bats, broke into a car yard and within minutes did more than $100,000 worth of damage to the cars. He also began collecting explosives, intending to blow up public buildings. Fortunately he didn't go that far because God mercifully saved him.

'George' developed building and mechanical skills and was using these in a volunteer capacity with a mission where Phyl and I were teaching. One lunch hour he sat with a crowd listening to Phyl speak on childrens' problems. She spoke for more than one hour, and 'George' was so fascinated that he sat immobilised the whole time. An uneaten sandwich was still in his hand when she finished speaking. He then put the sandwich down, went up to her and asked whether he could give her a hug, saying, 'Lady, you have just told the story of my life.'

Some considerable time later our paths crossed again at the same location where the young man was attending a counselling course. His rejection was still causing him big problems. He was still withdrawn. Each time he felt threatened by a lecturer, he mentally switched off and fantasised about being back in the mountains again. His grades were not good, and his relationships little better.

Several days after he had received deliverance, we happened to sit behind him in a church service. His response to praise and worship was spontaneous and genuine. When he saw us at the end of the service he rushed up and embraced us both, kissing us both on the cheek.

The journey back to self-acceptance and right relationships with others had begun. He could understand and remember what he was being taught more easily, and could even dialogue with his lecturers without retreating into unreality.

Like the previous case history, the Lord's releases through deliverance were but the first phase of inner healing, self-acceptance, and the establishment of wholesome relationships. These always take time and persistence. God's human miracles are usually conditional. He will do what he alone can do, as long as we trust him, make right choices, and obey him fully. Limit faith, and you limit God.

> '*He could not do any miracles there, except lay his hands on a few sick people and heal them. And he was amazed at their lack of faith.*'
> (Mark 6:5, 6)

We have not seen this young man again, so we cannot say how far he has progressed, but he certainly was set free.

On the 9th August 1987, a shock wave which started in Hoddle Street, Melbourne, reverberated throughout Australia. A mass-killer had acted out his fantasies behind the sights of a rifle. Seven were dead, and dozens lay injured. Julian Knight was judged not to be criminally insane, but was jailed for a period of seven life-times, plus four hundred and sixty years on forty-six charges of attempted murder. The judge ruled that the twenty-year old must spend at least twenty-seven years in prison, by which time 'he might no longer be a danger to the community'.

In the court's opinion, Knight was not a psychopath, but the victim of his own background and disordered personality. His violence had obviously erupted from emotional pressures which had been building up for years. Three factors can be identified: people and circumstances continually rejecting him, his own deep self-rejection, and a growing fear that things wouldn't change.

There is a clear pattern leading to the climax of the Melbourne blood-bath:

- Julian's first rejection came when he was adopted at birth by an army major and his wife. As he grew older he found this hard to accept. Adopted children sometimes feel antagonism towards their natural mother for having given them away. These feelings are often expressed by bitterness, hatred and rebellion towards the adopting mother.

- When Julian's parents were divorced, he was only thirteen years of age, and very vulnerable to the emotional fall-out. He lived with his mother from then on, but lacked the guidance, encouragement, and restraint of a father.

- His adult educational programme ended in one rejection experience after another. He enrolled in an Arts degree course at La Trobe university, but he lasted only six weeks. The following year (1987) he went to the Royal Military College at Duntroon, but being younger than most of the intake, he soon felt he was being badly treated. His rejection and low self-image soon showed, and climaxed when he stabbed one of his superiors in a Canberra night club. He resigned on request.

- A seventeen month relationship with a Melbourne young lady had been terminated by the shift to Canberra. The ex-fiancee later spoke of Julian's excessive tearfulness, and his difficulty in coming to grips with his adoption, and with his parents' divorce. At one point she suggested that he seek psychiatric help.

- The events preceding the night of mass-murders pushed Julian's massive rejection past the critical point of control. Firstly, he first slighted because he had not been invited to a party at his ex-girlfriend's house. Secondly, around 5 pm on the afternoon of the shootings, the gearbox in his car broke down after he had left a friend's house. That depressed him because he had planned to sell the vehicle to repay debts. Thirdly, he tried to obtain solace by drinking for several hours at a hotel bar, and during this time he was rebuffed by a barmaid. This finally triggered his emotions into mindless fury. Returning home, he went straight to the cache of arms he kept under his mother's bed, and took an M14 rifle, a pump action shotgun, and an automatic carbine. The rest, tragically, is history.

His rejection, resentment, bitterness, and hatred had turned him into an anti-social monster, now caged for the community's protection.

At the time of writing two men have been charged with the murder of their estranged wives in Sydney. One is alleged to have poured petrol over his ex-wife and set her on fire as she waited with their five year old daughter for an elevator in an apartment block. The blazing woman travelled down twelve floors by elevator, and ran screaming into the lobby where the flames were extinguished by the janitor. She received burns to 100% of her body, and could only be identified by dental charts.

The other man is alleged to have stabbed his wife at least twelve times as she lay in bed. Neighbours found her, barely conscious, lying on blood-soaked bedding. She died in hospital shortly afterwards.

Unhappy marriages are breeding grounds for rejection. While some couples stick together for the children's sake, or keep up appearances in front of their friends, others head straight for separation or divorce. So often, the marital atmosphere is tense with resentment and bitterness. Some partners withdraw, and privately express their hurts, in weeping and depression. Others burn with suspicion, or jealousy, and become openly aggressive particularly if the other partner confesses to infidelity, or is proved to be unfaithful. Jealousy sometimes turns into a compulsive desire for revenge, even murder, despite the guilty party knowing he or she will be a prime suspect. '... *for jealousy arouses a husband's fury, and he will show no mercy when he takes revenge'* (Proverbs 6:34).

Violence and murder can therefore be the direct descendants of rejection. While the world focuses on punishing offenders, the church's role is to deny Satan grounds for rejection by winning lives to Jesus Christ.

Chapter 7

Rejection and Onions Have
a Lot in Common

The first (and facetious) comment is that they can both produce
tears! But the real comparison is that rejection can also grow layer
upon layer, tightly compacted like the concentric rings of an onion.
The multi-layered rejection syndrome is far more pungent and long-
lasting than an onion, unless Jesus Christ stops the process and heals
the victim.

'Sue's' testimony, is supplemented by my case notes. It illustrates
both the layering process and the total freedom Jesus Christ gives,
and is used by special permission.

The core of rejection

'I was an only child. My mother's health was so bad that she was
advised against having any children . . .'

Layer 1

'I had a bad instrumental birth, and still carry scars on my thigh. The
doctor thought my mother had died, and expressed his preference
for my death rather than my mother's . . .'

Layer 2

'I broke my leg at sixteen months and my mother was blamed for it,
so she kept me from walking for a long time after my leg healed . . .'

Layer 3

'My father was a perfectionist, and expected me to be perfect. Whenever he saw me do something wrong, he really punished me ...'

Layer 4

'I hated school. Every day at a certain time the boys would corner me, hold me on the ground, and molest me. When that didn't satisfy them, they inserted objects into me. This went on for four years, and I was scared to tell anyone because I had been threatened ...'

Layer 5

'Because I was left-handed, my teachers constantly humiliated me in the classroom, and I was forced to use my right hand ...'

Layer 6

'When I was 7, my father became very ill with cancer. The last time I saw him was on my 8th birthday. I carried my cake into his room and found him in tears. He told me it broke his heart that he wouldn't see me grow up. I used to plead with God not to take him, even threatening not to love God if my father died ...'

Layer 7

'As my father lingered on I was sent away from home for six months and seldom saw my mother during that time. I began to have bad nightmares. I started to wet the bed frequently and was punished for it. I felt a wreck, and desperately wanted love, but no one reached out a hand to me. The boys continued their torment ...'

Layer 8

'When my father died, I was not allowed to go to the funeral, but was made to attend school where the kids mocked me.

I hated God for taking my father from me. Hadn't I constantly prayed for him, and even threatened not to love God if he died? In my misery I reasoned that God could not be a God of love. Mum wanted to commit suicide. In my hatred, I tore my Bible into shreds trying to kill the god within me. Then a demon had sex with me one night as a seal on what I had done ...'

Layer 9

'After returning home from visiting Dad's relatives overseas, an older female cousin sexually molested me, which caused me to dislike her intensely ...'

Layer 10

'At the age of 9 I was alone so much that I began to talk to an imaginary friend. I later found that I had made contact with a familiar spirit. By the time I was 10, I realised I had occult powers but my mother warned me against using them. A friend later hypnotised me without my knowing it, and told me I wouldn't be able to use the powers any more ...'

Layer 11

'When I was 11 years old I began to menstruate heavily, and lose weight. Then I was raped by a supposed family friend. When I told Mum she nearly killed him. He was charged with the offence but only received a fine, although he had had 16 previous convictions for the same offence. After the court hearing he saw me in town, and threatened to kill me if he ever saw me again ...'

Layer 12

'When I was 12, I was sent to a church boarding schol. The headmistress told me that because I had been raped, I would never again be clean and pure in God's sight. So I hated myself. The girls in the school found out what had happened, and asked me cruel questions about sex. They thought I was strange as I often woke up screaming. They didn't know that "something" was having sex with me. One night I saw a dark object leave my bed, then I knew that I had not just been dreaming ...'

Layer 13

'My mother had lots of men-friends. One molested me, and when I told her, she wouldn't believe me. She defended the man involved, and told me I had caused her enough trouble as it was. What hurt me so deeply was the rejection I felt when she said she wished she had never had me. In my case I was supposed to have been a boy, not a girl! ...'

Layer 14

'From the age of 16 to 17, things didn't improve. My mother's ten month marriage came to an end when my step-father died. Later, another man moved in. Then our greatly respected family doctor molested me badly, and told me some awful things about sex. Since then I just have not been able to consult a male doctor ...'

Layer 15

'When I was nineteen I was brutally raped in my flat. I was scared to tell my mother because I feared that she might go to the police, after what had happened previously. I could no longer live alone, so shifted to another city and flatted with a girl friend, getting into drugs and alcohol ...'

Layer 16

'To get away from the drug scene I moved in with a much older guy who was very jealous. If another man just looked at me when he was drunk, he would kick me, beat me up mercilessly, then demand sex. One night it was so bad I thought I was going to die. The next day I was so bruised all over that the "de facto" told me to tell people that I had had a car accident. I left him, fearing that he might kill me in a tantrum ...'

Layer 17

'From that time onwards I mixed with people who were involved in spiritism, and learned everything I could about the black arts, from tarot cards to mind reading. I consulted many palm-readers and mediums. I found I could use mental telepathy to get my mother to call me any time I wanted. I also learned how to do "astral travel" in my dreams. The night before my step-father died I "visited" two people in another city and told them I had dreamt of his death. Two months later these two people went to my mother and told her that I had come to them as a "ghost", and had spoken to them ...'

Layer 18

'By the time I was 21, I was so starved of love that I had had sixteen relationships with men, most of whom turned out to be into some form of perversion which I hated intensely. One fellow caused me to be physically sick by forcing me to have sex with his best friend while he took photographs.

I left, and moved in with a Christian woman whom I learned afterwards had been praying for me. Two days later, I went with her to church and trusted Jesus Christ to be my personal Saviour. Then began a period of discipleship training which took me overseas ...'

Layer 19

'In a place where I worked as a telephone counsellor, another Christian girl and I became close friends. This made me feel safe because of my hatred of men. But then I found that I had been trapped by a lesbian. The relationship lasted for a short time. By now I was 23. After further travel, I returned home to my mother who was going through her latest divorce ...'

Layer 20

'Even after becoming a Christian, in my mid and late twenties I was raped twice. On two occasions I have loaned men considerable sums of money, and not a cent has been repaid. Because I was never able to know my father, I have struggled with being able to understand God's love as a heavenly father.'

Because 'Sue' had a strong aversion to men, Phyl obtained the information she needed, and commenced to pray for her. The demonic forces which had gained more and more control over her soon showed intense opposition during the time of deliverance, despite the fact that she had been genuinely born again and longed to be free. Phyl then invited me to join her in what turned out to be a three-hour fight in the powerful name of Jesus Christ against forces of darkness.

First of all 'Sue' said dreamily 'I'm on another planet.' This was of course a diversionary tactic by a spirit of astral travel which was forced to leave. Then 'Sue's' fingers became twisted and rigid causing her considerable pain. This normally indicates that demons of lust are active, but in 'Sue's' case, strong spirits of anti-Christ were also manifesting themselves because those fingers had torn up a Bible under their influence. Then she tried to throttle each of us in turn, but told us afterwards that we both seemed to be protected by what she thought were protective steel bands around our throats. The Lord was indeed our strength and shield, and when the time of deliverance, cleansing, and prayer for wholeness was ended, she felt totally forgiven, clean, and a new person inside. She walked outside the house, then came back and told us 'Everything looks so different to me'. She then slept for two and a half hours, and during this time the Lord revealed himself to her saying that she had been a beautiful rose whose petals had been plucked, as she was slowly being dragged into hell. In his open hand were the fallen petals which he had picked up, one at a time, as he had waited to give her eternal life. When we saw her later that night she looked radiant, and her eyes were shining.

'Sue' has kept in touch with us since then. She very unexpectedly turned up at an advanced deliverance seminar in a city not far from where she was living and told us that she had been raped twice since we had seen the Lord free her. It was obvious that she was still bound by a spirit of the 'lust of man'. (I had come across a case like this once before in Japan when a trained nurse told me that she felt unclean. Although other nurses had given way to some doctors' sexual demands, she had refused their advances because she was a Christian. After the Lord revealed to me the nature of this oppressive spirit, and I had broken the bondage of the 'lust of man' in the name of Jesus Christ, she immediately cried out, 'That's it. I feel clean again.')

So we prayed with 'Sue' and the Lord freed and cleansed her from a sense of defilement, guilt, and the fear of man. By the grace of God, thirty years of tragedy gave way to a future of companionship with Jesus Christ.

Multi-layered rejection can also be likened to a compost bed in which many other seeds grow, and produce fruit. Demon powers will quickly take advantage of every negative, hurtful, or unfortunate experience. They either bind their victims with guilt, hopelessness, and a conviction that they will never be forgiven and made clean again, or drive them relentlessly to do whatever the demons desire even if the sufferers hate what they are being forced to do.

Satan always takes the greatest advantage of rejection's fallout – low self-image, withdrawal, guilt, and desperate feelings of being forever trapped in a state of hopelessness and despair. Daily living soon becomes downgraded to mere painful existence.

The tragedy of this situation is that the person being crushed by the tightening rings of rejection did not personally initiate the syndrome, but simply became enmeshed in a succession of circumstances from which there were no clearly marked exits. At the lower levels of self-evaluation sound reasoning disappears, and the victim often is unconsciously deceived. For example, the benign front-window display of occultism offers spiritual powers for self-realisation without having to worry about sin and repentance associated with traditional religion. A blurred perspective of self-worth also causes some women to seek the approval of men by offering them sexual favours which they imagine will transform their deep feelings of rejection into self-worth and self-acceptance. Regrettably, this is wishful thinking, and greater guilt and self-rejection always results, sometimes forcing them into greater bondages such as prostitution, lesbianism or trans-sexuality. The transitory euphoric relief they may gain in their emotional prison does nothing to shorten the sentence they serve. Only Jesus Christ can set them free.

Most of us scan the faces of the people we pass in the street, but we neither know, nor could we possibly imagine, some of the human tragedies they have possibly passed through.

Here is another example of the growing and overpowering effects of the rejection syndrome.

'Pam's' mother left home when she was two years of age. Because her father was a shift worker, she slept in a different home almost every night. She was blamed for her father's desire to commit suicide, and even for the death of her step-brother who was really her only friend, protecting her from the unfair treatment of other family members. From a child she hated herself, and when she was 12 or 13 years old, her mother kidnapped her from school and took her to a city hundreds of kilometres away from her father. She was forbidden to write to him, and was virtually kept a prisoner for around fifteen months.

From the time she was 3 years old her brothers and cousins started having sexual experiences with her. When she was 5, they forced her to do sexual acts with a family pet. She told us she felt physically sick and wanted to die (and that always causes the entry of spirits of rejection and death). Her father had had sexual intercourse with her on two occasions, and from the age of 10, a sister had forced her into acts of lesbianism. She had also been raped twice.

It was no wonder she grew up rebellious, defiant, and prone to the

71

same violence the family had experienced for generations. She had attempted suicide three times, and murder three times. One attempt very nearly succeeded.

In adulthood, 'Pam' turned to alcohol, drugs, gluttony, psychiatry, occultism and witchcraft for solace, but the sexual degradation by men and demonic domination only increased.

By the time 'Pam' came for ministry she had been a Christian several years, and had even been a Bible school student. Despite that, she had no assurance of salvation, was loaded with rejection, self-rejection, fear of rejection, and was still dominated by occult spirits which openly challenged us during her time of deliverance. Since being saved, she had continued to drag around the spiritual carcass of her past, because no one had either been sensitive to her desperate need, or knew how to free her from the evil forces which dominated her. Since finding freedom, 'Pam' has become a strong Christian intent on seeing others set free, as she herself had been.

These last two case histories do not establish a standard multiple-rejection pattern. Firstly, some people may have a lesser number of incidents causing rejection, yet they may be more deeply affected. Secondly, sexual experiences, and occultic or witchcraft involvements are not necessary for a person to have suffered from multiple-rejection.

Here are some further 'onion-skin' examples of people whom the Lord has set free:

Example 1
'Peg's' father remained single for 50 years, then married a widow with five children. Her mother was very sick when she was born, so her first six months were spent in a children's hospital. Because her mother made no pretence of liking her new daughter, she left home when she was 16. As a parting shot, her mother cursed her saying, 'I hope your kids do the same to you one day, and you end up with a knife in your back!' After 'Peg' was married, her husband's mother kidnapped her two children when they were aged 3 and 4, and she saw little of them for the next 20 years, during which time court battles were fought over custody rights.

'Peg' came for prayer in her fifties, carrying the accumulated pressures of rejection which began in utero, and continued through childhood and teenage years into married life.

Example 2

'Kate's' mother had had 21 pregnancies of which only seven children were born, (one dying later). Fourteen of the pregnancies had been terminated by medication. The six living children were girls, much to the chagrin of the father, who openly expressed his displeasure by calling each daughter 'son'. When 'Kate' was 13 years old, her mother died, adding another layer of rejection. She grew up hating men, particularly after she became a single mother. She withdrew, and had difficulty in restraining her anger towards her child. She was also relentlessly driven to smoke and gamble by compulsive hereditary spirits which further increased her self-rejection. Although she was an attractive looking woman in her mid-thirties when she came to see us, 'Kate's' accumulated layers of rejection, from childhood onwards, had robbed her of any degree of self-worth. She was convinced that other people felt the same about her as she thought about herself. In this way she had robbed herself of any anticipation of future fulfillment.

After deliverance, she forgave herself for her self-restricting attitudes, and willingly committed herself to a biblical programme of self-adjustment to live as God intended she should, as a daughter of the King of Kings.

Example 3

One of the most distressing cases of multi-layered rejection I have dealt with was a young lady who had been so constantly rejected and dominated by her alcoholic mother that she was forced to leave school at an early age to become a wage earner. 'Jean's' mother took all her wages and used most of them to buy alcohol. She lay idly around the house all day, ordering 'Jean' around like a dog, and forcing her to do all the housework. Her mother also took a sadistic delight in tormenting the girl by threatening to commit suicide. Occasionally she would sneak outside and discharge a firearm just to enjoy the panic she caused.

After the Lord had freed 'Jean' from the many layers of rejection in her past, and given her mental and emotional wholeness, she spontaneously and joyfully said, 'The Lord has shown me that the future has nothing to do with the past.' What a powerful statement!

Example 4

'Butch' came for deliverance with a written list of past events which had preceded an unstable marriage and the birth of five children. The ever growing and tightening rings of rejection were obvious:

1. 'My mother considered my conception was too close to my elder brother ...'

2. 'My birth was precipitated by my mother having a fall two weeks before I was due to be born. It was a very quick delivery ...'

3. 'My parents were extremely poor at the time...'

4. 'I suffered from traumatic and terrifying dreams in early childhood ...'

5. 'My earliest recollections were of feeling rejected and being full of fear. When my next sister was born I was not much more than two years old, and still remember the feelings of absolute devastation on being separated from my parents for three weeks ...'

6. 'For 10 years I was a middle child, then another sister was born ...'

7. 'I was a very insecure child, always demanding attention and generally being difficult. For punishment I was usually shut in my bedroom until I was prepared to be nice ...'

8. 'I thought my rejection and punishment were caused by being caught, rather than being the result of bad behaviour ...'

9. 'Although I had no problem coping with my schooling, I constantly felt socially inadequate ...'

10. 'As a boy I was a petty thief, although I never needed what I stole. I was never caught, and lied shamelessly to avoid any possibility of blame. In fact, I still have difficulty in confessing wrong ...'

11. 'In early adolescence I indulged in sexual fantasies, initially to cope with the assorted fears which ruled my life and made sleep difficult. This led to masturbation and a lustful pre-occupation with the female form. Even now I have to battle constantly against lustful thinking.'

One of the most interesting features of 'Butch's' rejection syndrome was that it was not deliberately caused by his parents. 'My parents were good living, loving, nominal Christians who treated their family well. My father was a kind, gentle, sensitive person. My mother administered the discipline.'

His growing sense of rejection came from three sources. Firstly, he was an innocent victim of the timing and circumstances of his birth and early life. No one was to blame. Secondly, his own introvertive reactions to each rejection experience added further layers. Thirdly, his attention-seeking activities of naughtiness, stealing, and lying, together with his sexual fantasy and masturbation only added to his self-rejection and fears.

Example 5

One final instance of this childhood through adulthood increasing syndrome comes from 'Henry', a 40 year old who reluctantly came for help:

1. His father was murdered and his mother 'slept around'. As a boy he lived with his grandmother who died when he was 7 years old. He then returned home to a step-father whom he believes was 'demon-possessed' and who used to physically abuse the family.

2. At 9 years of age, 'Henry' tried to murder his step-father with a knife, but his intended victim rolled over in the bed, just as he struck.

3. He kept running away from home, and lived in a railway station for six months. At 10 years of age he responded to an altar-call and felt God was there to help him.

4. At the age of 12, he was committed to the care of a minister of religion who turned out to be a homosexual. When propositioned, he refused.

5. Vietnam was a heavy experience for 'Henry' and he suffered the rejection all the veterans felt on returning home. His sexual experiences with the Vietnamese bar-girls and other women is not suitable to print.

6. He admitted to having been a 'hit-man' and a social and religious rebel. Some of his confessions must remain confidential.

'Henry' had previously had some bad experiences when people tried to help him, and was wary of further ministry. But God did a real work in him. Regrettably, I lost contact with him after a week. I later learned that he had returned to one of his more frequent places of residence – prison, but a recent report was that he is again facing up to spiritual realities. Satan never gives in easily. Unless his victims are deeply repentant, and equally determined to follow Jesus Christ in true discipleship, the roots and fruit of rejection may need to be dealt with more than once.

Conclusions

1. Rejection which commences in utero or at birth often provides a basic core around which layers of rejection will continue to grow and consolidate.
2. Rejection does not disappear just because its crippling effects have been diagnosed. It controls attitudes, relationships, and conduct.
3. Attempts to alleviate the pain of rejection may lead to addictions such as overeating, drugs, alcohol, lust, or occultism. They in turn add yet more to the rejection syndrome.
4. Hopelessness and despair are very often the most bitter fruit of rejection, and may cause suicide, or murder.
5. When two rejected people marry, they often cause and receive further rejection. Unless this growing problem is counteracted, adultery may occur, and the marriage end in separation, or divorce.
6. Deliverance from the fruit of rejection such as fear, rebellion, anger, withdrawal, addiction to food, or lustful behaviour, will not remove the three-fold root systems of rejection, self-rejection, and fear of rejection.
7. Like onions, rejection may grow layer upon layer, but methodical deliverance will destroy the entire evil structure.

Chapter 8

'The Basement, Please'

Withdrawal caused by rejection was likened, in part one, to a snail disappearing inside its shell when danger is sensed. Illustrations were also given to show how people act similarly.

Although the number of rejection sufferers who withdraw deeply is small compared to the number who show other manifestations, this syndrome needs closer examination. There may be readers who will identify with the problems which will emerge in further case histories.

When teaching participants in deliverance seminars about deep withdrawal, we have used the term 'mole syndrome'. Although the mole is not native to Australia, few will not have read about its underground life. In fact, we often call exaggeration 'making a mountain out of a mole-hill'.

In this chapter we will add a further description – 'basement living'. This rejection pattern applies to men and women who withdraw to the safety of their own inner world whenever they feel threatened. They usually look no different to anyone else, but when you ring their communication 'door-bell', no one answers. This makes them characteristically different from those who merely withdraw.

Victims of 'basement living' usually guard their private lives carefully, and may even 'switch off' in the middle of general conversation, if they feel their privacy is being threatened.

Basic causes

(1) Hereditary apathy
The Concise Oxford Dictionary defines 'apathy' as 'Insensibility to

suffering; passionless existence; lack of interest or desire'. Its root is the Greek word *apatheia* – without feeling. It is particularly a male characteristic and comes down from one generation to another.

While physical inactivity may be the most noticeable symptom, the avoidance of decision-making and the lack of authority or discipline in a family home seriously affect the children of intensely apathetic fathers. In reviewing case histories we have frequently found that this spirit has come down from the paternal grandfather, through the father to the grandson. The bad home example makes each generation think it is normal living.

(2) Crushing by a dominant or manipulating person

A permanent state of unresponsiveness may be a defensive reaction to over-possessiveness. Parents may cause this in their children, or in one another, but more frequently an insecure, jealous, or self-protective wife may 'smother' her husband, leaving him unable to express a personal opinion or initiate anything that does not have her approval. Casual observers may conclude that the couple are ideally suited to one another because they appear to be in love. But careful attention to the husband's conversation may suggest that the relationship is not all that it appears. 'Yes dear; no dear; I agree with you dear; what do you think dear?; I'll do whatever you say, dear'. Suddenly a picture in your memory bank lights up – that very large woman you once saw waddling down the road with a diminutive and meek little man trotting at her side. Very occasionally roles are reversed, and the male dominates.

(3) The only child, or spoilt child syndrome

The only child is often a spoilt child, but a spoilt child may not be an only child.

Loving mothers are a delight to watch, but doting mothers are a danger to society. Pampered children never seem to grow out of expecting to receive special treatment, even as adults.

An ordained minister, a medical practitioner, a highly qualified nurse, and a watchmaker/jeweller all came for ministry over a period of time. They all had similar backgrounds, and problems:

- Each one had, or had had a strong manipulating mother, and most of their fathers had been passive.

- Each one had a time-consuming activity which they used as a convenient form of escapism.

- Each one had a withdrawn personality, although outwardly appearing to be friendly.
- Each one had difficulty in effective one-to-one communication, particularly those who were married.
- Each one was grossly self-centred.

Evident symptoms of 'basement-living'

As with all physical and psychological problems, the range and severity can vary considerably. Here are some descriptions of 'basement people':

1. They may be egocentric, self-protective and selfish, keeping anyone or anything at arm's length which threatens to unsettle them.
2. They are very insecure, but may appear to be proud, arrogant or 'have their act together'.
3. Most are passive, and are lacking self-motivation and self-discipline.
4. Apathy, lethargy, laziness and complaints of excessive tiredness are usually apparent.
5. Many are ambivalent, therefore indecisive.
6. Most are full of self-pity, and wilfully insensitive to others.
7. They are unwilling to communicate, or do so on their own terms and conditions.
8. Most will protect themselves with excuses, excuses and more excuses. They frequently express disappointment in others.
9. Fear of the future, and fear of old age are frequently shown.
10. Deep apathy may freeze any display of emotion, so that others may think they don't care. To get 'kicks' some of them flirt with death.

This type of rejection may not afflict as many people as other syndromes, but it may begin in childhood and be quite devastating in later life.

Illustrations of the syndrome

- 'Campbell' was born prematurely by Caesarian section. His parents were reserved English folk and had no real friends. As the lad grew up, he withdrew, became rebellious, a loner, and anti-social. He wore long hair, joined a hippy commune, and used drugs. His grandfather had been a follower of Rudolph Steiner's philosophy. He investigated Hinduism, then became a Hare Krishna devotee.

Sometime later 'Campbell' became a Christian. He came to see us at the request of his pastor. We found him extremely passive, lazy, lacking in both motivation and enthusiasm. He answered our questions listlessly, endlessly repeating the words, 'a little ... a little'. Fortunately the Lord helped more than 'a little'. He was re-vitalised.

- 'Jack' held a respected professional position in a country town. He was married and a father, but lived a double lifestyle. At work he was efficient, highly respected, and diligent. But at home, he changed from the moment he opened his front gate. The long grass and weeds didn't disturb him in the slightest. He just didn't notice them or the obvious repair jobs crying out to be done in and around the house. After all, he was just too exhausted because of his exacting workload. He probably had never been overtired by using a dishtowel, because he wouldn't allow anything to come between himself and his obsession – restoring a vintage car. This involved a few hours work and endless hours talking with his car-buff friends, at their place, of course.

  Then the Lord changed him, and put his marriage back together again. In an open testimony session at his church he introduced himself to the congregation as 'the new me'. Jesus Christ had been put first, his wife and family second, becoming useful in the kingdom of God, third. I believe an unrestored vintage car is still around, somewhere!

- 'Jack' intrigued me the first time I saw him while lecturing a counselling class. He sat in one corner separated from all the other students by the ring of chairs he had carefully arranged round himself. I had seldom seen such a 'mole-hill'. That made me determined to try to help the man. It turned out to be a much more difficult and time-consuming task than I had anticipated. He did some journalling for me which was certainly helpful but what he wrote was disjointed, time-wise.

  'My mother has verbally abused me from the age of four, and

thirty-two years later is still at it. She was very critical of my failures, short-comings, friends and girl friends. I was openly criticised, punished, and demeaned by vile comments in front of those I cared about.

For eight years, until I was twelve, I was beaten almost daily. It was unprovoked, and often vicious. I was whipped from head to foot, often on my face, and the welts showed for days. I was also punched, strapped, and made to stand still while my mother threw objects at me. She favoured my younger brother, and refused to stop him stealing from me.

After my mother's beatings stopped, my father showed me his hatred, and constantly put me down until he died. I was twenty years of age, by then. I had recurring nightmares that my father was a black man trying to kill me. He made me stay around the house and help him entire weekends, week after week. He was cold, incommunicative, and disinterested in me as a person. I spent hundreds and hundreds of hours with my father, and during that time I recall only two in-depth conversations, one after he had ground out a cigarette in my hand, then apologised in remorse. The other was just before he died when he apologised from the "bottom of his heart" for having been such "a lousy father".

My twin sister had excessive fears, and clung to me. I was made to take care of her, and she attracted me sexually. I felt responsible for the nightmares she continually experienced, and felt very guilty about it.'

'Jack' also wrote of:

- a homosexual teacher who dominated and humiliated him, but who did not touch him sexually.
- some fourteen people or organisations who had hurt him, or from whom he had received rejection. God was included.
- constant masturbation for self-comfort.
- a brother who had rejected him by trying to kill him.
- a self-image which was 'the scum and offscouring of the earth'.
- being gripped by fears, dominated by nightmares, and cursed by the fortune-telling and witchcraft activities of his father. (He had also dabbled in evil powers himself.)
- the rejection which had been in his family for many generations.

In spite of all this background, 'Jack' was a believer in Jesus Christ, and although he was a defeated Christian, there was a sound basis to work on. Every one of his long list of problems had come from heredity and the ceaseless rejection to which he had been subjected. Up to that point, 'Jack's' whole life had been spent in 'basement living'.

It took many hours of deliverance ministry, counsel, prayer, and sharing the love of Jesus Christ to see him freed. When we parted, he was rejoicing, and knew he was free. But he was also well aware that to maintain his freedom he had to constantly make right choices to break well established habits. When God does his part, he expects us to do our part, otherwise we simply mark time, spiritually.

Before moving on to the next phase of rejection, we need to understand that there is at least one physical cause of 'basement living' (or the 'mole syndrome'). People who suffer from acute kidney dysfunction, and who depend on dialysis are often severely restricted in their lifestyle, and find themselves forced to live semi-isolated lives. Rejection is a natural by-product which can produce the same symptoms as those outlined for the other listed causes. These people need special love, care, and attention, particularly if their physical condition remains unchanged. Unlike those whose root systems can be released solely by deliverance, these sufferers need special spiritual help to become, and remain overcomers.

Chapter 9

Who Needs Parents Anyway?

When 'June' was four years old, her father developed meningitis. Because he was so ill, she was not allowed to see him, and because her mother spent all her time nursing her dad, she was virtually cut off from her mother also. An eight year-old sister was left to look after her. As a result the four-year old rejected her parents, and began to live in her own fantasy world. But more of that later.

In *Deliver Our Children From the Evil One*, special attention was given to rejection experienced in the womb, by babies because of traumatic births, or through the events of early childhood. In this chapter we will look at the effects on children who reject their parents during their developmental years and the results that extend right on into adulthood.

Childhood rejection of parents opens a 'Pandora's box' of problems

In Greek mythology this box allegedly contained 'Hope'. But when it was rashly opened, all other blessings were lost, or all kinds of ills were let loose on mankind, (Concise Oxford Dictionary). Greek mythology is hardly suitable for Christian teaching, but the principle is a sound one. All the hope and aspirations which parents may have for each child may vanish, and be replaced by a growing number of life-changing difficulties and problems if a child believes that he or she has been rejected. Whether that rejection has been open, is implied, or just imaginary, the results will be the same. Many adults have confessed to having rejected one or both of their parents in their early years, either as an act of retaliation, or self-protection. In every case, the feelings of rejection became an emotional 'compost-heap' from which associated problems and other evil seeds have germinated, and become reproducing.

'June' illustrates both of these points. From the time of her perceived rejection, she began to assert her own independence, and concentrated on music and playing tennis. She reached grade eight in her violin playing. When both her music teacher and tennis coach committed suicide, she was devastated and wanted to die. She had thought seriously of suicide, read books on psychic phenomena, embraced abstract art, and rock and roll. She had also read extensively about pyramidology and UFO's, and became obsessed with insects, bats, snakes, and frogs. She had searched museums to look at shrunken heads.

'June' was aggressive, violent, swore constantly and used obscene language. As a perfectionist in some activities she was uncompromising. She was also apathetic, passive, lazy, and depressed. She masturbated daily, imagining incest with her father, and indulged in some very gross sexual activities including demonic experiences. She felt tormented, suffered ulcers, pain and sickness, and was full of fears.

When she was twenty years of age Jesus Christ totally freed her as we prayed and ministered deliverance for two hours. After sixteen turbulent years of a chaotic lifestyle, the roots of her childhood feelings of rejection and her unilateral independence from her parents were removed, and she started again as a submissive child of her heavenly Father.

God obviously intended parents and children to blend harmoniously in a mutually respecting partnership called a family. When difficult circumstances severely strain that relationship, or it is broken by illness, death, or divorce, it is the children who suffer most. Parent rejection often understandably follows, but its effects on a child can be dramatic, and life-changing.

God accused Israel of having rebelled against him, and rejection of him. The great Old Testament prophets Isaiah and Jeremiah both commenced their writings with God's indictment against his people for having rejected him, and for their unfaithfulness in doing whatever appealed to them. By the time Jeremiah's ministry ended, his generation were either dead or in captivity; the land had been devastated by war, and over-run by foreigners.

The Word of God makes it very clear that children and their parents, and God's children and their heavenly Father are bonded together by a special covenant of love to which children are required to submit. When a child of either family rejects this relationship, the parenting process and the protection it brings can no longer function effectively. At that stage children who reject their parents will attempt to set their own boundaries and guidelines even though they continue living in the family home. By doing so they unknowingly expose themselves to Satan. Just as marauding animals and birds will attack an injured and defenseless member of their own kind, so the evil one will swoop on any child who tries to go it alone.

Some of the symptoms of the 'mole (or basement) syndrome' also apply to the 'I'll-go-it-alone' syndrome. They include:

Emotional immaturity
Children need to have behavioural boundaries for their well-being and security. Those who have inwardly declared their independence from parental control will find that their emotional hurts (real or imaginary) will be greatly increased and will accumulate with time, hindering full emotional development. Without openly declaring their parental rejection, their attitudes and conduct will cause family criticism and possible punishment, as they grow. But this only increases their feelings of rejection, and in their own eyes further justifies the step they have taken. Self-defensive actions include anger, accusations of injustice, stubbornness, disobedience, emotional coldness, hardness, pride, and a self-protective screen of indifference.

'Beware – this animal bites!'
Some children, teenagers, and adults should display a notice like this on their personality cages. They want to be left alone; will attack in self-defence; spit critical tirades at anyone who says one word out of place; and growl defensively if anyone gets closer than they ought. Parent-rejecters are usually more defensive or verbally offensive than those who suffer from the normal type of rejection.

'Don't call me a child – I'm grown up now'
If a ten year-old were to say this, it would seem entirely out of place, but some of them do, and believe it to be true. Children in this

category actually may also reject their own childhood. When a three year old child says (as one did to us), 'When I was a little girl', something has obviously gone sadly wrong.

Some children will deliberately set themselves the goal of learning and doing what older young people do, either to make themselves appear more mature than they actually are, or because they genuinely believe that they have reached that level of sophistication.

'I'll prove that I'm OK'
Mention has been made of the use of education in the 'mole-basement' syndrome. It is also a feature of teenagers and adults who have rejected parental advice, or refused to accept approval if given. They feel compelled to prove their own ability to themselves and to others. Reaching for academic excellence sometimes becomes an obsession, but it does little to establish emotional maturity.

The appeal of the supernatural
Supernatural experiences can exhilarate a child or teenager who has begun to 'manage' his or her life. The false self-worth received amounts to a sense of power, but the new friendships gained only create more problems. The growing fears, delusion and relentless demonic control are often not realised until it is too late to withdraw. Only God knows how many witches were rejected children who in turn rejected their parents, and found comfort and 'family' in supernaturalism.

Becoming sexually active
Rejected children are an easy prey for lustful adults who offer 'love' with gifts of money, or drugs for sexual favours. God designed sexual relations as his beautiful wedding present to married couples. Sadly, today's society regards it as the friendliest thing any two people can do together. So perverts and paedophiles drag 'love' through the lustful sewers of their sexual desires and corrupt unprotected children. Some ghouls even get rich by forcing them to 'perform' for debased pornographic film-making.

The tragedy is that illicit sex usually ignites an unquenchable fire of lust which often leads to prostitution or the vile sexual practices of Satan worship.

So what begins with child-rejection and counter-rejection may balloon into tragedies of the greatest magnitude. It is no wonder that many turn to drugs to cope with their feelings of worthlessness, shame, and abject hopelessness. Some commit suicide.

The redeeming power of Jesus Christ is the only permanent way of escape for those trapped people. Lauren Stratford became the sexual pawn of her mother in exchange for favours of dirty old men when only a small child. Johanna Michaelson, author of *The Beautiful Side of Evil* was greatly used by God in reclaiming her in adulthood from ritualistic sexual abuse. She encouraged her to write her tragic story. It can be read in *Satan's Underground* (Harvest House).

Living in fantasy land

Escapism often becomes a life-long 'art-form' to children who reject their parents. The fantasy inspired by fairy tales, comics like 'Batman' and 'Spiderman', and children's games simply grows to adult-size. Day dreaming becomes a time-wasting habit, while the excitement of space exploration games, films and books, together with demonic play-acting as in 'Dungeons and Dragons' (and many similar games), are waiting to trap them in a world of dangerous, but exciting demonic delusion.

People of all ages who are trying to escape the rejection syndrome they have helped to create may also search for a personal hero in comics, books, or film and video viewing. When one is found they will either intentionally or subconsciously adopt that character (whether real or fictional) as an alter-ego role model. Problems arise when their thinking becomes so divided that they really don't know which person they are. Some of our counsellees have had to be delivered from false personality demonic spirits such as 'Don Juan' or 'Don Quixote', and then receive spiritual healing, before being able to become undivided personalities once again.

Some people have a combination of problems, as the following case histories illustrate. Names have of course been changed, and identifying factors removed to prevent embarrassment to the real persons. Praise God, he liberated every one.

- 'Jock', a teenager was saved at the same time as his parents. Because they opened the family home to reach neighbours and friends for Jesus Christ, he felt neglected, so he rejected his parents, and embraced withcraft and immorality. His life continued to deteriorate until the Lord had mercy on him, and freed him from many oppressive spirits.

- 'Sonia' rejected her father because her mother disliked him. She stopped playing with dolls, and determined she would protect her mother from her father. She spurned her femininity, played aggressive outdoor sports, and rode horses. All this affected her hormonal balance, and by fourteen years of age her menstruation was irregular, and she had a lot of facial hair. She completed a music degree, and had feelings of sexual stimulation in astral travel caused by constantly listening to classical music. 'Sonia' enjoyed being an intellectual, and had one brush with lesbianism, but it didn't last. She experienced some deliverance, but because it had been ineffective, was fearful of never being freed. But she had underestimated the Lord's love and power, and publicly and joyfully testified to the complete change he brought about.

- 'Marguerite' was an only child. Her mother was an alcoholic, so she idolised her father, following him around the farm as much as possible. She rejected her femininity, and dolls, and refused to do household chores. She had great problems in accepting menstruation, and was devastated when her father died while she was still a teenager. Her rejection, loneliness, and insecurity caused her to seek fulfillment in education, and she finally graduated with her doctorate. But she remained emotionally starved, and went into long-term lesbian relationships for comfort. One of these lasted for over ten years until the Lord rescued her. The changes brought about by her freedom have come gradually, but despite remaining single, Jesus Christ is satisfying her emotional needs. Her many Christian friends are giving the companionship she lost when her father died, and which she never had with her mother. However, because 'Marguerite' has forgiven the wrongs in the past, she and her mother now relate well together.

- 'Donna' was born after her mother had lost twin boys. Because her parents had desperately wanted a 'replacement' boy, she was confused in her identity from early childhood, and rejected herself as a female. She also rejected her father, hated all men, and grew up wanting to murder her dad. She found satisfaction in intellectualism, and tried to surround herself with intellectual people. She was arrogant during deliverance sessions, and wanted ministry only from those with whom she felt intellectually compatible. The Lord soon changed that. When she was freed, everyone could see a softness in her eyes, and a total change of attitude and behaviour.

- 'Bronwyn's' parents were alcoholics. The father was a homosexual, the mother, a lesbian. She never had the carefree joys of childhood, and at the age of eight years was virtually parenting her mother and father who had separated, and was fulfilling adult entertainment responsibilities. All this caused her to age prematurely, so that when she was only a teenager she was as sophisticated as an adult. She had no idea how to relate to young people her own age. 'Bronwyn' had rejected her parents and their life-styles very early in life, but when Jesus Christ saved her as a teenager, he also freed her from a host of hereditary problems, as well as her whole double-rejection syndrome.

- 'Georgina's' mother became jealous of her relationship with her father when she was only 3 years old. She said to her constantly, 'You're a spoilt little bastard, you are a reincarnation of your dead older sister.'

'Georgina' naturally rejected her mother because of this. As a child she practised telekinesis, and was highly delighted when she was able to move an object with only the use of her eyes. As she grew older she used voodoo against another girl, and indulged in occultic and witchcraft practices as much as possible. Later, as a trained nurse she and another nurse used to place curses on geriatric patients. One night, she walked into a 'wall of cold' in one of the hospital corridors and felt that a spirit of terror had entered her. She began to fear snakes were in her bed, and often jumped out of bed during the night because her imagination was so vivid.

'Georgina' had been sexually molested at the ages of six, and ten, but was still a virgin. Her mother had told both her and her sister that she hoped that neither of them would have children. As a result both daughters had had to take drugs to ovulate. 'Georgina' soon dropped the drug-taking, and by the time she received deliverance she had not had a period for thirteen years. Her mother's antagonism to her father was very evident in her hatred for men. When Jesus Christ set her free, everything changed, and she publicly confessed this to a large group of her friends – with one arm around my waist!

The case histories could continue, but we need only enough to illustrate the 'double-rejection' syndrome. We have used one male testimony to this point, but we could speak of:

- 'Frank', who was beaten so badly that he left home when he was nine years of age and became a criminal.

- 'Franklin', who had lived in so many homes and attended so many schools that he became fed up with it all, and started running his own life. He became a homosexual. That is until Jesus Christ freed him, adjusted his sexual imbalance, and made him a first class husband and father.

- 'Hank' rejected his parents at fifteen because of his intolerable frustrations. He withdrew, became extremely angry, and although so intellectually gifted that he achieved every goal he aimed for, he gradually sank into a morbid state of self-rejection and hopelessness. His recovery after deliverance has been arduous, but is still continuing.

- 'Alfonso' did not overtly reject his parents, he was just so profoundly deaf that he curled up in his own fantasy world. At school he was regarded as 'dumb', and even a sister told him he was 'thick'. When he came for deliverance he was deeply apathetic, defeated, and very troubled sexually because of what his mother had done to him as a boy. The Lord helped him greatly, but regrettably Phyl and I had to move on before his freedom become established.

It may be that some very hurtful childhood memories have surfaced as you have read the contents of this chapter. Some parents and grandparents may also now understand why there were such sudden and inexplicable changes in their children, or grand-children, in their early years.

Although some causes of parent-rejection have been given, this chapter has concentrated more on how children are affected after spurning their parents. But one particular cause does need mentioning – the father who sexually molests or sexually penetrates his own daughter. The tragic long-term results are listed in *Deliver Our Children From the Evil One*. In many cases much greater damage is inflicted on the child if he or she tells the mother what 'daddy has done', and is not believed. It becomes much worse if the child is punished for 'making-up' lies about the father. Parental rejection always follows.

These illustrations come from counselling sessions with people in many countries. More could be given, but because of lack of space, and requests by some that we do not publicise their tragic stories, it is neither possible, nor needful. The syndrome has been clearly established.

One final important point. When ministering deliverance to anyone who rejected one or both parents as a child or teenager, we ask them to forgive the parent responsible, and repent of their rejection. When possible, (and advisable under the circumstances), we also suggest they ask for forgiveness. Some beautiful cases of reconciliation have taken place.

Chapter 10

Homo-sapiens, Rejection, and Homosexuality

The word 'homosexual' has two meanings according to the Concise Oxford Dictionary. The one more commonly known implies sexual activity between two people of the same sex. The other is 'relating to the same sex'. Both males and females mutually associate for genuine reasons such as accommodation, transport, missionary or social work, financial economy, a common love of the arts, music, sport, hobbies, or the great out-of-doors. With these people nothing could be further from their minds than sex.

Obviously the major thrust of this chapter is not about men or women in the second category, but of some people (often from Christian homes), whose homosexuality was the direct result of rejection received in early life. Each subject of the following case histories has claimed to be a born-again Christian.

Not many years ago, 'homosexuality' was almost a conversational 'no-no', or spoken of only in whispers. And little was known about lesbianism or feminism. Today, lesbians openly confess their sexual preference, and make constant demands with male homosexuals for public acceptance as an alternative lifestyle. Heterosexuals, and most Christians find themselves unable to agree, and it is generally remembered that the AIDS killer-virus was initially introduced to the Western world by homosexuals. But more of that subject later.

First of all we need to look quickly at some well-known causes of homosexual conduct, then concentrate on rejection as the first cause.

Hereditary spirits of homosexuality

Family spirits of this nature are very strong, and can cause homosexual tendencies to appear in even the smallest children.

Homosexual molestation

When older people indulge their sensual appetites by handling the genital areas of children or teenagers of the same sex, this usually causes a similar sexual urge to begin in their victims. Should this produce a sexual orgasm, cause an ejaculation, or involve oral sex, the homosexual desires will increase considerably. In cases of anal penetration by males, and vaginal insertion of objects by females, a demonic urge is certainly implanted in the victim to do the same to others, even to their own children if they marry and have a family. Despite initial shock and repugnance, the driving spirit will sooner or later torment its victim with fantasy temptations, or cause such acts to take place.

If children fall victim to paedophiles, or are shamelessly used for pornographic films, despite their incessant guilt and shame, they will be irresistibly driven to molest others as they themselves have been molested.

Deliberate choice

Even without the influence of heredity or molestation, some adults personally choose a homosexual lifestyle simply because it appeals to them. Others associate with their own sex for sport, recreation, or similar interests, and men and women quite innocently find themselves drawn into mutual friendships which in time develop into full homosexual relationships.

The unfortunate victims of hereditary homosexuality or molestation, will of course show every symptom of rejection, but that is not the basic cause of their homosexuality. The fact that the perpetrator may have been a rejected person does not mean that spirits of rejection are passed on with the homosexuality because there is no transfer of genes. The implications of the unnatural acts will be sufficient to cause the rejection syndrome to commence.

From now on, we will focus on these cases in which rejection, or hereditary rejection, cause homosexual activity. To give explicit details of the cesspit into which some have fallen would be in bad taste, so case histories will be appropriately 'sanitised'.

1. The influence of a passive or weak-willed father

Every boy and girl needs the security of strong fatherhood. When fathers are weak-willed, indecisive, and express no opinions at all, the children may feel ashamed of them in front of their friends, and develop rejection. It is also an hereditary condition. Boys find this harder to cope with than girls, particularly when the male parent shows little or no interest in their educational or sporting activities. In their longing for fatherly support, these boys are vulnerable to homosexual males who bait their traps with special attention, gifts, or offers of 'comfort'.

2. The case of 'the missing Dad'

Some fathers have employment which keep them away from home for short or long periods when children most need them. Unfortunately, these absences often coincide with events which are important to the child such as birthdays, graduation ceremonies, awarding of trophies, sports fixtures, holidays, and even times of sickness. Because some children cannot be expected to understand the reasons behind a father's absences, they may feel hurt, and rejected. The danger is that if any 'fill-in' male comfort comes the worst can happen. The father whose vocations may cause this problem are commercial travellers, airline pilots, seamen, permanent nightshift workers, or professionals and businessmen who spend long hours at work and who are required to travel extensively.

3. The dominating or manipulative mother

Some mothers are really 'smotherers'. It may commence quite innocently. When a child is sickly, is an 'only-chick', or the mother has a fear of something happening to her little one, the protective instinct may get out of control. Again, when a mother is a single parent, a widow, a divorcee, or has been deserted, over-protectiveness often develops. This may mean that a growing girl becomes so used to female companionship that her only friends are those of her own sex; this may lead to lesbianism. Boys with manipulating mothers sometimes seek male companionship, particularly if their fathers are absent or passive, not realising the potential dangers. They become so fed-up with 'petticoat-government' that they become anti-female. If a girl or a boy stumbles into a homosexual net because of these circumstances, it would be under the influence of the rejection they were trying to escape.

4. *Unloved children, or adults*

When small children are deprived of much needed parental-love, they will naturally turn to dolls, teddy bears (and other cuddly toys), or animal pets for comfort. But as each child grows older their friends (sometimes also rejected and starved of love), often supply the love they long for. In the process of sharing, mutual sexual stimulation sometimes spontaneously commences, and makes these persons more vulnerable to homosexual approaches in later life.

Numbers of adults, particularly women, have told us that they had moved in to live with one or more members of their own sex, prompted only by their feelings of rejection, loneliness, and desire for companionship. Without being aware of the subtle changes which were taking place in their expressions of affection to one another, casual homosexual experiences have occurred, sometimes developing into full sexual partnerships. Those who have come for deliverance have been deeply repentant, full of guilt, and usually fearful of going back into sin again unless they are set free. We have certainly seen the Lord do wonderful works of grace in freeing both men and women who have been caught in this trap.

5. *Parental favouritism*

Occasionally a mother will focus all her love on an only child, or one particular child in a family to the exclusion of everyone else. This may even be instituted as a form of punishment to a husband.

- 'Arthur's' mother had never felt fulfilled by her husband, so she made her middle-child her 'soul mate'. Once she casually exposed her breasts to him, and on many occasions had 'Arthur' photograph her in a brassiere or bodice with her hair hanging loosely over her shoulders. His touch was very healing to her. The maternal grandmother had been a witch and 'Arthur's' mother qualified for the term 'white witch' because she controlled every movement made by her favourite son.

'Arthur' became attracted to men at eleven years of age, being obsessed with male nudity. He used to frequent male toilets, exposing himself to masturbating men. His homosexual relationships went no further than mutual masturbation. He flew thousands of miles to have deliverance when a friend told him that Phyl and I would see him. He felt very deeply rejected, hated himself, was full of shame and guilt, and his mind was obsessed with homosexual thoughts. The Lord freed him, and gave him accommodation and a job in another city. His lifestyle totally changed.

6. Sibling rejection

Being an only boy in a family of girls may become a recipe for rejection if a brother is made to feel unwanted, or is swamped with attention. In trying to escape a feminine household, some boys have become caught in the web of homosexuality.

* 'Trevor' was a rejected twin. Looking for comfort he became obsessed with ghost stories, horror films, heavy metal rock music, and astrology. He bought fashion clothes, dressed in women's underwear and painted his nails to be accepted as a female in the homosexual world.

7. Abandoned, unwanted, or parentless children

The common factor between them all is that each one has been denied the personal warmth and guidance of parents. Orphanages and foster homes usually become 'de facto parents' for babies who were abandoned at birth, were never wanted, or who have become 'parentless' through the death, disappearance, or mental instability of their mother or father. Although these young ones are usually adequately fed, clothed, and housed, they always feel lonely, and naturally look for comfort from those around them, particularly those of the same sex. This often leads to mutual sexual stimulation with the possibility of forming permanent preferences. In any form of communal living, younger children are always subject to domination by older and stronger boys and the possibility of stand-over tactics by fellow inmates or even staff, is obvious.

8. Children evicted from the family home

The Human Rights Commission's findings about homeless Australian children make sickening reading. Rejected by their parents, and in turn rejecting their parents, children and teenagers live in what they term 'squats', railway carriages, and refuges, or sleep on park benches or under hedges covered only by newspapers. Tragically, in order to get money for food, drugs, and other necessities, they sometimes sell their bodies for casual homosexual or heterosexual experiences. Some of them end up as homosexual prostitutes. Without doubt, rejection is the explosive force which blows families apart. The ingredients are supplied by both parents and children, but it is the latter who are the most disadvantaged and exposed to the dangers of sliding helplessly into the sub-culture of homosexuality.

9. The homosexual twist of feminism

Some homosexual men wear female clothing (particularly underwear) to make themselves more attractive to their partners. In the entertainment world, many female impersonators take hormonal drugs to stimulate breast development. Ironically, some have died from breast cancer.

From time to time we also read of trans-sexuals who endure years of drug treatment, psychological counsel, and painful surgery to become fully identifiable as members of the opposite sex. Much is made of hormonal imbalance, and the irresistible urge to be different, but little or no thought is given to the possibility of driving out demonic forces of rejection, feminism (or masculinity), sexual fantasy, unreality, and self-centredness. It is surely grotesque when a biological father becomes a 'mother' or 'aunt' by a sex-change.

When children are unfortunate enough to be born with the sex opposite to what their parents wanted, their sexual identity often becomes very confused.

- 'Dora's' father was bitterly disappointed with a daughter, so to please him she became a 'tom boy', and tried to do everything a son would have done. When she came to us for deliverance, she was a middle-aged woman, dressed in men's overalls, and wearing a man's watch. Her hair was short, her voice was mannish, and her occupation was truck-driving. After the Lord had set her

98

free, she wore frocks, make-up, dressed attractively, grew her hair longer, and wore feminine trinkets. Some six months afterwards, I met her in another country and did not recognise her because she had changed so much. She had to re-introduce herself!

- 'Charles' didn't become a homosexual, he just lived in a female fantasy world. He told me that because his mother had been so disappointed in her husband, she had lavished all her love on him. She had dressed him in frilly clothes, and smothered his body with kisses after bathing him. She used to partially undress in front of him, and quite frequently put her skirt over his head. He grew up with an obsessive desire to look under women's skirts, dress in female clothes and parade around shopping centres. When the Lord released him from his spirits of rejection, femininity, perversion, and lust, he also broke his habits and freed him of guilt, shame, and self-rejection. He was able to accept himself as a normal heterosexual.

10. Feminism, an introduction to lesbianism

Not all feminists are lesbians, but all lesbians are certainly feminists. Much has been written on this subject and the writer certainly believes that the present clamour for female equality at every level of life (a thinly veiled synonym for superiority), is rooted in Eve's deception of Adam in Genesis chapter three. Satan was then, and still is, the unrecognised driving force.

Christianity has been responsible for improving the social status of women worldwide, although there are some under-developed countries where women are still made to gather fuel, carry huge loads, do all the garden cultivation, and wait on their menfolk hand and foot.

Regrettably the world-wide religious community has been very slow in giving the women-folk biblical status and recognition. But surprisingly perhaps, there has been a positive 'kick-back' of feminism in Christian circles. Attitudes to women are changing. At one time many authoritarian husbands caused their homes to become female prisons where wives were:
- expected to remain on call at all times,
- regarded as live-in domestic helps with little financial reward,

- required to be first class cooks, entertainers, and gardeners,
- made responsible for all children's needs, around the clock,
- assumed to be sexually responsive twenty-four hours per day,
- taught to be submissive to the head of the house, and not to voice their own opinions.

The pleasures and blessings of mutual partnership in the home and in the church are at last beginning to stem the tide of rejection, unhappiness, and oppression which have caused both single and married women to embrace feminism as a means of self-expression. Because the homosexual dangers are often not realised, we share some 'insider' evaluations by a married Christian ex-feminist whom the Lord has set free. 'Cantrelle' has given written permission for the use of relevant portions of her testimony to highlight the dangers of feminist philosophy.

'I had always been fearful of women. My mother and even more so, my sister, loomed large as threatening and domineering figures in my childhood world. My sister openly hated my father, and destroyed any respect I may have had for him. He had appeared to me in disposition like a woman, and my mother like a man. Consequently I was confused in my sexual identity, as well as fearful of my own femininity.

When I arrived in ... without my usual support in this "brave new world", it was to women's groups that I gravitated. I needed nurturing. I was in the grips of anorexia and a severe emotional depression. They understood my position and laughed and cried with me, shared, hugged, and talked over endless cups of tea. I not only survived, but grew in that atmosphere, and performed in a women's theatre group before audiences, frequently made up only of women. A regular "contingent" turned out to be a group we called "the radical feminist lesbian separatists". To my horror, I found myself secretly identifying with them. At the time I was a-sexual, but "butch" in hairstyle and dress. I moved in and shared a house with an overpowering young feminist who was often scathing about men, and I found myself being influenced by her, and increasingly confused in my attitude to men. My friend was a masseuse, and I found my body responding to her sexually. From that time onwards I increasingly fantasised about sexual exchanges with women. When I later fell in love with, and married the man of my life, I continued to be plagued and tormented by confusion and distortion of my sexual identiy.'

'Cantrelle' continues:

'The feminist world has far reaching overtones. It enters the emotional, the political, the social, sexual, and spiritual spheres.' She wore their sloganed T-shirts, marched in their rallies, sang their songs but never felt totally at ease.

'I remember attending a workshop called "Reclaiming the Feminine" where we shaped our "goddesses" in clay, watched slides of Kali and numerous other goddesses, and "re-worked" the Garden of Eden "myth". The aim was to link the Genesis serpent with the snake which was an ancient symbol of women's wisdom, thereby reclaiming the Garden of Eden story as a wise fall rather than an evil one caused by a vulnerable and manipulating woman.

I gradually became steeped in the world of goddesses, and read of, and revered, those ancient matriarchal societies where women made the decisions by intuition, and where the men acted on them.

I was also aware of the movement within some churches advocating that women play a greater "up-front" role. I attended one group keen to re-write the Scriptures and liturgies in non-sexist language, to define God as "Mother" as well as "Father", and speak of "she" as well as "he". Some became extreme in their views. On one occasion a cup was passed around, as in communion, and we all drank. Then a "Christian" woman jumped up and denounced Christ, and I realised the gathering was like a witches' coven, and I had opened myself to anti-Christ spirits and powers. The anger expressed towards a patriarchal church proved later to be a major hurdle in asking Jesus Christ to be Lord of my life.'

'Feminists use the herbal folklore medicines for which their predecessors were burnt at the stake by male academics and developers of new medical techniques. They also worship Demeter, the great earth mother, symbol of women's struggles to save the world from ruin, and total destruction by a male-dominated chemical and nuclear technology. I too looked forward to having goddess divinity within me, and tried to apply myths of Aphrodite and Psyche to myself. I used a set of women's tarot cards – so colourful, soft, with rounded edges (not like the traditional harsh "male" rectangular ones which I had always found "ugly"). I leaned heavily on the cards for decision-making, and pressed on into the world of goddesses and witches. I had great difficulty in letting them go when I realised their deceptive anti-Christ nature.

My re-parenting with God as a **father** led me through the antithesis of female-male identification rather than my previous female-female identification. I am free of my past. I am forgiven, and have forgiven myself. I am glad I am a woman and I am becoming a more and more beautiful one.'

'Cantrelle's' final summary was:

'Feminism, at its best, offers to redress the injustices perpetrated aginst those women in our society who have been abused, maltreated, or denied human rights and privileges, simply because they are women. At its worst, I believe feminism offers a breeding ground for "man-eaters" – women who are consumed with hatred and anger for men, and are thus separatist, and often lesbian by preference. Progression from the first position towards the second is a subtle transition. I was almost unaware it was happening.'

When rejection dominates a person's life, almost anything can happen. Tragically, homosexual preferences and lifestyles are being more and more accepted socially, even amongst rabbis and ordained ministers of many denominations.

Both rejection and its evil fall-out of homosexuality, occultism, and witchcraft practices are undeniably demonic. Only deliverance destroys root systems.

All liberated homosexuals need godly, sensitive, and mature 'role-model' re-programming for several reasons. Firstly, they need to recover full acceptance of their true sex identity after having been involved in a deceptive life-style. Secondly, where rejection has been the basic cause of the development of homosexual desires, behaviour, or relationships, there is a need for some guidance in re-adjusting to normal heterosexual attitudes and friendships. Thirdly, when natural parents have been responsible for the rejection which led to homosexual activity, healthy attitudes to, and relationships with adult authority figures need to be restored. This is particularly so if the released person marries (or returns to a marriage), and children are involved, or may be born. Fourthly, unless parental perceptions and relationships are normalised, it will be more difficult for released people to relate to God as their heavenly Father, and to enjoy the relationships involved in the Spirit filled Christian life.

Finally we need to consider God's attitude to the whole subject of homosexuality.

God expressly hates, and forbids every kind of homosexual behaviour between members of the same sex, and will punish it most severely. Note, the Concise Oxford Dictionary includes sex acts between humans and animals (bestiality), in its definition of 'sodomy'.

(1) Biblical statements on homosexual activities:

(a) **Men.** *'If a man lies with a man as one lies with a woman, both of them have done what is detestable. They must be put to death; their blood will be on their own heads'* (Leviticus 20:13).

(b) **Boys.** *'I will gather all nations ... I will enter into judgement against them ... for they ... traded boys for prostitutes ...' (Joel 3:2, 3).*

(c) **Women.** *'Even their women* (in early history) *exchanged natural relations for unnatural ones.'* (Romans 1:26). Together with the *'men who ... were inflamed with lust for one another ... (and) committed indecent acts with other men'* (v. 27), God had this to say. *'Although they know God's righteous decree that those who do such things **deserve death**, they not only continue to do these very things but also approve of those who practise them'* (Romans 1:32, emphasis added).

(d) **Clothing.** *'A woman must **not** wear men's clothing **nor** a man wear women's clothing for the L*ORD* your **God** detests anyone who does this'* (Deuteronomy 22:5, emphasis added).

(e) **Bestiality.** Both men and women were put to death for this variation of homosexuality under Old Testament law (Deuteronomy 27:21; Leviticus 18:23).

(2) The Bible clearly states that all homosexual activities are:

- a wicked thing (Genesis 19:7).
- a vile ... disgraceful thing (Judges 19:23).
- the abandonment of natural relations – indecent acts – perversion (Romans 1:27).
- depravity of mind (Romans 1:28).
- deserving of death (Romans 1:32).
- filthy living of lawless men (2 Peter 2:7).
- lawless deeds which torment the righteous (2 Peter 2:8).

(3) Practising homosexuals do not have eternal life:

*'... the **wicked will not** inherit the kingdom of God. Do not be deceived: Neither the sexually immoral nor idolators nor adulterers **nor male prostitutes nor homosexual offenders** ... will inherit the kingdom of God.'*

(1 Corinthians 6:9, 10, emphasis added)

4. Repentant homosexuals can be released, cleansed, and receive eternal life:

*'And that is what some of you **were**. **But** you were **washed**, you were **sanctified**, you were **justified** in the name of the Lord Jesus Christ and by the Spirit of our God.'*

(1 Corinthians 6:11, emphasis added)

Summary

1. Homosexual preferences and practices may commence through a number of factors, of which deep rejection is a major cause.
2. Unless these deep roots of rejection are removed, homosexuality will continue to be a strong temptation.

3. Deliverance is the only thorough and lasting means of resolving problems of homosexuality, and lesbianism, whatever the basic cause may be.
4. Social acceptance of homosexual lifestyles will never change God's righteous judgement against those who practise it.
5. The power of the Gospel, the name of Jesus Christ, and the Spirit of God offer hope to victims of rejection and to those who practise forbidden lifestyles.

NOTE: Christians who abhor homosexuality in its broadest sense on Scriptural grounds should remember to show Christian love to the people involved, for whom Christ died.

Chapter 11

Wherever Did This Curse Come From?

This chapter has been written for the more investigative reader who would like to know why Satan is the father of rejection. Any person who would prefer to commence with the subject of the contamination of the human race should feel free to turn to the next chapter.

One thing is certain. Rejection was not there when God saw his creation was *'very good'* (Genesis 1:31). Neither was it in Adam and Eve's garden honeymoon accommodation after they had moved in, and where God was a frequent visitor. His glory filled them personally and flooded their surroundings.

But all that changed the day a very crafty and smooth-tongued serpent unexpectedly dropped in for a chat. What the snake said, and the devastating effect it has had on world history, make it essential to find out all we can about this incident.

Adam and Eve were not naive when this incident took place; they were innocent and guileless, which is quite different. Obviously they were unprepared for the serpent's subtle reasoning and would have remained innocent had they remained loyal to God. He not only threw doubts on what they were forbidden to eat, but brazenly contradicted God's warning that disobedience meant death. The snake even hinted that God had not told them about 'evil' for purely selfish reasons, and that Adam and Eve could actually become like God himself by following his advice. His evil objective was so cleverly disguised that Eve fell into his skilfully covered trap, and Adam deliberately jumped in after her (Genesis 3:3–6). The snake was delighted, and the guilty couple fled in fear hiding from the God. The death penalty was inevitable (Genesis 2:17; 3:3).

So who was it that began the process of human and environmental pollution which has reached crisis levels today?

The complete picture

Our aim is to examine biblical pointers to the snake's true identity from the time he was created (only God is self-existent, immortal, and eternal). This will include his position and personality; possible causes of his total reversal of character and subsequent change of name; and how God judged him. Finally, when each piece of information is correlated we should have a much greater understanding of the grand-master of evil who orchestrated man's fall from grace.

The first piece of the jigsaw

There are two Old Testament prophecies which non-liberal theologians believe apply more to a pre-history spiritual being than to the earthly kings to whom they were first directed. The relevant Scriptures are Isaiah 14:3–20 (circa 712 BC), and Ezekiel 28:12–19 (circa 588 BC). Each prophecy is believed to be a corollary. In other words, the writings have hidden meanings.

For example, the revelations are addressed to the kings of Babylon and Tyre, but they are more applicable to a spiritual being who was not born as humans are, but was created, and ordained to fill a very special appointment in heaven.

Consider the following descriptions (Ezekiel chapter 28). That angelic being was:

- absolutely blameless from the day he was created (v. 15).

- a model of perfection, full of wisdom and beauty (v. 12).

- personally commissioned by God to the highest office of a *'guardian cherub'*, possibly a presiding archangel (v. 14).

- named *'Lucifer, son of the morning'* (Isaiah 14:12 KJV). Other translations include: *'morning star, son of the dawn'* (NIV); *'light-bringer and day-star, son of the morning'* (Amplified Bible).

The second piece of the jigsaw

It is obvious that in eternity past Lucifer planned a revolt in order to seize God's throne. The usurper's secret desires are listed in Isaiah chapter fourteen.

'You said in your heart,

- *I will ascend to heaven* (v. 13);
- *I will raise my throne above the stars of God* (v. 13) (angels, according to Revelation 1:20);
- *I will sit enthroned on the mount of the assembly, on the utmost heights of the sacred mountain* (v. 13);
- *I will ascend above the tops of the clouds* (v. 14);
- *I will make myself like the Most High.'* (emphasis added).

These five declarations clearly identify evil forces we all know, only too well!

- **Pride**, or self-importance.
- **Covetousness**, or self-seeking.
- **Idolatry**, or self-worship.
- **Independence**, or self-sufficiency.
- **Rebellion**, or self-determination.

Lucifer's unilateral declaration of independence and rebellion against God is undoubtedly the first recorded act of REJECTION.

The third piece of the jigsaw

God's immediate response was to himself reject, then pass judgement on the angelic rebel.

Firstly, he named his actions as *'sin'*, *'wickedness'* and *'corruption'* (Ezekiel 28:15–17). From then onwards, Lucifer was known as *'Satan'* (the hater, accuser).

Secondly, God dismissed him from office and threw him out of heaven (Ezekiel 28:16,17). I believe Jesus Christ was referring to the personality of the evil one when he said in Luke 10:18 *'I saw Satan fall like lightning from heaven'*. At Calvary's cross he destroyed the work of the evil one and his demonic hordes by triumphing over sin's nature, power, and consequences (Colossians 2:11–15; 1 John 3:8).

Deprived of title, position, and totally rejected by God, Satan left heaven to share his exile with a number of other rebellious angelic beings subsequently called *'angels'* (Job 1:6; 2:1), the *'sons of God'*

(Hebrew for *'angels'* Genesis 6:4), and *'demons'* in the New Testament (Luke 4:41). Jesus Christ always rejected their confession of his identity (Mark 3:11,12).

Thirdly, Hell was created for the eternal imprisonment and punishment of the devil (or Satan), and his angelic following (Matthew 25:41).

The composite picture therefore shows that *'Lucifer'*, *'Satan'*, *'the devil'*, and *'the serpent'* are all one and the same person.

> *'An angel ... seized the **dragon**, that ancient **serpent**, who is **the devil**, or **Satan**, and bound him for a thousand years. He threw him into the Abyss ... and **the devil** who deceived them, was thrown into the lake of burning sulphur where the beast and the false prophet had been thrown. They will be tormented day and night for ever and ever.'*
>
> (Revelation 20:1, 2, 10, emphasis added)

Jesus once gave the devil an unsolicited character reference. He called him *'a murderer from the beginning'* ... with *'no truth in him'*; *'a liar and the father of lies'* (John 8:44); and a *'thief who comes only to steal, and kill, and destroy'* (John 10:10).

The curse of following bad advice

Adam and Eve did not realise that the snake costume was a disguise for 'Mr Evil' himself, the implacable enemy of God, and of every person and created thing reflecting his glory.

It should be no surprise then, that under his influence, they also rebelled against God and lost their special position and authority just as Satan did. The similarities between their behaviour and Satan's are certainly not just a coincidence. They too had become:

- **Proud**, by putting their own interests before God's.
- **Covetous** of what the serpent hinted that God had denied them.
- **Idolatrous** in wanting the 'good things' of life instead of being satisfied with the best things God had already given them.
- **Independent**, by acting unilaterally and failing to check the serpent's credentials with God.

- **Rebellious**, by flagrantly over-stepping the only restriction God had made.

- **Rejected** by God. With their innocence in tatters, their ruling authority in the hands of the evil one, and their nakedness shamefully obvious because God's glory had left them, it is no wonder that they were immediately overcome with guilt, shame, fear caused by sin, and feelings of rejection.

- **Evil** by nature. The knowledge of evil which the snake had so deceitfully promised, (as if it were a treasure beyond value), had itself become a monster which now dominated their own lives, and would continue to do so for generations.

Within 1656 years, the descendants of Adam and Eve (except eight righteous people) were indicted by God, and wiped off the face of the earth.

> '.. The LORD saw **how great** man's **wickedness** on the earth had become.'

> '... and that **every inclination** of the thoughts of his heart was **only evil all the time** ... Now the earth was **corrupt** in God's sight and **full of violence**.' (Genesis 6:5, 11, emphasis added)

What Satan had been unable to do in heaven, he had done successfully on earth. His claim to be God's credible alternative is probably more widely accepted today than it has ever been. Prophecy becomes history before our eyes as this false messiah edges closer to being universally acknowledged as the solver of world problems. That 'snake' is as insidious today as he was in the Garden of Eden, and his 'New Age Movement' is only an update of Baalism, or Satan worship, with the same old hackneyed promise to make people 'gods' by following his advice.

Question – Why didn't Adam and Eve die physically? After all they had done the unthinkable by flagrantly disobeying God's only rule: '... *you must not eat from the tree of the knowledge of good and evil, for when you eat of it you will surely die*' (Genesis 2:17). Did God renege on his word, and give the rebels another chance? By no means. His character made that impossible. His word had to be fulfilled.

History has made much of the seven wonders of the ancient

world, of which relatively little remains today. But the two greatest wonders of all time, are not material, but spiritual. On not one, but two occasions in history God has personally come to earth to deal with the consequences of sin. The first occasion was after the grievous sin of Adam and Eve. The second was when he lived here for thirty-three and a half years, and ended up being crucified by those he had come to save.

The parallels between these two visitations emphasise God's eternal plan of love to redeem fallen mankind from the deceit and domination of Satan.

1. *God is always merciful to sinners*
(a) In Eden, he personally searched for Adam, calling aloud to him. When the frightened couple finally came out of hiding, God listened to what they had to say before passing judgement.
(b) In Israel, Jesus Christ said: *'For I have not come to call the righteous, but sinners'* (Matthew 9:13). And, *'Come to me, all you who are weary and burdened ...'* (Matthew 11:28).

2. *Death is God's unvarying sentence for committing sin*
(a) In Eden, he himself sacrificed animals to obtain skins to cover the bodies of Adam and Eve. Sin had already cut them off from God and caused them to die spiritually. Many years later, they experienced a second death. They died physically. While not specifically stated, the animal blood obviously established a precedent for atonement for sin. *'For the life of the creature is in the blood, and I have given it to you to make atonement for yourselves on the altar; it is **the blood that makes atonement for one's life'** (Leviticus 17:11, emphasis added).*
(b) At Calvary, Jesus Christ (*'... the Lamb of God who takes away the sin of the world'* (John 1:29), was sacrificed to wash away the sins of the whole world (Hebrews 9:28). *'... you were redeemed ... but with the precious blood of Christ, a lamb without blemish or defect'* (1 Peter 1:18, 19). Sins were only covered in Eden, but now sinners can be made clean, and their ugly record, obliterated.

3. *God preserves those whose sins he has dealt with*
(a) In Eden, God took the skins of the sacrificed animals, and

112

shaped them into clothes for Adam and Eve for modesty, warmth, and protection (Genesis 3:21).

(b) Since Calvary, the righteousness of Jesus Christ becomes the spiritual clothing of every person to be born again. Isaiah explains the principle: *'I delight greatly in the LORD, my soul rejoices in my God. For he has clothed me with the garments of salvation and arrayed me in the robe of righteousness ... so the Sovereign Lord will make righteousness and praise spring up before all nations'* (Isaiah 61:10, 11). *'... when the day of evil comes ... stand firm then with the breastplate of righteousness in place ...'* (Ephesians 6:13, 14).

4. God replaces rejection with affirmation

(a) In Eden, blood was shed, but the rejected sinners were banned from God's presence. Until Jesus Christ came, rejected people could only approach God through sacrifices made by a priest on their behalf.

(b) At Calvary, Jesus suffered the curse of sin and rejection, in order to reconcile repentant sinners with God so that they could become his adopted children, and he could become their loving heavenly Father. As a result, no genuine believer needs to suffer any longer from rejection. Freedom is a personal choice. Not God's, but ours.

Summary

1. Lucifer was the first to experience rejection because of his attempt to overthrow God.

2. As Satan, he deceived Eve, and caused Adam to rebel against God, causing rejection to become a bitter human experience. Since then, man has used it as a weapon against his fellow man and even God himself (1 Samuel 8:7; 10:19).

3. Old Testament sacrifices provided limited access to God for rejected sinners.

4. Jesus Christ offers repentant sinners reconciliation with God, removal of rejection, and a 'Father–child' relationship.

Chapter 12

The Saddest, Loneliest, and Most Rejected Family on Earth

They were an extremely sad couple. They had just been evicted from the luxurious living quarters which had been 'home' for so long. And they had been permanently banned from ever entering its beautiful garden setting again. Even the memory of the angelic guard blocking the entrance with his fearful flaming sword must have sent cold shivers up and down their spines.

They were lonely because God no longer dropped by, and there was no one else to talk to. The world's first married couple only had each other in their new environment, and it grew nasty thorns and briers.

They were rejected because God had turned his back on them, and their clothing sombrely reminded them that they were alive only because God had killed animals to clothe them. Whether they realised it or not, the countdown to their physical death had also begun. Adam did not reach it until he was 930 years old (Genesis 5:5). Eve's death is not recorded.

But life had to go on, and in due course two sons were born. Cain was the first person born by natural means, and his mother acknowledged God's help: *'With the help of the LORD I have brought forth a man'* (Genesis 4:1). Abel was next, and obviously others followed but were not mentioned in biblical history because of its selective record. For example, Cain's wife was referred to (but not previously mentioned), after God had sentenced him for murder (Genesis 4:17). But the event we need to focus on concerns the two sons.

How could two brothers be so different?

This is a question many parents ask today. When the two boys offered their first personal sacrifices to God, Cain did his own thing and was rebellious, argumentative, and defiant. Abel showed a submissive and obedient spirit, and received God's approval.

The writer suggests that Cain may have inherited his mother's strong disposition, while Abel was more like his fther, quiet and submissive. In the events of the previous chapter, Eve was obviously strong-minded, while Adam appears to have been quieter and more pliable. The 'Yes Dear, if-you-say-so-Dear' type. Had this not been so, Eve would have asked her husband to talk to the serpent when he began to question God's word. After all, Adam had been forbidden to eat fruit from the tree of the knowledge of good and evil, before she existed (Genesis 2:16, 17). But he did not interrupt her conversation, protest at her obvious intentions, or stop her from disobeying God. Instead he meekly did as she suggested, eating the offered fruit, without protest. By obeying his wife instead of God, God judged Adam's action to have been outright rebellion. For this he received the greater punishment. *'Because you listened to your wife,'* God said, *'and ate from the tree about which I commanded you, "You must not eat of it,"* Cursed is the ground because of you'* (Genesis 3:17, emphasis added).

Both young men must have been well taught on the type of sacrifice God wanted. The youngest son offered *'fat portions from some of the firstborn of his flock'* which pleased God (Genesis 4:4). Maybe he understood the principle that only blood covers sin.

But Cain was as determined as his mother. As she had coveted and taken attractive looking fruit to satisfy her appetite, Cain grew food and offered the best to God. Eve did what she pleased, and so did her eldest son.

Evangelicals believe that this event also indicates that God accepts blood sacrifices for sin offered by faith (as in the case of Abel), but rejects offerings of sweat and hard labour (good works) like Cain's. The former illustrates justification and salvation, the latter, rejection, and judgement. But there is something more sinister about those two offerings which is often overlooked. *'... Cain belonged to the evil one ...'* (1 John 3:12, emphasis added). The Scriptures do not say when or how this came about, but it is obvious that everything Cain said and did in this chapter was controlled by the evil one.

Cain's parents had committed what is generally called 'original sin'. So all the children born to them and their descendants had sin as a 'spiritual gene' turning 'original-sin' into 'hereditary-sin'. Subsequently, the whole human race has had that same sinful nature, and the death penalty has passed on down to them through the process of conception (Romans 5:12).

Because Cain was the first naturally born child, Satan may also have claimed him as the spiritual firstfruits of the fallen Adamic nature, which he 'fathered'. Cain certainly spoke to God in the same impudent, brazen, and offensive manner as his spiritual father, the devil (note Job chapters 1, 2).

The word 'firstborn' is also significant to God. Jesus Christ is called *'the firstborn over all creation'* (Colossians 1:15), showing his divine priority over all created things. He is also *'the firstborn from among the dead'* (Colossians 1:18), indicating his resurrection victory over death caused by original sin.

God also regarded the Israelites as his inheritance, his *'spiritual son'*. Moses was told to say to Pharaoh: *'This is what the LORD says: Israel is my firstborn son and I told you "Let my son go, so that he may worship me." But you refused to let him go, so I will kill your firstborn son."'* (Exodus 4:22, 23, emphasis added).

Egypt's final judgement occurred the night the Hebrews brushed animal blood over their doorways and offered passover sacrifices. They alone survived the visitation of the angel of death. At midnight the LORD struck down all the firstborn in Egypt, from Pharaoh, who sat on the throne, to the prisoner in the dungeon, and all livestock. *'... and there was loud wailing in Egypt, for there was not a house without someone dead.'* (Exodus 12:30).

From then onwards, yearly passover sacrifices became a permanent memorial so that every Israelite would be reminded that the firstborn of every family and cattle were God's by redemption. Satan claimed the first human child to be born, but God reclaimed a whole nation as his 'son'.

'"You are to give over to the LORD the first offspring of every womb. All the firstborn males of your livestock belong to the LORD. This is why I sacrifice to the Lord the first male offspring of every womb and redeem each of my firstborn sons." And it

*will be like **a sign on your hand and a symbol on your forehead** that the Lord brought us out of Egypt with his mighty hand.'*
(Exodus 13:12, 15, 16, emphasis added)

It is little wonder that Satan will stamp his own evil symbol on people in the same two places in the last days.

*'He also forced everyone, small and great, rich and poor, free and slave, to receive a mark **on his right hand or on his forehead**, so that no-one could buy or sell unless he had the mark which is the name of the beast, or the number of his name.'*
(Revelation 13:16, emphasis added)

But why murder innocent Abel?

As Satan already controlled Cain, he may have feared that Abel would become the generational link to the promised 'seed of the woman', whom God said would crush his head (Genesis 3:15). With Abel out of the way, Satan may have thought he had sabotaged God's purposes, and consolidated his own kingdom.

Satan would also have been keen to stop Cain's atoning animal sacrifices. They were contrary to his 'Eden-philosophy': *'Listen to me, do what I say, and you will be like God himself'* (Genesis 3:5).

The clear distinction between the children of each kingdom is emphasised in the New Testament Scriptures.

● The Jews who opposed Jesus claimed to have God as their Father because they were Abraham's descendants (John 8:32,41). But Jesus Christ said, *'You belong to **your father, the devil** and you want to carry out your father's desire'* (v. 44, emphasised).

● *'This is how we know who the children of God are and **who the children of the devil are**. Anyone who does not do what is right is not a child of God; neither is anyone who does not love his brother'* (1 John 3:10, emphasis added).

Because Cain, the first child to be born in the human race *'belonged to the evil one'* (1 John 3:12), any consideration of how Satan is able to manipulate humanity must commence with him.

THE 'CAIN-SYNDROME'

This subject was introduced in *Evicting Demonic Intruders and Breaking Bondages*, but needs to be examined in greater detail.

Cain was born with hereditary rejection

His parents had suffered the maximum impact of rejection. Stripped of God's glory, evicted from their garden sanctuary, and wearing animal-skin clothing, the stark reality of their new environment and change of lifestyle must have still been acute when the two sons were conceived. They were both born with hereditary rejection, but it was Cain who appeared to have been most affected.

Cain's character analysis

Firstly we will define each characteristic, then at the end, place each on one of the three branches of rejection symptoms described in both our previous books – 'aggressive reaction', 'self-rejection symptoms', and 'measures to counter the fear of rejection'. Each one is easily distinguishable:

1. *Pride.* Cain was arrogant in his dialogue with Almighty God.
2. *Covetousness.* As the eldest brother, he was peeved by the approval Abel's offering had received.
3. *Self-idolatry.* He was certainly into self-worship, and pleasing himself was more important than honouring God.
4. *Independence.* Cain refused to offer sacrifices, and gave God his best home-grown produce. Without doubt Abel would have gladly bartered animals for produce had he been asked, but apparently he wasn't.
5. *Rebellion.* Although God tried to reason with Cain, he wouldn't budge.
6. *Jealousy.* He ignored God's promise of acceptance if he offered a suitable sacrifice (v. 7). He was so eaten up with jealousy that he sulked.
7. *Anger.* In fact the more he mulled over it, the madder he became. Finally, he was *'very angry'* (v. 5).
8. *Moodiness and depression.* *'His face was downcast'* (v. 5). Cain's feelings became so obvious that God asked him why he was so angry and why he looked so miserable. (It is very difficult to mask feelings of rejection.)

9. ***Stubbornness***. If Cain was really listening to what God was saying, he neither gave any indication of it, nor did anything about it.
10. ***Unforgiveness***. The issue had become entirely a personal one in the older brother's eyes. He just could not tolerate 'Junior' getting approval before himself.
11. ***Resentment*** was the next additive to Cain's emotional cauldron which was beginning to over-heat. The more he thought about it, the more he resented Abel and his 'goody-goody' lifestyle.
12. ***Feelings of injustice***. Cain had obviously convinced himself that God was treating him unjustly by ignoring what he considered were his rights as the eldest son. His imagined **in**justice was in effect a flimsy cover-up for his self-idolatry. The more he thought about it, the madder he must have felt because he was being denied the 'I'-justice to which he felt entitled.
13. ***Bitterness*** followed, and Cain's hatred began to bubble. It was already being slowly poured into the worst possible expression of rejection – murder.

GOD'S UNBELIEVABLY GRACIOUS PLEA FOR SANE THINKING AND A RIGHT RESPONSE

We will put our consideration of Cain's rejection-controlled behaviour on hold briefly, and think about one of the most remarkable verses in all Scripture:

> *'Then the LORD said to Cain ... If you do what is right, will you not be accepted? But if you do not do what is right **sin is crouching at your door**, it desires to have you, but you must master it.'* (Genesis 4:7, emphasis added)

Firstly, God's gracious attitude towards the young rebel emphasises that he is infinite in love, mercy, and reason. He speaks with frankness but in gentleness, without threatening Cain. Isaiah later emphasises this aspect of God's character by writing:

> *'"Come now, **let us reason together**" says the LORD. "Though your sins are like scarlet, they shall be as white as snow; though they are red as crimson, they shall be like wool. **If you are willing***

and obedient you will eat the best from the land; but if you resist and rebel, you will be devoured by the sword.'' For the mouth of the LORD has spoken.' (Isaiah 1:18, emphasis added)

Cain was being offered a second chance, but refused to accept it.

Secondly. The first time the word 'sin' appears in the Bible, God uses it. He told Cain it was 'crouching'. This surely compares sin to a predatory animal waiting to pounce on its prey. And who of us has not at some time or other experienced this 'devouring'?

Thirdly, God said that sin was crouching at Cain's 'door'. In other words, each one of us can open ourselves up to, or shut out, any person or temptation we choose. Jesus Christ confirms this:

'Here I am! I stand at the door and knock. If anyone hears my voice and opens the door, I will come in and eat with him, and he with me.' (Revelation 3:20, emphasis added)

Some Christians have objected to that verse being used in personal evangelism because it was written to the Laodicean church. But when both God and Jesus Christ speak of a door to the heart (or inner life) its use is validated.

Fourthly. God told Cain he alone was responsible to stop sin from entering: '*. . . but you must master it*'. The Hebrew word '*marshal*' translated as '*master*' (NIV), '*rule*' (KJV) is no passive attitude. It means 'to have dominion, reign, have power' (No. 4910 Strong's Exhaustive Concordance). Paul emphasises this truth in Christian living: '*Do not offer parts of your body to sin, as instruments of wickedness, but rather offer yourselves to God . . . For sin shall not be your master . . .*' (Romans 6:12–14, emphasis added).

But Cain made no positive response to God's warning because he had become obsessed with his plan to murder his brother. As soon as God finished speaking, he sprang into action (v. 8). So let us return to Cain's behavioural symptoms.

14. *Impatience.* Frustrated by having to 'mark time' while God talked, Cain's impatience must have been obvious, because he did not try to hide his feelings when his offering was rejected.

15. *Unrepentance.* Cain's mind was now like concrete, permanently set. God's appeal and warning had failed to change him.

16. *Fighting rejection with rejection.* Cain committed the greatest possible sin by rejecting the Holy One who had mercifully warned him that sin was self-destructive. It was his final 'NO' to submission, humility, and obedience.

17. *Hatred.* Abel's righteousness appeared to have had the same effect on Cain as a matador's red cape has on a bull. It stirred him up and made his evil nature the more obvious (1 John 3:12).

18. *Revenge.* Cain was the first person to use the 'pay-back' system. Abel totally undeserved what he received, but his brother's mind was so distorted by poisonous emotions that his reason no longer functioned.

19. *Deception.* Like his serpent-mentor, Cain was also smooth-tongued, saying to his brother, *'Let's go out to the field'* (v. 8). There wasn't the slightest hint of the planned homicide.

20. *Violence.* As soon as they were out of sight, Cain's rage erupted in physical violence on Abel (v. 8).

21. *Murder.* He only stopped when the younger brother no longer moved, his blood staining the soil underneath his body.

22. *Callousness.* If Cain felt even a twinge of guilt, he kept it to himself. He sauntered around as if nothing untoward had happened.

23. *Defiance.* When God asked Cain where his brother was, he refused to tell him.

24. *Self-protection.* He stood up to God in a vain attempt at self-defence.

25. *Lying.* *'"I don't know," he replied . . . '* (v. 9). Cain entered a plea of 'not guilty' in a deliberate attempt to evade self-incrimination. Regrettably, this has since become common practice.

26. *Evasiveness.* *'. . . Am I my brother's keeper?'* (v. 9). Cain now deliberately attempts to bluff his way out of trouble. But that never has, and never will work with an omniscient God. The Lord read the charge, *'What have you done? Listen! Your brother's blood cries out to me from the ground'* (v. 10).

The inescapable consequences of sin. (v. 11, 12). God convicts Cain of fratricide, and sentences him:

- Firstly, he was placed *'under a curse and driven from the ground'* (v. 11).

- Secondly, he was told that he would no longer be successful in working the soil because it would not produce crops for him (v. 12).
- Thirdly, the rest of his days were to be spent in restless wandering (v. 12).

Had Cain been an Australian, we would say that he then began to 'whinge' (complain) about his penalty.

27. *Self-pity.* The guilty brother's only concern was for himself. He expressed no remorse, but appealed against the harshness of his sentence. *'My punishment is more than I can bear'* (v. 13).

28. *Accusing God of over-reacting.* *'Today you are driving me from the land* (my occupation), *and I will be hidden from your presence'* (v. 13, 14a).

29. *Fear of rejection.* *'... I will be a restless wanderer on the earth ...'* (v. 14). By now, Cain was beginning to realise something of the impact of his life-sentence. He also showed:

30. *Fear of victimisation.* *'Whoever finds me ...'* (v. 14). Cain's memory was troubling him. He obviously considered the possibility of being hunted by those out to revenge Abel's death. And there were other fears:

31. *Fear of death.* *'... will kill me'* (v. 14). The possibility of being killed himself was beginning to dawn on him. Cain hadn't heard the saying, 'sow a wind, and reap a whirlwind', but he acted as if he had.

Again we see the mercy of God. Cain was promised protection, and physically marked to warn would-be murderers that God would punish anyone who sought to kill him.

32. *Fear of abandonment.* God's presence had obviously meant something to Cain because he expressed concern at the prospect of losing this. *'I will be hidden from your presence'* (v. 14). *'So Cain went out from the Lord's presence ...'* (v. 16), marked for life. His other brother was dead, and now he himself was separated from his parents and his God, being crushed by the very wheel of rejection he had first rolled on his brother.

But it was Adam and Eve who probably suffered the most. They were alone again. Their youngest son dead, and their eldest, banished.

When Adam was 130 years old, Seth was born. Instead of being in the image and likeness of God, as his father had been created, he was the replica of his father's fallen nature (Genesis 5:1–3). Since the flood, all humanity had descended from Seth through Noah and his three sons, and every single one has inherited that rejection-prone sinful nature.

The 'Cain-syndrome' helps us understand the range of symptoms from which rejected people suffer today. Cain's diagrammatic tree should be compared with the tree in chapter 21. It is also obvious that present day symptoms of rejection run in the same general pattern as those first shown in Genesis chapter four. In fact the first tree could be updated by the extra Cain symptoms, marked *.

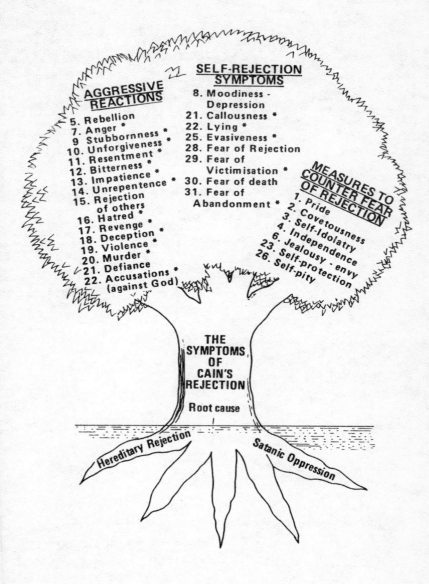

AGGRESSIVE REACTIONS

5. Rebellion
7. Anger *
9. Stubbornness *
10. Unforgiveness *
11. Resentment *
12. Bitterness *
13. Impatience *
14. Unrepentence *
15. Rejection of others
16. Hatred *
17. Revenge *
18. Deception *
19. Violence *
20. Murder *
21. Defiance
22. Accusations * (against God)

SELF-REJECTION SYMPTOMS

8. Moodiness - Depression
21. Callousness *
22. Lying *
25. Evasiveness *
28. Fear of Rejection
29. Fear of Victimisation *
30. Fear of death
31. Fear of Abandonment *

MEASURES TO COUNTER FEAR OF REJECTION

1. Pride
2. Covetousness
3. Self-Idolatry
4. Independence
6. Jealousy - envy
23. Self-protection
26. Self-pity

THE SYMPTOMS OF CAIN'S REJECTION

Root cause

Hereditary Rejection

Satanic Oppression

125

Chapter 13

The Bible's 'Who's Who' of Rejected People

There are many biblical examples of rejection. Some are obvious, others more obscure. The following list is by no means exhaustive, and includes only one people-group. It provides us with some understanding of the variety of rejection-causing incidents, and the degree to which some well-known Bible personalities suffered from its symptoms. In many instances, only basic details are given, such as who or what initiated the rejection experience.

A

ADAM by God, for listening to his wife and breaking his commandment (Genesis 3:17–19).

ABEL by his brother Cain, for righteous living (1 John 3:12).

ABRAM by his wife Sarai, because her servant Hagar despised her when she fell pregnant with Ishmael (Genesis 16;4,5).

ABAH, (King)
- by Naboth, for refusing to sell the king his family vineyard. He went home angry and sullen, and lay on his bed, sulking (1 Kings 21:1–4).
- by God, through Elijah, for practising evil (1 Kings 21:19–25).

ANANIAS (with his wife Sapphira), by God through Peter, for lying to the Holy Spirit. As a result they both died (Acts 5:1–11).

B

BELSHAZZAR   by God, in the message of judgement which appeared on the palace wall. And by Daniel, for pride, and having ignored the lesson God taught his father (Daniel 5:20–30).

C

CAIN   by God, for rejecting his advice, and murder (Genesis chapter 4).

CALEB   (and Joshua), by the Israelite congregation, for believing God (Numbers 14:1–10).

CANAAN   by Noah, for the sin of his father Ham (Genesis 9:22–25).

D

DANIEL   by the Babylonian administrators, for his devotion to God, his prayer faithfulness, and refusal to be idolatrous (Daniel chapter 6). Even the lions rejected him! (v. 22).

DAVID, (King)
  • by his father Jesse, in not including him with the other sons when the prophet Samuel invited the family to a special sacrifice (1 Samuel 16:1–13).
  • by his eldest brother Eliab, because of his interest in Goliath at the battle-front (1 Samuel 17:28,29).
  • by his rebellious son Absalom, who stole the hearts of the people and caused his father to flee for his life (2 Samuel chapters 15–17).
  • by Shimei, who cursed David and threw stones and dirt at him and his supporter as they passed a small village after leaving Jerusalem (2 Samuel 16:1–14).

E

ELIJAH   by the wicked Queen Jezebel, because of the slaughter of 850 prophets of Baal and Asherah (1 Kings 19:1–3). Elijah fled in fear.

ELISHA   by the young louts of Bethel (2 Kings 2:23–25).

ESAU   by his brother Jacob, who bought his birthright and stole his blessing as the eldest son (Genesis 25:31–34; 27:34–36, 41).

G

GOD
- by Adam and Eve, through disobedience (Genesis chapter 3).
- by Pharaoh, in stubbornly refusing to let his people go to worship him (Exodus chapters 7–12).
- by the Israelites, in demanding an earthly king so that they could be like the other nations (1 Samuel 8:7, 8, 9).
- by his earthly people before and after the captivity (Isaiah chapter 1; Jeremiah chapter 2).
- by an unbelieving world (Revelation 21:8).

H

HAGAR   by her mistress Sarai, for despising her after giving birth to Abram's child (Genesis 16:4–6).

HANNAH
- by Peninnah, Elkanah's second wife, because she was unable to conceive children (1 Samuel 1:6). Although Hannah's husband loved her deeply, and was twice as liberal with her, Peninnah continued her open provocation (v. 6, 7). The rejection symptoms are evident:
  - **Low self-esteem** and feelings of **uselessness** and **hopelessness** in being unable to have children.
  - **Tears of frustration** and **loss of appetite**, caused by constant vexation and her own feelings of self-rejection (v. 6, 7).
  - **Bitterness.** Hannah was unable to forgive Peninnah. Unforgiveness, jealousy, envy, resentment, and the hurt of being victimised, soon established a root of bitterness which hindered her prayers from being answered (v. 15; Hebrews 12:15).
  - Hannah **could not respond** to her husband's love, despite his generosity and personal appeal (v. 8).
  - **Depression.** Elkanah admonished her for not eating, and being down-hearted (v. 8).

- **Self-pity.** Her tears and prayers were self-centred, *'O Lord Almighty, if you will only look upon your servant's misery and remember me, and not forget your servant but give her a son ...'* (v. 11).

● by Eli the priest, who sharply rebuked her because he assumed she was drunk when he saw her lips moving, but could not hear a sound (v. 14). Hannah explained that she was not a wicked woman, **but was** praying in great anguish of soul (v. 16). When Eli blessed her, everything changed. She ate, cheered up, worshipped the Lord, and went home (v. 18, 19).

With her deep-seated rejection gone, the Lord answered her prayer. She conceived and gave birth to Samuel whom she gave to the Lord as she had promised (v. 11). At Samuel's dedication ceremony at Shiloh, Hannah gave a Spirit-anointed testimony:

'My heart rejoices in the LORD; in the LORD my horn is lifted high. My mouth boasts over my enemies for I delight in your deliverance ...'   (Chapter 2:1, emphasis added)

Following her freedom, and healing, she had five more children (chapter 2:20, 21).

HERODIAS   by John the Baptist, for being the de facto wife of her husband's brother, Herod the tetrarch of Galilee. She resented it so strongly, that she finally had John beheaded (Matthew 14:1–11).

HOPHNI   (and his brother Phineas) and their descendants, by God, for their wickedness as priests (1 Samuel 2:12–25).

I

ISAAC
   ● by his wife Rebekah (who was younger than he was), when he was old and almost blind. To protect her favourite son, Jacob, she eaves-dropped while Isaac instructed Esau to hunt game and prepare his favourite food as a prelude to giving him the customary eldest son's blessing before he died.
   ● by Jacob, whose mother helped him to deceive his father by impersonating Esau, and steal his blessing (Genesis 27:1–29).

ISHMAEL

- by his father Abraham, in allowing Sarai to ill-treat Hagar, his Egyptian wife, who then ran off into the desert with his son (Genesis 16:4–6).
- by those around him, because of his lifestyle God said to his mother before he was born that he would be (chapter 16):
  - a wild donkey of a man (v. 12).
  - aggressive by nature, and consequently, the target of aggression by others (v. 12).
  - the father of twelve sons who would be hostile to one another (v. 12). They certainly were (chapter 25:18).
- by Sarah, who caught him mocking Isaac during his weaning celebrations, and who ordered her husband to *'Get rid of that slave woman and her son.'* Sarah couldn't tolerate the thought of Ishmael sharing any inheritance with her own son (Genesis 21:8–10).
- by his father Abraham, who although greatly distressed by her demand, sent Hagar and his son Ishmael away after giving them food and a skin of water (chapter 21:11–14).
- by his mother, when their water supply ran out in the desert of Beersheba. She left Ishmael under a bush and sat sobbing some distance away because she couldn't bear to watch him die. God heard the boy crying, and showed Hagar where to find water (chapter 21:15–19).

NOTE: This explains why all Arabs (Ishmael's descendants irrespective of where they are born), constantly show their hereditary ethnic rejection, by:

- bitterly disagreeing with one another – reflected in OPEC oil quotas and prices, and their unashamed financial exploitations of world economies for their own profit.
- aggressively countering Christianity, and mounting Islamic fundamental evangelistic zeal which has caused problems in many countries.
- belligerently opposing their half-brothers (the Jews). Their 'Six day war' was disastrous for them. The continued military and propaganda posturing of both parties certainly makes world peace a very fragile commodity. And the root cause is ethnic rejection, and counter-rejection.

J

JACOB

- by his father who favoured his brother. *'Isaac, who had a taste for wild game, loved Esau, but Rebekah loved Jacob'* (Genesis 25:28).
- by having to leave home because Esau had planned to murder him for stealing his blessing (Genesis 27:41–45).
- by Laban, his prospective father-in-law who switched brides on his wedding night after he had given seven years free labour for Rachel (Genesis 29:21–26).
- by Leah, his first wife who bore his children but knew she was not loved (v. 31–35).
- by Laban, through his meanness, deceit, and poor wages (Genesis 3:41,42).
- by the Canaanites and Perizzites, when his sons Simeon and Levi deceived and slaughtered the defenceless Schechemites. He said,

'You have brought trouble on me by making me a stench to the Canaanites and Perizzites, the people living in this land. We are few in number, and if they join forces against me and attack me, I and my household will be destroyed.'

(Genesis 34:30, emphasis added)

- by his eleven sons, when they showed him Joseph's ornamental robe dipped in animal blood, and caused him to presume Joseph had been killed by a wild animal (Genesis 37:31–35).

It is little wonder that the Israelis (his descendants), not only suffer from hereditary rejection, but international rejection.

JEREMIAH   by the inhabitants of Jerusalem and Judah who refused to believe that his words were from God:

- he received beatings and imprisonment (Jeremiah 37:15–21).
- he was thrown into a muddy pit (chapter 38:6–10).
- he was taken in captivity into Egypt, despite his warning against it (chapter 43:6, 7). His book of Lamentations reflects his deep feelings.

JEROBOAM (son of Nebat, first king of Israel after the breaka-
way) by God through a prophetic word for gross idolatry to
golden calves (1 Kings 12:26–13:5).

JOB
- by Satan, in suggesting to God that he only lived a moral and
  upright life for self-protective reasons. God then permitted
  Job's moral integrity to be tested. Satan caused the death of all
  of his children and most of his servants; had his livestock
  butchered or stolen; and made Job break out in boils from head
  to foot (Job chapters 1, 2).
- by his wife who advised him to curse God and die (chapter 2:9,
  10).
- by his three philosopher friends (chapters 3–31).
- by his family, friends, and the community at large because of
  his repulsive condition and appearance (ch 1:8; 2:3).

JONAH
- by God for trying to evade his commission to preach repentance and judgement in the city of Ninevah (Jonah 1:1–4).
- by the sailors who threw him overboard in the middle of a fierce
  storm (chapter 1:11–17).
- by the whale which found him hard to digest and vomited him
  up on the beach (chapter 2:10).
- by God, for self-pity and lack of compassion for the repentant
  city of Ninevah (chapter 4).

JONATHAN by his father King Saul, for his protection of his
soul-mate David

> *'You son of a perverse and rebellious woman! Don't I know you
> have sided with the son of Jesse to your own shame and to the
> shame of the mother who bore you?'*   (1 Samuel 20:30, 31)

JOSEPH
- by his brothers because of their jealousy for the special love
  and favouritism of their father (Genesis 37:4).
- by his brothers, and Jacob his father who rebuked him as a
  dreamer because none of them believed that one day they
  would bow down and worship him (v. 5–11,19).
- by his brothers, who, because of their intense hatred, sold him
  as a slave to Ishmaelite traders who took him to Egypt (v. 25–
  28).

- by the lying wife of Potiphar the Egyptian, who, being unable to seduce Joseph, falsely accused him of rape (Genesis 39:6–19).
- by his lengthy and unjust imprisonment on a fabricated charge (v. 13–19).
- by Pharaoh's cup-bearer who promised to speak to the king on his behalf when released, but forgot him for two years (chapter 40:12–15; 41:1).

Joseph's preservation from the evil effects of rejection (as a type of Jesus Christ) was because the Lord was with him at all times (Genesis 39:2, 3, 9, 23; Psalm 105:19).

JUDAS, (Iscariot)
- by Jesus Christ, for planning to betray him (Matthew 26:21–25).
- by Satan, through suicide, after having treacherously used him (Matthew 27:3–5; Acts 1:18).
- by the chief priests and elders who refused to accept the return of the thirty pieces of silver he was given to betray Jesus Christ. He threw the conscience money onto the temple floor for having betrayed 'innocent blood'. A burial field for strangers was purchased, and named 'the Field of Blood' (Matthew 27:3–10; Acts 1:19). The Old Testament prophecies about him were totally fulfilled (Psalm 109:4–16; Zechariah 11:12, 13).

L

LAZARUS by the chief priests, for the glory brought to Jesus Christ by being brought back to life (John 11:46–54; 12:10).

LEAH by her husband Jacob, who was deceived by Laban into marrying her instead of her sister, Rachel (Genesis 29:31–34).

LOT
- by the men of Sodom and Gomorrah for his opposition to their homosexual behaviour (Genesis 19:3–9).
- by having to flee for his life for his home, possessions, and wife, when God destroyed his evil city (v. 15–17).
- by having to live in a cave in fear for his life (v. 30).
- by fathering sons to each of his two daughters while in an alcoholic stupor (v. 31–38).

M

MARY, (Mother of Jesus)
- by the prospect of the fulfillment of Simeon's prophecy, when Jesus was dedicated in the temple.

> *'This child is destined to cause the falling and rising of many in Israel, and to be a sign that **will be spoken against**, so that the thoughts of many hearts will be revealed. **and a sword will pierce your own soul too.'*** (Luke 2:34, 25, emphasis added)

- by her son's 'absence without leave' in Jerusalem at 12 years of age (Luke 2:48).
- by the lack of family life with Jesus because of the constant demands of his ministry (Matthew 12:46, 47).
- by Jesus Christ being crucified for being who he was in reality, the Son of God. She, more than any other human, knew this was true (Mark 15:26).

MIRIAM   by God, with leprosy, for criticising Moses' marriage to an Ethiopian, and for questioning his right to hear God's voice before her and Aaron (Numbers 12:1–15).

MOSES
- by his mother when he was three months old. She abandoned him in a papyrus basket among the bulrushes in the river Nile (Exodus 2:3).
- by having to act as an Egyptian, knowing all the time that he was really an Israelite (Exodus 2:5–10).
- by a fellow Hebrew, after killing an Egyptian who was beating him, *'Who made you a judge and ruler over us?'* (v. 11–14).
- by Pharaoh who wanted to kill him when he heard about what had happened, causing Moses to flee from Egypt (v. 15).
- by having to live as an exile among the Midianites (v. 22).

Moses suffered a lot of self-rejection. His forty year stint as a shepherd was a complete reversal of his Egyptian luxurious lifestyle, and the honour he received because of his highly successful military career (according to historians). The comedown from the highest educational and social circles of Egypt to leading sheep around a desert had obviously shattered his self-image. This is clearly seen in the objections he raised when told to return to Egypt and lead his fellow Hebrews out of captivity. God even had to perform a miracle to get his attention and stimulate his interest (Exodus 3:2,3). He later wrote about his dialogue with God. In this we clearly see his:

- **Low self-image.** *'Who am I that I should go to Pharaoh and bring the Israelites out of Egypt?'* (chapter 3:11).
- **Insecurity.** Despite God's promise to be with him all the way, and that he would lead the people out of captivity to worship on the very spot where he was standing, Moses had no confidence in his own ability (chapter 3:13).
- **Fear of man.** *'What if they do not believe me or listen to me and say, "The LORD did not appear to you?"'* (chapter 4:1). In reply, God gave him three remarkable signs to use: his rod for power over the devil and witchcraft practices; his hand to become leprous, then be healed; and the ability to turn water into blood (chapter 4:1–12).
- **Sense of inferiority.** *'O LORD, I have never been eloquent neither in the past nor since you have spoken to your servant. I am slow of speech and tongue'* (chapter 4:10). Even when God promised to give him all the ability he needed, Moses made one last desperate attempt to opt out. *'O LORD please send someone else to do it'* (chapter 4:13). This tells us that:
  - he was a reluctant conscript because of his own basement-level self-evaluation,
  - he didn't want the responsibility because he felt so inadequate, and
  - he had a strong fear of failure because of his rejection.

This defeatist attitude made God angry (v. 14). One cannot but wonder just how many people (readers included), have also made God angry by failing to trust and serve him because they are dominated by rejection!

- by the elders of Israel, because slavemasters were ill-treating the people more than ever, and the promises of deliverance Moses had made were wearing very thin (chapter 5:20, 21).
- by the continual hardness of heart shown by Pharaoh and his court in rejecting every request he made for the people to be allowed to go and worship the Lord (chapters 7–11; 10:28).
- by the Hebrew congregation, time and time again. For example, when:

- they faced the Red Sea with the Egyptians closing in behind them (chapter 14:11, 12).
- they complained about missing the good Egyptian food and faced the prospect of starving to death in the desert (chapter 16:3).
- they grumbled so much about the lack of water at Rephidim that Moses feared for his life (chapter 17:3, 4). They complained even more bitterly, at Kadesh, (Numbers 20:2–13), causing Moses to 'loose his cool', and dishonour God by striking the rock (instead of speaking to it), and shouting at the people in anger. He later died and was buried within sight of his objective (Deuteronomy 32:48–51; 34–5).

Some 1500 years later, Moses the first deliverer, appeared on the mount of transfiguration, and spoke to Jesus Christ, the greatest of all deliverers (Luke 9:30, 31; Romans 11:26, 27).

N

NAOMI   by the death of her husband and two sons during the family's stay in Moab. When she returned to Bethlehem with Ruth, her Moabite daughter-in-law, she said,

> *'Don't call me Naomi ... call me Mara, because the Almighty has made my life very bitter. I went away full, but the Lord has brought me back empty.'*   (Ruth 1:20)

NOAH   by the evil people around him during the 100 years it took to build the ark (Genesis chapter 6; Matthew 24:37–39; 2 Peter 2:5).

P

PAUL, (apostle)
- by the believers at Jerusalem after his salvation. They were afraid of him, and doubted his sincerity (Acts 9:26).
- by Elymas the sorcerer because the proconsul, Sergius Paulus was interested in hearing the gospel (Acts 13:8).
- by the crowd at Lystra. Stirred up by the opposition of the Jews who followed Paul, they stoned him, and dragged him out of the city thinking he was dead (Acts 14:19, 20).

- by the owners of the demon-possessed fortune-telling slave girl whom Paul set free. Paul and Silas were severely beaten and thrown into a dungeon without a fair trail (Acts 16:16–24).
- by jealous Jews in Thessalonica (Acts 17:5–8).
- by the Epicurian and Stoic philosophers in the Areopagus (Acts 17:18–32).
- by Demetrius and the silversmiths at Ephesus (Acts 19:23–41).
- by the wild mob in Jerusalem (Acts 21:27–40); continuous accusations, and trials, his shipwreck experience, and his final imprisonment in Rome (Acts chapters 22–28).

PETER

- by Jesus Christ, for letting Satan speak through him (Matthew 16:22, 23).
- by himself, with tears, when the crowing of a cock reminded him that he had broken his promise to Jesus Christ. He had denied knowing him, with oaths and curses when accused of being a Jesus-follower (Matthew 26:33–35, 69–75). Peter's rejection, self-rejection, and guilt were removed after meeting Jesus privately (Luke 24:34), and being reaffirmed in the presence of the other disciples (John 21:15–19). As a confirmation, the Spirit of God filled him and spoke through him at Pentecost (Acts 2:1–41).

PRODIGAL, (Son)   The story told by Jesus illustrates rejection in a family situation. The older brother rejected the young prodigal for profligate living and the squandering of his share of the family inheritance. He also rejected his father because he was jealous of the special treatment his young brother had received after returning home in rags and repentance (Luke 15:11–32).

Whether this is a parable or real life story, the process of rejection is clearly illustrated.

S

SAMSON

- by his fiancee for giving his Philistine enemies the answer to his riddle (Judges 14:15–18).
- by his lover Delilah, who incessantly plagued him for the secret of his great strength, then betrayed him for a bribe (Judges 16:4–21).

138

- by the Philistines who gouged out his eyes, bound him with bronze shackles, and forced him to grind corn in the prison-house (v. 21). Later they made fun of him at a sacrificial festival in honour of their god Dagon, and a great many of them died when Samson regained his strength and revenged his rejection (v. 23–30).

SARAH, (Sarai)

- by her husband, when they were in foreign countries together. Abraham (Abram), for fear and self-preservation twice told her to deny her married status by saying she was his sister (Genesis 12:11–13; 20:2–13).
- by herself, because she was unable to bear children (Genesis 16:1–2).
- by Hagar, who gave birth to her husband's child, Ishmael (Genesis 16:4).

SAUL, (Israel's 1st king)

- by God, through the prophet Samuel for being presumptuous in offering sacrifices, instead of waiting for Samuel (1 Samuel 13:6–14).
- by God, through Samuel, for arrogance and rebellion in not killing every Amalekite and animal. '... *Because you have rejected the word of the Lord, he has rejected you as king'* (1 Samuel 15:22, 23, emphasis added).
- by the giant Goliath, who dismayed and terrified him in his rejected condition (1 Samuel 17:11).
- by the Holy Spirit, who left him and sent an evil spirit to torment him (1 Samuel 16:14–23).
- by his own jealousy because of his son Jonathan's loving relationship with David, whom Saul feared and hated (1 Samuel 20:30–33). His rejected state became so intolerable that he finally disguised himself and consulted the witch of Endor. But when God revealed Saul's true identity to her, his alibi collapsed, and Samuel's message of ultimate rejection by death, shattered him (1 Samuel 28:7–20).

SOLOMON, (King)

- by God, because of his failure to obey the laws governing kings set out in the laws of Moses. Kings were not permitted to:
- – accumulate great numbers of horses, or send buyers into Egypt to purchase them (Deuteronomy 17:16). Solomon broke both commandments (2 Chronicles 1:16,17).

– take many wives, in case they led them astray. Solomon
certainly did that in grand style with 700 full-timers and 300
stand-bys; they certainly did lead him astray (1 Kings 11:3).
- by God, for doing evil, and encouraging idolatry.

*'The LORD became angry with Solomon because his heart had
turned away from the LORD ... Although he had forbidden
Solomon to follow other gods, Solomon did not keep the LORD's
command. So the LORD said to Solomon, "Since this is your
attitude and you have not kept my covenant and my decrees,
which I commanded you, I will most certainly* **tear the kingdom
away from you***, and give it to one of your subordinates ...'*

(1 Kings 11:9–11, emphasis added)

From then on Solomon's rejection became more and more
obvious, as reflected by much of the contents of the book of
Ecclesiastes.

T

TAMAR, (daughter of King David) by her lustful brother
Amnon, who deceived and brutally raped her despite her desperate appeal to him to marry, but not force her. An even greater
rejection followed when she was thrown out, and the door
locked. She spent the rest of her life in her brother's house, *'a
desolate woman'* (2 Samuel 13:1–20).

U

UZZIAH, (King) By God, for pride, unfaithfulness, and presumption in burning incense in the temple. He was struck with
leprosy, and forced to live in isolation, unable to enter the temple
again (2 Chronicles 26:16–21).

V

VASHTI, (Queen) by her husband King Xerxes (Ahasuerus), in
a fit of pique and anger inflamed by alcohol. She had refused to
obey his order to parade before his guests wearing her royal

regalia (Esther chapter 1). Her rejection was well publicised to prevent *'no end of disrespect and discord'* among the wives of the Mede and Persian nobility (v. 18).

Z

ZACCHAEUS, (the tax collector)   by his fellow countrymen, for being a Roman quisling (Luke 19:1–10).

These biblical examples may shed more light on why some people have suffered rejection. The examples given have many parallels in modern living. Of course no two situations will be exactly the same, but there may have been a familiar ring to any reader who has:
- wilfully sinned, or dishonoured the name of the Lord. Paul warns us that because of this, some people have become weak, sick, or have died. (1 Corinthians 11:27–30).
- been rejected as a Christian, by family or friends.
- suffered rejection for witnessing about Jesus Christ in cultures where religious or demonic practices oppose the gospel.

Irrespective of the source of rejection and the extent of its effects, every rejection sufferer whether innocent or otherwise, can receive deliverance and healing through Jesus Christ, provided right choices are made.

Chapter 14

The Most Rejected Person
Who Ever Lived

Secular historians may have difficulty in deciding who this person would be, but when biblical history is considered, it soon becomes obvious that there has never been a more rejected person than Jesus Christ. He was rejected because of who he was, what he said and did, how he lived, and particularly because of the way in which he died.

His coming to earth was a closely kept secret before time began. It was God himself who broke the news to the serpent in the Garden of Eden: *'I will put enmity between **you** and **the woman**, and between **your offspring** and **hers, he** will crush your head, and you will strike his heel'* (Genesis 3:15, emphasis added). Isaiah later expanded that revelation, *'**The virgin** will be with child and will give birth to **a son**, and will call him **Immanuel**'* (Isaiah 7:14). *'For to us a child is born, to us **a son is given**, and the government will be on his shoulders'* (Isaiah 9:6).

*Jesus Christ fulfilled each scripture – Immanuel – the given son – born to a virgin. When he asked his disciples, '**Who do people say the Son of Man is?**'* (Matthew 16:13, emphasis added) Peter answered, *'You are the Christ, **the Son of the Living God**'* (v. 16, emphasis added). *Jesus then said, 'Blessed are you Simon son of Jonah, for this was not revealed to you by man, but by my Father in heaven'* (v. 17).

'Son of man' ... *'Son of God'*, a living expression of God's love to sinful, rejected mankind. As *'Son of Man'*, he was *'tempted in every way, just as we are – yet was without sin'* (Hebrews 4:15). As *'Son of

God' – 'Although he was a son, he learned obedience from what he suffered and, once made perfect, he became the source of eternal salvation for all who obey him ...' (Hebrews 5:8). We need to examine the rejection of Jesus Christ from two perspectives.

Firstly, to what extent did he have to identify with our rejection in order to fully represent human experience? Secondly, why is it that rejection did not have the evil effects on him that it has had on the rest of humanity?

The extent of the rejection Jesus Christ suffered in his lifetime

The greatest difference between the 'Son of Man' and us, the 'sons of men', is that **He chose** to be rejected; we didn't.

1. His early life

In choosing to be born of a woman, Jesus Christ knew that it would mean a jolting, swaying in-utero 112 kilometre journey to the 'maternity hospital' by donkey; it would mean the lack of pre-natal care because local accommodation would be unavailable; that his delivery was going to be in a cattle stall among the animals he himself had created; and that a pile of hay in a feeding-stall was to become his first bed.

He chose to be born to a betrothed but unmarried virgin, and to live for a while as an alien in a foreign land to escape a ruthless Roman megalomaniac who wanted to kill him (Matthew 2:16).

He also chose to become an apprentice carpenter, which caused problems with the locals in Nazareth where he had been brought up. They didn't understand the source of his wisdom without special education, or the basis of his power to do miracles (Matthew 13:55–57). In fact, their unbelief and rejection were so strong that he could only heal a few sick folk among them (Mark 6:1–6). Later on, these very people became furious when he read a well-known prophecy from Isaiah in their synagogue and applied it to himself. They rushed him to a nearby cliff-top intending to hurl him to his death, but he simply walked unnoticed through them, and went on his way (Mark 6:1–5; Luke 4:16–30).

144

Even his family put him down. His mother and step-father didn't take too kindly to their eldest son remaining in Jerusalem after their celebration of the Feast of the Passover (Luke 2:42–46). *'His mother said to him, "Son, why have you treated us like this? Your father and I have been anxiously searching for you"'* (v. 48). Neither of them understood what Jesus meant by saying he had to be in *'his Father's house'*, but Mary kept these words amongst her treasured memories (v. 51).

His step-brothers also gave him a hard time. They cynically suggested that if he wanted to become a public figure, he ought to stop acting so secretly and do his thing publicly by performing more miracles for his disciples. In other words, they were saying, 'We don't believe you either, brother' (John 7:2–11).

2. His brief three and a half year public ministry

(a) The religious and political Jewish leaders rejected him

From the very beginning they were suspicious, envious, jealous, openly antagonistic, and finally, murderous. Their rejection included:

- accusing him of blasphemy for forgiving sins (Matthew 9:2–6).
- claiming that he cast out demons through Beelzebub the prince of demons (Mark 3:22; Matthew 12:22–28).
- constantly demanding signs of his authority and power (Matthew 16:1–4).
- turning his Father's house (the temple) into an animal market, and a den of thieves (Matthew 2:12, 13; John 2:16).
- always trying to trick him into making a mistake, or contradicting himself (Matthew 22:15–21).
- complaining about the respect and praise the people gave him on Palm Sunday (Luke 19:39).
- objecting to him healing on the Sabbath day. Their stubbornness deeply distressed Jesus (Mark 3:2–6).
- blaming his disciples for not conforming to the traditions of the elders (Mark 7:5–13).
- becoming angry when parables were spoken against them (Mark 12:1–12).
- behaving discourteously when he was the guest of Simon the Pharisee (Luke 7:36–50).

- plotting his death (Mark 3:6).
- arresting him as if he were leading a rebellion (Mark 14:42–49).
- using false evidence to have him condemned by the Sanhedrin (Mark 14:53–64).

(b) The Jewish population at large rejected him

Because of the oppressive and heavy-handed religious leadership during the Roman occupation, many people were fearful of reprisals if they displayed public approval of Jesus Christ, even though he had done many miracles in public. Many of their reactions to Jesus Christ and his ministry were expressions of rejection. These include:

- muttering disdainfully because he went to the home of Zacchaeus, whom they branded *'a sinner'* (Luke 19:7).
- claiming that God was their Father because they were Abraham's descendants, while they were plotting to kill his Son. Jesus revealed their spiritual heritage by saying, *'You belong to your father, the devil, and you want to carry out your father's desire. He was a murderer from the beginning, not holding the truth, for there is no truth in him ...'* (John 8:44).
- being rebuffed by a Samaritan woman – from a different culture (John 4:9).
- pressuring him to leave the Gadarene coast after some 2,000 of their local swine had rushed down a steep bank and drowned in Lake Galilee as a demoniac was delivered and healed (Luke 8:26–37).
- demonstrating noisily outside Pilate's judgement hall, shouting for Jesus to be crucified, and demanding the release of the murderous mobster, Barabbas (Mark 15:11–15).
- taunting him to come down from the cross, on which he had been securely nailed. They twisted the truth by saying that if he was going to destroy the temple and rebuild it in three days, he could surely prove he was the Son of God by freeing himself and saving his life (Matthew 27:39–40). The mob was backed up by the chief priests, elders and teachers of the law (v. 41–43).
- even the two thieves who were crucified with him insulted him (v. 43). One later repented, and asked to be remembered by Jesus. He received the promise of life that day (Luke 23:39–43).

(c) The Roman overlords also clearly rejected him:
● in the cruel mockery of their soldiers (Matthew 27:28–30; Luke 23:36).
● in Pilate's unjust death sentence made in fear of Caesar (John 19:1–16), despite a last minute plea by his wife (Matthew 27:19).
● by public crucifixion which automatically placed a curse on Jesus according to Jewish law (Luke 23:33; Galatians 3:13).

(d) Even his own disciples rejected Jesus
Despite his blameless life, his wisdom, his public and private teachings, his great power in deliverance, healings, miracles, and the obvious delight he gave his heavenly Father,
● they were slow to learn and quickly forgot the lessons he taught them (Mark 8:14–21; 16:14).
● many deserted him because they could not understand some of his teachings (John 6:60–71).
● Mary, Martha, and their friends just could not believe that Jesus intended to raise Lazarus from the dead before their very eyes. They were sure he was referring to the future resurrection of all the dead. Jesus was deeply moved in spirit, and troubled by their unbelief, he wept (John 11:1–35).
● Judas, the disciples' treasurer, betrayed him (Matthew 26:47–49).
● when Jesus needed most support in the Garden of Gethsemane during his agonised praying, his three closest disciples slept, despite being asked to remain alert and pray (Mark 14:32–41). The writer believes that the disciples were under demonic oppression because their heavy sleep was unnatural. Jesus had wakened them twice, urging them to keep watch with him, but both times they immediately returned to deep sleep (v. 34, 37, 40, 41).
● after his arrest, every disciple deserted him (Mark 14:50).
● despite fervent promises of loyalty, Peter denied he knew Jesus when challenged in the courtyard of the High Priest's palace (Matthew 26:70–75).

(e) Jesus Christ spoke openly about his rejection
His earthly life and crucifixion totally fulfilled Isaiah's prophecy, *'He was despised and **rejected of men'*** (chapter 53:3, emphasis added).

- he concluded a parable by saying: *'Have you not read in the Scriptures: "The stone which the builders **rejected** has become the capstone; the Lord has done this, and it is marvellous in our eyes?"'* (Matthew 21:42; Psalm 118:22, 23, emphasis added).

- *'He then began to teach them that the **Son of Man** must suffer many things and **be rejected** by the elders, chief priests, and teachers of the law, and that he must be killed and after three days rise again'* (Luke 9:22; Mark 8:31, emphasis added).

- *'For the **Son of Man** in his day will be like the lightning, which flashes and lights up the sky from one end to another. But first he must suffer many things and **be rejected by this generation**'* (Luke 17:25, emphasis added).

It is little wonder that when John wrote his gospel towards the end of the first century, he made it clear that the whole world had rejected him:

> *'He was in the world, and though the world was made through him, the world **did not recognise him**. He came to that which was his own, but **his own did not receive him**.'*
>
> (John 1:11, emphasis added)

(f) Finally, the awesome experience of the cross

This brief study of the rejection of Jesus Christ commenced by noting that he was the perfect manifestation of God's holy nature as *'Son of God'*, and sinless humanity as *'Son of Man'*. It is therefore appropriate that we conclude with the same two aspects of Christ Jesus:

(i) as Son of God

After the Roman soldiers had hammered jagged iron spikes through his hands and feet, Jesus prayed to his Father as 'Son of God': *'Father forgive them, for they do not know what they are doing'* (Luke 23:34).

As God's Son, he also extended mercy to the penitent thief – *'I tell you the truth, today you will be with me in paradise'* (Luke 23:43).

(ii) as Son of Man

Even in excruciating pain, Jesus was loving and graciously thoughtful towards his mother Mary, saying to her, *'"Dear woman, here is your son"*, and to the disciple (John), *"Here is your mother"'* (John

19:26, 27). From then onwards, the two became 'mother' and 'son' in John's household (v. 27).

About 3 pm on the afternoon of the crucifixion, in total darkness, a piercing cry came from the bloodied figure on the central cross, '"Eloi, Eloi, lama sabachthani?" – which means "My God, my God, why have you forsaken me?"' (Matthew 27:46; Mark 15:34). His cry was to the one to whom he was offering himself as an acceptable, sinless sacrifice on behalf of a world of sinners. By fully suffering God's judgemental wrath on sin, and making reconciliation with God available to sinners by repentance and faith, Jesus totally fulfilled his purpose in becoming 'Son of Man'. God confirmed that by raising him from the dead (Romans 1:4). Born amongst cattle, and crucified between criminals surrounded by a murderous mob egged on by fanatical religious leaders, Jesus, 'Son of God', 'Son of Man', has made it possible for us 'sons of men' to become 'sons of God'.

Explanatory note: The extent to which Jesus Christ suffered our rejection so that we might have his freedom will be the subject of the next chapter.

At present we need to consider briefly why Jesus Christ, as the most rejected person who ever lived, was never controlled by it. In fact, he was symptom-free.

The Scriptures give us the reason this is so:

3. His dedication to fulfil his divine commission

(a) He came to destroy every evil work of Satan
'But you know that he appeared so that he might take away our sins, and in him is no sin' (1 John 3:5). 'The reason the Son of God appeared was to destroy the devil's work' (v. 8).

The first two parts of this book supply ample evidence that rejection is indeed a major work of the devil affecting believers and unbelievers alike.

(b) He came to fulfil his Father's will
'"My food", said Jesus, "is to do the will of him who sent me and finish his work"' (John 3:34). 'I have brought you glory on earth by completing the work you gave me to do' (John 17:4). Nothing changed that objective. 'Jesus resolutely set out for Jerusalem' (Luke 9:51; Matthew 16:21).

(c) He brought release to rejection sufferers wherever he found a need:

- by healing a leper and touching him as a sign of his healing (Matthew 8:1–4).
- by his continuous ministry of deliverance and healing (Luke 4:40–41), and by authorising his disciples to do the same (Luke 9:1, 2).
- by inviting weary and burdened people to come to him and receive rest (Matthew 11:28).
- by giving the power and authority of his kingdom (symbolised by keys) first to Peter (Matthew 16:19), and later, to all the disciples (Matthew 18:18).
- by healing a woman whose sickness had made her a social outcast (Mark 5:25–34).
- by raising a young man from the dead, and restoring him to his grieving, widowed mother (Luke 7:11–16).
- by the deliverance and healing of a badly crippled woman, rejected by a pompous synagogue ruler (Luke 13:10–17).
- by promising that *'the Comforter'* would take his place (John 14:16).
- by reaching across cultural barriers to bless needy people – the Roman Centurion's servant (Luke 7:9, 10), the Samaritans (John chapter 4), and the Greek mother's daughter (Mark 7:24–30).
- by blessing a Jewish young man whom the Pharisees had publicly thrown out of the Temple because he insisted that Jesus must have been sinless (John chapter 10).

(d) He always lived in intimate fellowship with his Father

Neither Satan, his disciples, nor daily circumstances ever hindered this. *'But Jesus often withdrew to lonely places and prayed'* (Luke 5:16). *'One of those days Jesus went out into the hills to pray, and spent the night praying to God'* (Luke 6:12). Also Mark 1:35; Mark 6:46; Luke 9:28. His Father constantly affirmed his delight in his Son (Luke 3:22; Matthew 17:5; John 12:23–30).

(e) He was constantly filled, and controlled by the Holy Spirit

'For the one whom God has sent speaks the words of God; to him God gives the Spirit without limit' (John 3:34; also Matthew 12:18). Jesus Christ:

- was led by the Spirit (Luke 4:1).

- was empowered by the Spirit (Luke 4:14).
- cast out evil spirits by the Spirit (Matthew 12:28).
- offered his unblemished life as a sacrifice to God by the Spirit (Hebrews 9:14).

Summary

1. Jesus Christ came to earth knowing full well he would be rejected throughout his public ministry.
2. He was rejected by his family, his disciples, his nation, the Gentiles, and finally forsaken by his Father on the cross, all for our redemption and release from the works of the evil one.
3. Jesus Christ was never controlled by rejection, or showed its evil fruit.
4. His behavioural choices as 'Son of Man' provide us with a perfect example of a God-honouring lifestyle which will both release believers, and preserve them from rejection and its evil consequences. If we are to follow in his footsteps (1 Peter 2:21), we must also be prepared to be:
   - **dedicated** to God's pre-determined objectives.
   - **committed** to fulfil the Heavenly Father's will in daily living.
   - **constantly willing** to selflessly minister freedom and wholeness to others.
   - **live in unbroken, intimate fellowship** with the Father.
   - **always filled and controlled by the Holy Spirit.**

Chapter 15

How God Dealt with the Whole Rejection Problem

The last chapter focussed on what surely must be regarded as the most incredible event ever to have taken place in heaven or on earth. God himself fully identified with our rejection. His one and only son Jesus Christ was publicly crucified at mob insistence alongside two criminal insurgents. Nobody had offered to defend Jesus during the mock trials before either the high priest, King Herod, or Pontius Pilate . . . not one person whom he had healed, or delivered from demonic forces, or raised from the dead. And every one was living proof that He was indeed Immanuel (God with us). Even his disciples who had so fervently promised to support him, vanished. Peter later sneaked into the courtyard when Jesus was before the Sanhedrin, and warmed himself at the soldiers' fire. But when the crowing of a cock reminded him that he had broken his vow never to deny Jesus, he left in tears. Only John went to Calvary while it was still dark and joined Mary and a few of her close friends keeping silent vigil at the foot of the cross.

If we are to benefit from what Jesus Christ suffered, and gain the full release from the causes and effects of rejection, we need to consider just what did happen at Calvary. But firstly, a quick overview (Matthew 27:45–50).

1. During the hours of darkness, and by his death, Jesus Christ
- *paid God's ransom price to redeem us* (1 Timothy 2:6). Jesus willingly offered his life, choosing the place, means, and timing of his own death (John 12:32; 19:28–30).

153

- *made atonement for our sin* (Hebrews 2:17). He died as God's chosen sacrifice so that sinners could have their sins washed away (John 1:29, 36; Romans 5:11; 1 John 2:2).
- *reconciled God and man* (2 Corinthians 5:19). Now sinners could become children of God (John 1:12).
- *ended Satan's power to dominate us* (Colossians 2:15). Demon forces can now be overcome through the power of his name, and his shed blood (Mark 16:17; Revelation 12:11).
- *brought an end to the need for animal sacrifices, and became, himself, the only living way to God* (Matthew 27:51; Hebrews 10:19, 20, emphasis added).

2. In hell, Jesus Christ

- *announced his victory to the underworld* (1 Peter 3:19). Demons had so defiled the earth's population before the flood that God chained them in darkness for future judgement (2 Peter 2:4).
- *retrieved the keys to death and hell* (Revelation 1:18). Satan had afflicted mankind after his confidence trick on Adam and Eve (Genesis 4:8; 1 John 3:12; Luke 4:6).
- *liberated the righteous dead* (Matthew 27:52, 53; Ephesians 4:8). Some even walked around Jerusalem after the resurrection, and were taken to heaven by Jesus Christ.

3. Through his resurrection and ascension, Jesus Christ

- *became the King-priest of heaven's temple.* Through the blood of Melchizedek, we have cleansing, and power over Satan (Hebrews 7:17, 27; 9:11–28; Revelation 12:11).
- *was exalted above all created spirit-beings* (Ephesians 1:20, 21). In Christ we have been given authority to set people free from Satan's power, including rejection (Mark 16:17).
- *kept his promise and commissioned the Holy Spirit to replace him on earth* (John 14:16, 17; Acts 2:33). The subject of the Holy Spirit's ministry in us will be dealt with in a later chapter.

Now let us turn our attention to what the crucifixion, resurrection, and ascension of Jesus Christ should mean to every rejection sufferer.

The prophet Isaiah had a unique ministry. His vision of God, his prophetic writings about Immanuel (to be born to a virgin), and the details of his life, are without parallel in prophetic writings (Isaiah 7:14; 9:6; chapters 53, 61). In the 61st chapter of the book which bears his name, Isaiah outlines the future ministry of the anointed one (verses 1–3).

- He would preach the good news of God's redeeming love to those who humbled themselves (v. 1).
- He would bring spiritual healing to the hearts of all who broken-heartedly repented (v. 1).
- He would free prisoners from sin's slavery and consequences (v. 1).
- He would reveal God's purposes for man (v. 2).
- He would spiritually renew and comfort those whose sin caused them to mourn (v. 3).
- He would also make them as spiritually productive as oak trees (v. 3).

These priorities of Jesus Christ also establish a divine order for our present day ministry to people.

- salvation and reconciliation with God;
- deliverance from demonic bondages and oppressions;
- teaching from God's word;
- the comfort of healing and wholeness;
- discipleship and encouragement to grow spiritually and be reproducers.

This is God's salvation 'package-deal' for believers. If each person being led to a saving knowledge of Jesus Christ were to receive each interlocking piece of God's grace, new birth would mean what God intends it to mean. Churches would be filled with robust, loving, and reproducing believers not needing 'band-aid' counselling, or the support of friends, pastors, or even tranquillisers.

There are three other important principles in these three verses. Firstly, salvation normally precedes receiving God's healing grace. Secondly, deliverance should come before spiritual healing (including healing of the memories). If root causes are not removed, evil fruit will continue to grow. Thirdly, spiritual productivity is a must, not an option. Only at times of Holy Ghost revival will these experiences happen simultaneously.

It is now time to examine in detail Isaiah's other major revelation

– chapter 53. Apart from knowing that the 'son' to be given (chapter 9:6) was indeed God himself (chapters 7:12; 61:1), the writer was unaware of the personal name of the promised one. He used the pronouns 'he, him, his' forty times. The chapter shows how completely Jesus Christ identified himself with the roots and fruit of the sin problem, and the rejection it caused. In his humanity, Jesus Christ was affected by it, but never infected by it.

(a) 'He was despised ... ' (v. 3)
The Concise Oxford Dictionary defines 'despise' as 'regard as inferior, or worthless; feel contempt for'. This accurately describes how rejected people see themselves. The stronger the basic cause(s), the deeper will be the effects.

Low self-image is probably one of the greatest causes of failure. It is totally self-centred, based on feelings not facts, and certainly wrecks faith. Low self-image causes defeatism, stops positive thinking, and regards the future as being hopeless.

Jesus had none of these symptoms in himself otherwise he would have been an imperfect offering whom God would never have accepted (Hebrews 7:26). In his sinlessness, Jesus suffered the pain and punishment we deserved, and completely destroyed the power of inferiority and worthlessness. He freely gives us the victory for which he paid so dearly. One rejection sufferer had such a low self-image before he was set free that he could hardly bear to look at himself in a mirror. All has now changed.

(b) ' ... and rejected by men ... ' (v. 3)
The extent of his rejection was dealt with in the last chapter. The climax came when the chief priests, rulers, and their demonstrators shouted unanimously, *'Away with this man! Release Barabbas to us ... Crucify him! Crucify him!'* (Luke 23:18–21). This mob outcry was the basest act of rejection man could ever have displayed against God's grace.

In conquering Satan and his demonic hordes, Jesus Christ smashed the whole rejection stranglehold with which the evil one had crippled mankind from the Garden of Eden. Jesus now holds the keys to freedom (Revelation 1:18), and willingly offers to release victims from the emotional death and hell in which they are trapped. This is why the Gospel has such liberating power for human rejects who live furtively in our parks and city streets.

(c) '... a man of sorrows and familiar with suffering ...' (v. 3)

Rejection is certainly a chief cause of emotional suffering. The concept of 'pain' is expressed in 'sorrows' and 'suffering' in the NIV, rather than the 'sorrows' and 'grief' of the Authorised Version.

Is rejection painful? It most certainly is. Counsellees show it on their faces. They express it in words and tears. They reveal it by their grief, bitterness, and anger over the circumstances or people who have given them rejection. Some even walk around as in a fog, hopeless and melancholic. Hereditary rejection has the same effect.

No rejection sufferer should think of Jesus Christ on the cross without being able to say, 'He suffered that for me, to set me free!' Tragically, few see it that way. Their spiritual eyes are so often blurred by tears of self-pity. Some even get angry with God as if he were responsible for their rejection.

(d) '... surely he took up our infirmities and carried our sorrows.'
(v. 4)

The word translated 'infirmities' (AV 'griefs') means in the Hebrew 'sickness, weakness, pain' (Young's Analytical Concordance). Matthew said that when Jesus Christ *'drove out spirits with a word and healed all the sick', 'This was to fulfil what was spoken through the prophet Isaiah: "He took our infirmities and carried our diseases"'* (Matthew 8:16, 17).

The power Jesus Christ and his disciples used over demons and sickness now belongs to each member of his spiritual body (Mark 16:17, 18). This is particularly significant in the deliverance ministry. Those who have read either of the first two books in this series will remember that it has been constantly claimed that demonic powers are the causes of the root and fruit systems of rejection. This is why the problem cannot be just shrugged off, worked through, talked out, or cleared up by behavioural formulas or medication. Experience has proved that when the powers of the evil one are driven out, and spiritual healing received, rejection symptoms disappear. Deliverance and healing are just as powerful a combination in the 1990s as in the first century, because the atonement Jesus Christ made for us is timeless.

Without doubt, every Christian believes that 'God is still in the healing business' to quote a somewhat hackneyed saying. Everyone agrees that he may use healing as a sign to the world (Acts 28:7–9), or as a blessing to his people (Acts 20:7–12). Only the timing, manner, frequency, and extent of that healing are sometimes disputed. The writer firmly believes that no believer has the right to demand that God must heal, even if he is promised the glory. Sooner or later, someone is bound to get hurt, and lose faith.

Phyl and I praise God for the many times we have seen physical healings follow deliverance. In most cases, rejection has been the major cause of emotional and sometimes physical disorders. But it would be wrong to infer that every sickness disappears once a person is released from rejection. This is particularly so when the rejection process has commenced through becoming blind, bed-ridden, crippled, paraplegic, or quadriplegic.

Jay E. Adams in *Competent to Counsel* refers to another cause of sicknesses and problems. He states 'Psychosomatic illnesses are genuine somatic (bodily) problems which are the direct result of inner psychical difficulty. But illness caused by psychological stress must be distinguished from illness which causes psychological stress.' Deep rejection can indeed be a cause of psychical stress. Some very debilitating fears, anxieties and depression may arise from this. In such cases, deliverance from the spirits of rejection will release the psychical stress and enable healing to be received.

(e) '... But he was pierced for our transgressions, he was crushed for our iniquities ... for he bore the sin of many ...' (vv. 5, 12)
The psychical and physical sufferings of Jesus Christ ceased when he *'called out with a loud voice, "Father into your hands I commit my spirit." When he said this, he breathed his last'* (Luke 23:46).

Through the shedding of his blood, propitiation was made for the three major classifications of wrongdoings clearly named in verses 5 and 12, namely:
- **iniquity** – basically rebellion against God and his laws for right-eous living.
- **transgression** – defiance of God's boundaries, doing what he forbids and hates.
- **sin** – failing to measure up to God's requirements, similar to an archer missing a target. When used in the plural, the word 'sins' may also imply that each of these three offences has been committed. (For further references to the linkage between these

definitions see Exodus 34:7; Leviticus 16:21; Daniel 9:24; Psalm 103:10, 12.)

For readers who question what these three words have to do with rejection, there are two simple answers.

Firstly, to cause someone to be rejected is to sin against both God and the person he made to reflect his image. Whether we have deliberately rejected another person, or have done so unconsciously under hereditary influences, we need to repent and confess it before forgiveness and cleansing can be received. Secondly, if we have personally suffered rejection, we are still accountable for the ways we express it, such as anger, rudeness, rebellion, pouting, manipulation, offensive language, etc. Some also take self-comforting measures such as over-eating, sexual self-stimulation, drugs, alcohol, or move into occultism in order to counteract negative inner feelings. There must always be genuine repentance from wrongdoing, and a sincere willingness to embrace a new lifestyle before deliverance from the controlling demonic powers can be effective.

Even when people are innocent victims of rejection, they are still personally responsible for their defensive and offensive attitudes and actions. Repentance, confession, and forgiveness are very necessary if deliverance and healing are to be effective and permanent.

(f) '. . . the punishment that brought us peace was upon him, and by his wounds we are healed' (v. 5, emphasis added)

Jesus Christ, as the sinners' substitute, also made it possible for us to share fully in the blessings of his victory. Peace automatically follows freedom from demonic domination, and inner healing becomes real when our lives are cleansed and Jesus Christ is given his rightful Lordship in everyday living. Spiritual problems need spiritual remedies. The whole spectrum of medical and behavioural sciences may assist in the recovery process for Christians and non-Christians alike. However, the believer alone is able to receive the total and permanent release offered by the once crucified and now glorified Christ. What security is provided in verse 10b! '. . . *he will see his offspring and prolong his days, and the will of the Lord will prosper in his hand.*'

With a slight adaption, the well-known chorus could read:

'Turn your eyes upon Jesus,
Look full in his wonderful face,
And the freedom and joy that he gives
Will show others his glory and grace.'

When Christians are released from rejection, it may take time to establish the new habit of turning to Jesus Christ in all times of need. If anyone has previously relied on people-support, the dependence may be difficult to break. Jesus alone is our eternal security, and our faith in him should develop into an ever-deepening personal relationship. Heaven is where the action is, and always will be. So let's keep our eyes on Jesus Christ (Colossians 3:1, 2; Hebrews 12:2). By suffering rejection, Jesus Christ fully identified with this Satanic evil.

He ripped out its cancerous root system, and prevents the growth of its poisonous fruit. Slavery to sin is no longer the hopeless outlook facing every new-born child of God. The power of sin and rejection has been triumphantly smashed. Isaiah's description of our Saviour's sufferings shows that the very dregs of the cup he drank for us included the bitterness of rejection. But some reader will probably ask 'If this is so, why are so many Christians dominated by this dreadful thing?'. Here are some reasons:

- Many Christians think that rejection is a personal behavioural problem, not a spiritual one.
- Few believers understand that it has a Satanic origin, and operates under demonic influence. The problem is usually rationalized by seeking advice on how to alleviate its symptoms, without dealing with the source.
- Even when demonic involvement is recognised, the very word 'deliverance' often arouses prejudice, or causes fear of wild scenes and violence. So the real issue is avoided. Satan is a very successful propagandist.
- Believers who are effective in ministering deliverance are often not widely known, and those affected do not know where to find help.
- Sufferers learn to live with the problem, unaware that freedom is available.

In writing to Timothy, Paul said that the living God '... *is the Saviour of all men, and **especially those who believe**'* (1 Timothy 4:10, emphasis added). God is waiting to save every living person, but only a believer can call him '**my** Saviour'. He is also willing to free his people from every trace of satanic activity, but only those who trust him will be able to say, *'He is also, **my** Deliverer'* (Romans 11:26).

Chapter 16

There must be Something
Wrong Somewhere!

Several days ago, I received this letter from a young lady living in another State.

'Dear Mr Gibson, I've been listening to some of your teaching tapes on "deliverance" ... and I must say I was encouraged by your message. I have recognized the need for deliverance from the past ... but find there are not many Christians who see the necessity of this, rather they seem to believe we just cannot change; we are stuck with our warped personalities and stunted growth.

For two years I was involved with ... in Hawaii and Asia. They were years of growth for me in various ways, but since my return to my family and church, these last few years have been the most difficult of my 11 years as a Christian.

God has been teaching me much, and dealing with sins of which I have now repented. However, something is holding me back from becoming the person God wants me to be. I know I am still oppressed by Satan, and my family situation continues to be very difficult despite facing up to my shortcomings.

I desire to have the power of the Holy Spirit working in my life, and transforming me. I have great difficulty with many relationships despite my trying to overcome my personality defects, and I know this is a key area. Despite my feverish activity in the church scene, I am becoming very isolated and cut off from people, because of the lack of fellowship with Christians who also want to change ...

I have been trying to work through these problems for months on my own with limited success. I'm really tired of being a crippled Christian.

Hoping you can help in some way, or recommend another person who does really believe that Jesus can set us free from the defects that handicap us in life.'

Signed: 'Amelia'

The letter contains some interesting points.

- Although a committed Christian, 'Amelia' knows she still needs deliverance from the past.
- She receives little or no encouragement from fellow believers.
- Despite repentance from sin, she still feels its power gripping her.
- She concludes Satan is oppressing her.
- She longs for the transforming power of the Holy Spirit.
- She feels isolated despite being busy in church activities.
- Although having tried to 'work through' her problems, she still feels a crippled Christian.
- Although the word 'rejection' was not used, its symptoms were obvious – 'difficult family situation', 'great difficulty with many relationships', 'becoming isolated and cut off from people', 'lack of fellowship'.

In view of the perfect provision Jesus Christ has made for us, something is obviously very wrong with this young lady and the many who are like her. *'Now the Lord is the Spirit, and where the Spirit of the Lord is, **there is freedom***' (2 Corinthians 3:17, emphasis added).

This leaves us with an obvious question: 'Why is it that Christians are so vulnerable to demonic oppression, particularly rejection?' Of the many answers which spring to mind, two deserve special mention.

1. Christians are special targets for demonic oppression

In talking to Christians with problems, I have often said, 'I smell sulphur.' But this is no light-hearted statement. Many Christians have forgotten that:

(a) We all live in a world manipulated by the evil one (1 John 5:19).
Salvation is not a spiritual umbrella which keeps Satan off our

backs. We are given defensive spiritual weapons to use against his none too subtle oppression (Ephesians 6:10–18). Whenever we let down our defence, he wins by default.

(b) Jesus said that a Christian's good deeds are a light in a dark place, and bring glory to God (Matthew 5:16). We also know that the kingdom of darkness cannot extinguish that light (John 1:5). But the evil one does cause Christians to shade their lights and nod off to sleep (Ephesians 5:8–14).

(c) If we are not fully liberated from oppressive spirits when we are saved (Acts 26:18), we will continue to experience those miserable oppressions. For example, how many Christians do we know who are still troubled with anger, lust, fears, alcohol, occultic influences and rejection?

(d) When we are saved our souls are not put into automatic overdrive so that we can relax and enjoy spiritual blessings, without personal effort. Paul says: '... *continue to **work out** your salvation with fear and trembling, for it is God **who works in you** to will and to act according to his good purpose*' (Philippians 2:12, emphasis added).

(e) Careless Christian living may give lurking demon powers a foothold (Ephesians 4:26, 27). The Christian life is both a fight and a race. It also calls for hard work, discipline, and self-denial.

(f) The writer believes that God sometimes uses demons to punish disobedient Christians (1 Timothy 1:20; 1 Corinthians 5:5), as he used them in the Old Testament (Psalm 78:49; 1 Samuel 16:14). This subject is treated more fully in *Evicting Demonic Intruders and Breaking Bondages*.

(g) Satan hates God, and wants to destroy his creation, his spiritual kingdom and every believer in it (1 Peter 5:8).

(h) More than ever, the church's very existence is being challenged by Satan's own religious philosophy – the New Age Movement. It bypasses sin, repentance, and salvation by claiming to turn people into 'gods' by transcendental meditation. No wonder so many people try this deceptive self-help religious experience. Satan even promises the return of his demonic fake, 'The Christ'. The Bible warns that in the last days he will perform counterfeit miracles, wonders, and signs in profusion (2 Thessalonians 1:9).

(i)   Satan likes to afflict God's people with rejection to revenge himself against God. Most Christians have no idea that the devil causes their problems, and try to counteract them in their own strength.

(j)   If Jesus Christ himself was constantly targeted by Satan's destructive power, and his disciples suffered demonic oppression (one becoming possessed), why should today's Christians think they are immune? Towards the end of the first century, Satan was openly oppressing churches (Revelation chapters 2 and 3), and we may be sure that the closer the Church comes to the rapture, the greater will be the demonic pressures to which it will be subjected. It is no wonder that Paul's letters contain constant warnings about Satan's overt and covert tactics to undermine believers. 'The Spirit clearly says that in later times some will abandon the faith and following deceiving spirits and things taught by demons' (1 Timothy 4:1). Besieged on the outside, and betrayed on the inside, the Church is challenged to be alert and active in holy living (Romans 13:11–14).

(k)   As part of the Christian's defence system Paul advises *'praying in the Spirit'* (Ephesians 5:18, emphasis added). Jude confirms this *'... pray **in the holy spirit**'* (Jude 20, emphasised). Satan is certainly delighted when we overlook, refuse, or fail to obey this instruction. It makes his job a whole lot easier!

So far we have been considering the influences our unseen but powerful enemy can have on us. Let us now look at how we often help him.

2. Some Christians live like spiritual orphans

Being born spiritually into God's family is a special but often misunderstood experience. Many believers feel an inner glow and peace when they receive Jesus Christ as Saviour and Lord as the Holy Spirit's confirmation that a spiritual change has indeed taken place. But that should only be the beginning. As spiritual babies they need the post-natal care of some church 'nursery' to become strong healthy Christians. Otherwise they could develop spiritual 'rickets', and fail to grow healthily. Unfortunately there is no guarantee that even the best church follow-up system will make them mature; this depends on the converts' willingness to submit to the discipline of the Holy Spirit's control in developing the new lifestyle.

When a packet of seeds is sown, not every one germinates, and with those which do, the growth rate may vary significantly. Christians are the same. For example, during a sermon, everyone looks at the preacher, but every person is not necessarily listening. Family concerns, financial problems, disinterest in the subject matter, the use of words and terms unfamiliar to the hearer, and many other distractions easily sidetrack attention and hinder blessing.

Failure to show genuine friendship to a new believer is sometimes another hindrance. Unless he or she is made to feel welcome, church may be looked upon as just another club offering certain benefits for membership. Paul tells us that being in Christ means that old things have been left behind, and life becomes totally new (2 Corinthians 5:17).

This new-birth relationship with a heavenly Father and his earthly family should be a heart-warming experience. Unfortunately, the change-over from being a rejected, unregenerate spiritual waif, stray, or orphan, to participation in a warm, caring family relationship often takes some time. Some miss out entirely. There can be some very real hindrances:

- When anyone has suffered the trauma of rejection, there is often a fear of trusting people again.
- When love has never been warmly shown in the family home, some children grow up emotionally cold.
- When both parents work, a child has been neglected, comes from a large family, or has been told that he or she was not wanted in the first place, that person will not know how to give, or receive love.
- Sometimes a father does not, will not, or cannot express love, and a child is deprived of the 'Dad' they desperately need. Some fathers are loving, but are seldom home when most needed. Others spend too much time at the local 'pub'. On the other hand a father may have died, or deserted a mother, leaving her to bring up the family, single-handed. Some children still show the scars of their parents' messy divorce or custody battle, in adulthood.
- Even worse, there may be bad memories of a father's vicious temper, many beatings, constant parental shouting, violence, or the crushing indignity of sexual interference.

Constant criticisms and injustices can also keep people from relating to God as their heavenly Father, and to other Christians as brothers and sisters. Some don't know what a happy and united family is like, and find the new relationships difficult to handle. Other problems:

- There are those who feel so ashamed about the cause of their rejection that they avoid talking about it. Some people freeze emotionally because they fear more rejection if the past becomes known.
- Some carry such a burden of guilt that they feel unfit to get too close to happy and free brothers and sisters around them.
- Suspicion of the motives of Christians, and uncertainty as to how long their acceptance will last will cause some to hold back.
- Because some new believers have intellectualised and rationalised all their lives, they continue to do so as Christians, regarding warm loving relationships as totally unnecessary, maybe even slightly objectionable!
- Other people feel threatened by the whole Christian family concept. Being 'self-made', they show their independence by church adherence rather than membership.
- Then there are those whom a pastor, elder, or fellow Christian has hurt deeply, who react with self-protection and suspicion of others' motives.
- When extra-busy people are saved, their lives are often so full of activity that there is little time for prayer and Bible reading. This means they never come to grips with vital truths about Christian living, such as the Fatherhood of God or the family of God.
- Maybe the experience of rejection has been so hurtful that the new Christian automatically becomes a spiritual 'hedgehog' and curls up in self-protection, rather than accept love.

If none of these suggestions explain why you do not enjoy God being your loving Father, and why you don't relate well to your spiritual family members, please think it through carefully, then write the answer in the following paragraph.

'The reason I have not related to God as my heavenly Father, and his children as my brothers and sisters in Christ is
....
but I am willing to change my attitude with the help of the Holy Spirit.'

Now let us turn our attention to what is really missing.

God is a perfect father to each born-again child in his family. 'The Fatherhood of God', and 'the brotherhood of man' are well-known terms. Conservationists, nature-lovers, peace devotees, politicians, 'et al' quote them. They are true in a general sense because God did make man in his own spiritual likeness, and we all belong to what we call 'the family of mankind'. But the reality is only experienced by those who have been born again.

In the Old Testament God said, *'I am Israel's father'* (Jeremiah 31:9), and that *'Israel is my firstborn son'* (Exodus 4:22). Israel replied *'... you O Lord, are our Father'* (Isaiah 63:16). No other nation was given that honour. But hundreds of years afterwards, their descendants could not, or would not, understand that Jesus, the virgin's child, was indeed the very one Isaiah described as *'Mighty God, Everlasting Father'* (Isaiah 9:6).

King David also compared God's compassion to that of a father with his child (Psalm 103:13), and two of his most important statements are very significant to rejection-sufferers:

> *'**Though my father and mother forsake me**, the Lord will receive me.'* (Psalm 27:10, emphasis added)

> *'**A father to the fatherless**, a defender of widows, is God in his holy dwelling.'* (Psalm 68:5, emphasis added)

It was not until Jesus Christ came to earth and showed what his Father in heaven was really like, that the people of all nations were invited to join his special family.

It may well be that some reader will be thinking at this stage, 'I know all that, but it makes no difference.' Really? Perhaps this is because:

- you have never really understood just how much being a child of God influences everyday living.
- you have become so fixed in your views and lifestyle that you either don't want to change, or don't think it is possible to change.
- you don't want to get too close to God in case he starts ordering you around, and you couldn't stand that!
- the very thought of being sentimental or 'slushy' turns you off.
- you're a pastor or a Bible teacher and you know it all. But your head knowledge has never become a heart-warming experience.

This reminds me of a letter I received not long ago from an ordained minister who had done a lot of Bible teaching. She said that no one would believe she had a problem. Everybody kept telling her that because she was a pastor, she would never have to battle the ups and downs which affect 'ordinary' church members. To get the help she desperately needed for her rejection problem, she had to write overseas.

Pastors not only experience rejection, but they sometimes give rejection to others.

• Some preach inspiring messages, but avoid eyeball to eyeball contact with their hearers because they feel inadequate on a one-to-one basis.

• Some communicate excellently when preaching, but at home it is a different story. They take refuge in their studies for supposedly right reasons, but in reality they are covering their embarrassment and inadequacy in not being able to be the friendly dad their children need. Their behaviour is probably caused by their early childhood treatment.

• Some preach in glowing terms about Christians sharing love with one another, but at home, they freeze up and are unable to express love within their families. This of course is a rejection symptom.

• And then there are the pastors who sacrificially spend time in helping other families in need, but remain oblivious to the hurts they cause their own family by frequent and sometimes long absences 'for the ministry's sake'. From personal experience, I believe that a slightly varied Murphy's Law operates in all pastors' families. 'Anything that can go wrong will go wrong, and always when father is away.' Unfortunately it is possible for a pastor to be totally dedicated to serving the Lord, and at the same time be the major cause of his own family's rejection.

Every rejected believer (including pastors and preachers) needs to answer this important question: 'What do I have to do to turn my head knowledge into a heart-warming experience?' These suggestions may be helpful:

• Face up to the hypocrisy of using words which are untruthful.

• Repent from every attitude, action, and habit which is self-protective, hurtful to others, or disobedient to the clear teachings of Scripture. God is looking for total, not partial commitment.

Jesus Christ told one of the teachers of the law (quoting from Deuteronomy 6:4, 5), *'Love the Lord your God with **all your heart**, and with **all your soul**, and with **all your mind**, and with **all your strength**' (Mark 12:30, emphasis added). To obey in part, is to disobey in the whole.*

- Ask the Holy Spirit to fill and control you by breaking bad habits, and establishing new ones (Romans 8:14, Ephesians 5:18).

If you sincerely want to do this, please meaningfully pray the following prayer:

'Dear Father God,

Please forgive my formality, coldness, misunderstanding, or rebellion against you, and my attitudes and actions towards others which have not been loving and caring, particularly (name them) ....
Please remove every hindrance in me so that I will consciously come closer to you, and other members of your family. Amen.'

Remember:

- God is a perfect Father. He can never die, never be away when most needed, never keep us waiting when we call him, and never show favouritism.
- God is grieved when his children isolate themselves. Togetherness, love, mutual respect, and sharing one another's burdens are characteristics of his family.
- God expects every child of his to show the family likeness of Jesus Christ. Only the Holy Spirit can make us change.
- God destroys all records of the past.
- God will change only what we permit.

Chapter 17

How Well Do You and the Holy Spirit Know Each Other?

Even before these pages went to print, one reviewer challenged the inclusion of this chapter, suggesting it was beyond the scope of the book. In considering his viewpoint, two powerful reasons prevailed. (I trust this does not give him rejection.)

Firstly, every rejection sufferer needs to know why the development of the closest possible relationship with the Holy Spirit is essential to having victory over habits which can never be conquered just by good will, and discipline. Jesus Christ gave a timeless warning to his disciples, '... *apart from me you can do nothing*' (John 15:5, emphasised). Many of us have tried hard in our own strength, become disappointed, and finally, given up. This failure is largely due to a lack of understanding of the Holy Spirit's presence and power in the world to continue the ministry of Jesus Christ. Christians who walk by physical eyesight instead of spiritual insight make heavy weather of discipleship. Struggling and striving (as with the Mosaic Law) will never overcome habits established by rejection, but by the daily grace of the Holy Spirit, submission and obedience to Jesus Christ can become a continuous experience.

Secondly, because my personal release from rejection came through the sovereign work of the Holy Spirit and the Word of God, any omission of the subject could prevent some readers from receiving much needed freedom. Not everyone will agree with all that has been written, but open-hearted rejection sufferers will be encouraged to make themselves more available to the personal and powerful ministry of the indwelling Holy Spirit.

This is not about dry theology and doctrine, but a warm spiritual relationship. It is mainly biographical to avoid the obvious pitfalls of boredom, dogmatism, and controversy. It expresses my own pilgrimage from ignorance to enlightenment, legalism to liberty, and from prejudice to openness.

I was brought up so far right of doctrinal centre that I suffered from spiritual frostbite. The Authorised Bible was the only acceptable Bible translation in those days. The 'King Jimmy' version (as we rather irreverently described it), was by some, quite seriously claimed to be 'good enough for us because it was good enough for the Apostle Paul.' I was taught that other translations and paraphrase versions were definitely heretical. So it was the 17th Century use of English which started me down the wrong track.

The Holy Spirit was 'it', and 'the holy Ghost'. So I wrongly concluded that the Holy Spirit was some kind of influence. The term 'holy smoke' was heard frequently, and may have been caused by the English used in 1611. Satan's anti-God propaganda machine has probably never been more effective than its misinformation campaign against the Holy Spirit and his work in the world. It commenced with a wild rumour that the disciples were actually having a drunken spree (at 9.00 am in the morning mind you!), after God's Spirit came to his Church in an awesome demonstration of power (Acts 2:15). Since then, Satan's discreditation activity has only increased.

During the nineteen fifties and sixties, a tidal wave of fear swept through many churches sending shivers up and down the spine of every fundamentalist. There was gossip about 'holy rollers', wild demonic manifestations, and footprints up the walls and over the ceiling of those dreaded Pentecostal churches!

So I needed some spiritual dynamite to bring me out of my 'underground shelter', and disarm me of my offensive verbal weaponry. That took a long time, I can assure you. Like the Apostle Paul, I too persecuted the Holy Spirit. But that is in the past when I had an empty head, and a big mouth, and used them both overtime! (This reminds me of a card I once saw about some goon who wrote 'Wunce I coodint evin spel geeollagyst – now I are one.') So 'Wunce I was allerjick to karismaticks, but now I are one!'

How I needed to change! And how long-suffering God was during the process. In time I learned much more about the Holy

Spirit himself and how to dramatically update our relationship. In order for this chapter to be readable, I hope enjoyable, and above all profitable, I have itemised some of the important things I learned, and put them at the end of the chapter for more detailed study, if desired.

Important milestones that I passed include:

1. Learning that just as Jesus Christ was Immanuel (God with us), so the Holy Spirit is God within us (John 14:15–18). (See note 1 at end of chapter). I put down my spiritual binoculars and stopped searching for him. Instead I just believed what Jesus said, and began to enjoy the living presence of the Holy Spirit within me.

2. I learned that only God could teach me about himself, and fulfil what Jesus said, *'This is eternal life that they might know you, the only true God, and Jesus Christ whom you have sent'* (John 17:3, emphasis added).

It dawned on me that the Holy Spirit not only wanted to teach me, but change me. *'For those God foreknew he also predestined to be* **conformed to the likeness of his Son'** (Romans 8:29, emphasis added). That didn't appeal to me as I was quite satisfied with myself. But Gibson was no mere panel beating job; he also needed major renewal of gearbox, transmission, and engine. Finally, I gave in. Now, the 'new me' looks back with distaste on the 'old me'. Thank God I was able to attend my own funeral (Galatians 2:20) and throw the dirt of the past on the coffin!

3. I used to be scared stiff of anyone who suggested that a 'second blessing' was either possible, desirable or even essential. The problem was that just like a baby bird, I had swallowed someone else's pre-digested food. At that stage I didn't forage for my own. I later learned that although the Holy Spirit is indeed a person (and therefore cannot be received in instalments), it is possible to have endless experiences of being filled with his grace. Paul said '... *even be filled and stimulated with the (Holy) Spirit'* (Ephesians 5:18, Amplified Bible). The list of instructions which follow this verse certainly suggest that the number of fillings can be continuous. In fact this process affects social, family and work relationships (Ephesians 5:19–6:18). Quality comes before quantity every time. [Further comments on this subject appear in the second study at the end of the chapter.]

The disciples of Jesus Christ had their first infilling after the resurrection (John 20:22). Their second was at Pentecost (Acts 2:4). The third was at a prayer meeting (Acts 4:31). From both the Scriptures and personal experience, I soon learned not to limit the Holy Spirit's working to my preconceived ideas.

4. During my search for truth and reality I really choked over the term 'baptism of the Holy Spirit' – particularly when some over-zealous Christian challenged me by saying 'Brother have you been baptised with the Holy Ghost and spoken with other tongues?' I'm afraid I made a rather prejudicial and unloving reply, and walked away, in case I suffered from over-exposure to his 'evil' doctrine. But when I examined the whole subject of baptism more objectively, I was quite surprised at the number of baptisms the Scriptures mention.

(a) **Water baptism.** This was no problem because I had received 'believer's baptism' (as distinct from involuntary baptism as a baby). It was meaningful at the time because I knew it was a public witness to what I had already experienced in my heart.

- John the Baptist insisted on it as evidence of repentance (Mark 1:4). Jesus himself was baptised, although sinless (Matthew 3:13–15).
- As the disciples of Jesus travelled, they baptised people (John 4:2).
- It is an essential part of the Great Commission, not for salvation, but as a witness to it (Matthew 28:19).
- The early church obediently continued the practice (Acts 2:41; 9:18; 16:15).
- New Testament Christians who received the Holy Spirit had either been baptised, or experienced it immediately afterwards (Acts 2:41; 8:12, 17; 10:44, 47, 48; 19:5, 6). Water baptism is therefore important to anyone who has received deliverance and wants to be filled with the Holy Spirit.

(b) **The baptism of death.** Jesus Christ spoke of his distress at this prospect (Luke 12:50), and again confirmed its reality (Matthew 20:23 KJV).

(c) **The spiritual baptism of identification with Jesus Christ.** This is the nucleus of the experience of new birth, without which water baptism is meaningless. Any person claiming to be a Christian who does not sincerely believe that Jesus Christ was his or her personal substitute in suffering, dying, and returning to life again, and has not received him as Saviour is deluded if he thinks he is saved. Just as Old Testament sinners had to put their hands on the sacrifices the priests offered for them, so today, repentant sinners must identify with Jesus, God's offering for all sin. Any 'salvation-experience' which lacks this identification is empty and meaningless.

● The writer personally believes that when Paul speaks of baptism in Romans chapter six, he was speaking of identification with Jesus Christ's substitutionary work, not water baptism.

> '... *don't you know that all of us who were baptised into Jesus Christ were **baptised into his death?** We were therefore buried with him through **baptism into death** in order that, just as Christ was raised from the dead through the glory of the Father, we too may live a new life.*'
>
> (verses 3, 4, emphasis added)

The believing thief openly identified himself with the righteous Christ, and joined Jesus after death without having been baptised (Luke 23:40–43).

(d) ***Baptism by the Spirit into the body of Christ*** (1 Corinthians 12:13). This is our spiritual union with Christ, our head. The only evidence the person being born again may have of the experience is a new awareness and love for other members of God's family (1 John 3:14).

(e) ***Baptism with the Holy Spirit*** (Acts 1:5). This was to me **the** tricky one. I certainly suffered from fear of the spiritual unknown! John the Baptist had said Jesus would baptise people with the Holy Spirit and fire (Matthew 3:11), but I was quite sure that Pentecost had totally fulfilled that prophecy. Being then a rigid dispensationalist, I rested quite smugly in my self-induced delusion that everyone who claimed that all believers should be baptised with the Holy Spirit, were spiritual oddities.

Then the Spirit of Truth enrolled me in his special tutorial classes and gave me a lesson or two. I learned that Jesus Christ described being '*baptised with the Holy Spirit*' in various ways, such as:

177

- '... *the gift my Father promised*' (Acts 1:4, emphasis added, Luke 24:49). Peter's statement in his Pentecost sermon then convinced me that the Father's promised gift had no time restriction.

> *'Repent – change your views, and purpose to accept the will of God in your inner selves instead of rejecting it – and be baptised every one of you in the name of Jesus Christ for the forgiveness of, and release from your sins; and you shall receive **the gift** of the Holy Spirit. For the promise (of the Holy Spirit) is to and for you and your children, and **to and for all** that are **far away** [even] to **as many as** the Lord our God invites and bids come to himself.'*
>
> (Acts 2:38, 39 The Amplified Bible, emphasis added)

- '... *stay ... until you have been **clothed with power** from on high*' (Luke 24:49, emphasis added).
- '*But you will **receive power** when the Holy Spirit comes on you and you **will be my witnesses** ...* ' (Acts 1:8, emphasis added).
- In Acts 2:4, Luke said, '*All of them **were filled** with the Holy Spirit*' (emphasis added).
- Peter quoted Joel's prophecy '*In the last days, God says I will pour out my Spirit on all people*' (Joel 2:28, emphasis added).

By this time biblical truth was like a jack-hammer reducing my cherished prejudice to rubble. I had choked over one particular statement, ignored the rest, and missed the real meaning of each verse. It became obvious that I desperately needed the experience itself, call it what you may – a '*gift*', '*power for witness*', '*receiving a greater than Elijah's mantle*', the Holy Spirit '*being poured over me*', or even – yes – the previously dreaded term '*baptism of the Holy Spirit*'. A hunger began within me and produced repentance, openness and expectant faith until God answered. Now, I don't have reservations about the Holy Spirit's ministry, I just enjoy the love Jesus Christ shares with me.

(f) *Finally, the gifts of the Holy Spirit.* In a scale of one to ten measuring my doctrinal antagonism, I am sure I registered fifteen on this issue. I wouldn't budge. Hadn't I been taught that the sign-gifts had ceased by the end of the second century?

Didn't perfection come with the completion of the Bible and hadn't imperfection (supported by the sign gifts) disappeared? (1 Corinthians 13:10). And I had heard enough stories to be convinced that tongue-speaking must be of the devil.

Then I began to hear the gentle voice of the Spirit over and above the clamour of my own thinking. Step by step, the last of my fortress was demolished. He taught me:

- That his gifts were to be with the Church until Jesus had raised up every born-again child to be with him in heaven. Paul wrote to the Roman church, *'For in him (Jesus Christ) you have been enriched in every way ... Therefore you do not lack **any spiritual gift** as you eagerly wait for our Lord Jesus to be revealed. He will keep you strong **to the end**, so that you will be blameless on the day of our Lord Jesus Christ'* (1 Corinthians 1:7, 8, emphasis added). A further note (3) is at the end of the chapter.

  I also realised that God did not expect the Church to stand against the rising demonic power in the end-times by words alone, but by the power of the Holy Spirit (2 Thessalonians 2:3–7).

  And the claim that the sign gifts were only 'a form of scaffolding' around the early church soon collapsed when I remembered that scaffolding remains until construction is completed.

- I then realised that God's Word was indeed perfect as a record, despite explicit details of the sins of some of God's people which will obviously be blotted out in heaven. Secondly, Paul said that when tongues cease, so will knowledge (1 Corinthians 13:8). Daniel tells us that until the time of the end, *'Many will go here and there to increase knowledge'* (Daniel 12:4), so why should tongues have ceased if knowledge hasn't?

- Finally, through personal experience, the whole problem of tongues just disappeared. Since then, Phyl and I have certainly proved that Satan gives demonic tongues to his followers in the cults and in witchcraft, and even to a few Christians whom he has deceived. After all he only counterfeits genuine and valued gifts of the Spirit. We have often seen the delight on the face of believers for whom the Lord has taken away spurious things, and given the real thing.

So I repented of my presupposition that tongues were from the devil, because God doesn't give any unholy thing to his children. Jesus said he wouldn't (Luke 11:12). I know now with much assurance that he never has, and never will.

The subject of the Holy Spirit and his work is still a contentious issue to many. 'Charismatics' still get blamed for splitting churches. But often conservative leadership does not know how to handle them, and knee-jerk reactions precipitate divisions.

To sum up my personal experiences, God was indeed merciful to me, and the truth I once ignorantly rejected I now treasure. There are three aspects of the Holy Spirit's personality and ministry which must never be separated.

Firstly, because he is both the Spirit of God (Matthew 3:16), and the Spirit of Jesus Christ (Philippians 1:19), the Holy Spirit must be honoured as co-equal with the Father, and the Son. Some even claim that there can be no separate doctrine of the Holy Spirit. Jesus Christ never acted unilaterally. Neither does the Holy Spirit. They were and are equally dedicated to fulfil the Father's will both in timing and detail (John 5:19; 16:12–15). How true is the saying – 'I looked at the Lamb of God and the dove of peace flew into my heart. I looked at the dove of peace, and it flew away.'

Secondly, the experiences of being filled with *'the word of Christ'* (Colossians 3:16), and the *'Holy Spirit'* (Ephesians 5:18), will be seen to be synonymous when their results are compared. God planned it that way. Christ the living Logos (John 1:1), is the cutting edge of the written logos (Hebrews 4:12). The same Holy Spirit caused both the birth of Jesus Christ (Luke 1:35), and the writing and compilation of the written word of God (2 Peter 1:20, 21).

Thirdly, both the gifts of the Spirit (1 Corinthians 12:8–11), and the fruit of the Spirit (Galatians 5:22, 23), originate from the same person. If we accept one but reject the other, we do so at our spiritual peril, and dishonour God whose grace produces fruit and imparts gifts. Probably more verbal battles are waged over the 'fruit' versus 'gifts' controversy than any other ministry of the Holy Spirit. Personally, I have found that by earnestly seeking God's grace in order to produce fruit honouring to Jesus Christ, manifestations of sign-gifts flow as and when the Holy Spirit determines.

In summary, I commenced my search for truth about the Holy

Spirit with theological frostbite, a closed mind, and the fear of catching some dreaded spiritual disease. In reality, I have been brought into a much warmer relationship with God as my heavenly Father, a greater desire for Jesus Christ to be Lord in every detail of daily living; and an increased hunger for the Word of God. I also have infinitely more power and authority in the Holy Spirit than I had before. My attitude to all matters involving the Holy Spirit is rather like a man who in windy weather stands with his legs apart to brace himself against wind gusts. Sometimes I lean a little towards conservative thinking, and at other times I certainly have more open views. The Holy Spirit and God's word give me balance.

There have been other benefits. I now listen, and seek guidance from the Holy Spirit before making a judgement, or answering questions. I have also lost all fear of what other people think or say about what I believe and do in the Holy Spirit. (And believe me, some have said plenty!) Finally, rejection no longer troubles me. I trust that this account of my own search for truth may help many readers to enter into a warm and effective relationship with him. Deliverance from rejection can only be maintained through his indwelling presence and power.

Optional further studies

(At this point, some readers may prefer to turn to the next chapter.)

1. The person and work of the Holy Spirit

(a) He is co-equal with the Father and the Son (Luke 1:35; 3:22).

(b) He alone can reveal divine truth (John 14:16, 17; 16:8–15).

(c) He sovereignly controls Satanic and demonic activity (Ephesians 6:10–18; 2 Thessalonians 2:7).

(d) He glorifies Jesus Christ –
  • by enabling repentant sinners to be born again (John 3:5–6).
  • by sharing God's grace and power for godly living in the Church (Galatians 5:22, 23; Ephesians 1:19–23).

(e) He continues to reveal Jesus Christ to his Church (Revelation 2:7, 11, 17, 29; 3:6, 13, 22). Jesus himself said, '*I have much more to say to you, more than you can now bear. But when he, the Spirit of truth comes,*
  • *he will guide you into all truth.*

181

- *he will not speak on his own* ('authority' RSV); *he will speak only what he hears, and*
- *he will tell you of what is yet to come.*
- *he will bring glory to me by taking from what is mine and making it known to you'* (John 16:12–14).

(f) Like Jesus Christ, the Holy Spirit is totally dedicated to fulfilling God's predetermined will. He does not do anything that the Father and the Son have not agreed to. Isaiah said this would happen (Isaiah 61:1), and Jesus Christ confirmed it in the Nazareth synagogue (Luke 4:18–21).

2. *The clear distinction between the personality, and the ministry of the Holy Spirit*

The Greek New Testament clearly illustrates this. H.B. Sweet points out that when the Holy Spirit's personality is the subject of the text, the English translation is usually 'the Holy Spirit'. The Inter-Linear Greek-English New Testament does this over 50 times. For example:

> '... *Jesus was baptised too. And as he was praying, heaven was opened and the Holy Spirit descended on him in bodily form like a dove ...* ' (Luke 3:21b, 22)

Other occurrences are found in verses such as John 1:32, 33; 14:26; Acts 1:8; 5:3; Romans 5:5; Hebrews 3:7 etc.

On the other hand, when the subject of the Greek text centres on the empowering ministry of the Holy Spirit (as distinct from identifying him as a member of the Godhead), the English translation of each reference puts the definite article in brackets: *'[the] Holy Spirit'*. *'All of them were filled with [the] Holy Spirit'* (Acts 2:4). Some of the 34 uses include John 7:39a; Acts 4:31; 9:17; 13:9; 13:52 etc). It is a profitable study to examine New Testament references to the Holy Spirit in order to gain a deeper understanding of just when the personality or ministry of the Holy Spirit is conveyed in the text.

3. *The harmony within the Godhead in giving spiritual gifts*

As the Father, Son, and Holy Spirit are a divine unity, so their function within the Body of Christ cannot be divided,

- '... *different kinds of gifts* (Gr. *charisma*) *but the* **same Spirit**.
- '... *different kinds of service* (Gr. *diakonia*) *but the* **same Lord**.
- '... *different kinds of working* (Gr. *energema*), *but the* **same God** *works all of them in all men*' (1 Corinthians 12:4–6, emphasis added).

Paul follows these verses with a detailed list of the gifts of the Spirit, concluding with '*All of these are the work of one and the same Spirit, and he gives them to each man just as he determines*' (verses 7–11).

The 1989 Lausanne II Congress on World Evangelisation in Manila emphasised the present-day need for the miraculous ministry of Jesus Christ by resolving: 'Although the miracles of Jesus were special, being signs of Messiahship and anticipations of his perfect kingdom when all nature will be subject to him, we have no liberty to place limits on the power of the living creator today. We reject both the scepticism which denies miracles and the presumption which demands them, both the timidity which shrinks from the fullness of the Spirit and the triumphalism which shrinks from the weakness in which Christ's power is made perfect.'

Chapter 18

All About Re-programming Our Behaviour Computers

The times are certainly changing for us 'oldies'. Even primary school children are as computer conscious and efficient as the Chinese have been for centuries with their abacus. But whether it is an art-form, a special gift, or dogged determination I still need, I have yet to master this subject. It doesn't make 'Papa' feel very smart when his grandchildren do it with such ease!

But I have mastered my electronic typewriter, at least enough to make it respond to my finger-tip instructions. Unlike my word processor at present, 'it' is my obedient servant. When I activate the keys correctly, the response is excellent.

Computers and human personalities have one important principle in common. They both need to be programmed correctly to get the best results. The same principle applies to both – 'GIGO', or 'garbage in, garbage out'. No wonder a wise king once said *'Above all else, guard your heart, for it is the wellspring of life'* (Proverbs 4:23). Good drinking water does not come from contaminated wells. So we need to identify areas of inner pollution, and re-program our hearts and minds so that Isaiah's word will be fulfilled in us – *'With joy you will draw water from the wells of salvation'* (Isaiah 12:3).

If you really want freedom from your rejection problems your sincerity will be measured, firstly, by your perseverance in reading this chapter to the end without skipping anything. Secondly, by your determination to obey the Lord and permit him to program necessary changes to your thoughts, desires, and habits.

One of the most common mistakes made by people wanting deliverance is to believe that counsellors do everything, and that they, the counsellees, will walk away with a euphoric feeling that every problem has been completely and permanently solved.

Deliverance is certainly a miracle, because Jesus Christ said so (Mark 9:38, 39), but its full and permanent effect depends upon the total co-operation of the one being set free. This chapter, and others which follow will deal with the subject of human responsibility in the freedom experience. So if you are a candidate for release from rejection, these are the keys you will need to use to re-program yourself to receive and maintain the deliverance you desire. The preparation for deliverance and the follow-up steps are as important as the experience itself. These steps need to begin **now**.

1. Give daily Bible reading a high priority

The word of God is full of up-to-date answers to life's complex problems. Its rules, warnings, and challenges are fully illustrated by human case histories, and its promises are fully road-tested and fulfilling. Reading and studying it may be as dry as eating peanuts in their shells, or as refreshing as cold fruit salad on a hot day. What makes the difference? Discipline, and an intimate knowledge of its author, are probably the most important keys. Translations in modern English are easy to read, and paraphrases can certainly be of help.

Surveys constantly show that the average time Christians spend in God's Word daily, is only a few minutes. To reduce the average so drastically, this means that many believers never read at all. Bible reading, study, and meditation, are very similar to an athlete running a hurdle race. There are barriers to be cleared such as busy schedules, unavoidable interruptions, over-tiredness, and just plain excuses like the one a pastor once gave me – 'I know it all anyway!'

Satan hates God's Word. He opposes it every way he can. He misquotes it, and builds error around a single nucleus of truth by isolating it from its context, or from other interlocking teachings. If Jesus Christ at the age of twelve amazed people by his knowledge of God's law (Luke 2:46, 47), and successfully resisted the Tempter by quoting Scriptures (Luke 4:2–12), how much more do we need to be filled with the Word of the Lord.

Psalm 119 is the greatest encouragement to do this, particularly verses 97–100.

> *'Oh, how I love your law! **I meditate on it all day long**. Your commands make me **wiser than my enemies**, for they are ever with me. I have **more insight than all my teachers** for **I meditate** on your statutes. I have **more understanding than the elders** for I **obey** your precepts.'* (emphasis added)

Here are other significant reasons for gaining a good Bible knowledge:

(a) *Jesus Christ said it was essential to daily living.* '*Man does not live on bread alone, but on every word* (Gr. *rhema*) *that comes from the mouth of God*' (Matthew 4:4; Deuteronomy 8:3). The words of some great men are often quoted long after their death, but God's written word (Gr. *logos*) is always as living and up-to-date as when the Holy Spirit caused it to be written. In times of special need he will bring an appropriate verse or passage to mind (*rhema*). The prerequisite of this is that our memories are filled with the Scriptures. Paul advised young Timothy to study it to become spiritually mature (2 Timothy 2:15).

(b) *It is God's plumb-line of truth* (Acts 17:11).

(c) *His word is like a hospital emergency ward.* It diagnoses, operates, and heals 'heart' problems (Hebrews 4:12).

(d) *It is like chewing the 'spiritual cud'.* '*Blessed is the man ... (whose) delight is in the law of the Lord, and on his law he meditates day and night*' (Psalm 1:2).

The 're-cycling' of verses of Scripture is the best antidote for mental fantasy and over-active minds. Campbell McAlpine, a special friend of the writer has written an excellent book on the value and practice of meditation – *Alone with God* (Harvest House). It will greatly help any rejection sufferer wanting to bring the mind under control.

Warning. Meditation is also an activity of the New Age Movement. Basically it is associated with Yoga, Hinduism, and Buddhism, and devotees are often seen meditating in public places, in the 'lotus' position. Regrettably, some of its deceptive principles have been taught in theological colleges and have been used by Christians, unaware that meditation must centre on Jesus Christ alone.

2. Make sure you have a 'faith-lift'

Many people have 'barometer faith'. Remember seeing that little house hanging on a wall? The woman comes out with her shopping basket when it's fine, and the man comes out dressed in a yellow mackintosh and hat when it's due to rain.

'Fair-weather' faith will neither honour God, nor help us when we are in need. There are many reasons why our faith sometimes fails under test:

(a) *We place ourselves on a starvation diet.* Only a regular diet of God's word will increase faith (Romans 10:17).

(b) *Our Christian living is mainly based on a weekly event.* You probably know the routine. We make attending church a big deal. With a large Bible under one arm, we give plenty of 'Amens' and 'Hallelujahs', hug everyone, and bubble with enthusiasm. But on Monday the scene changes. With a quick Bible verse, and a bless-me prayer, it's off to work again with the latest 'Christian' rock and roll pulsating in our eardrums. And before you know it, the next weekend has arrived. God never intended Christians to live under a roster system.

Life in Christ is like a garden where the carefully cultivated fruit and flowers give enjoyment to all who see it. It is no wonder that Paul suggests that the Holy Spirit is like a first-class orchardist who tends our spiritual trees to make them bear excellent fruit (Galatians 5:22, 23). It is only through deliverance that a rejection sufferer's old root-fruit system can be destroyed and the right fruit be allowed to grow and mature.

(c) *Faith sometimes ebbs away through damaged emotions.* Christians whose rejection makes them feel insecure usually have difficulty in making judgements. Like a weather vane in variable winds, they swing from one opinion to another, and by listening to the conflicting advice of friends often end up confused, and make no decision.

God does not expect his children to blunder their own way through life. He led his people out of Egypt by the unseen angel of his presence, who later appeared physically in New Testament times, asserting that he was *'the way, the truth, and the life'* (John 14:6). Before Jesus returned to heaven, he promised that God's Spirit of Truth would take over the invisible leadership of the Church. *'But when he, the Spirit of Truth comes he will guide you into all truth . . . '* (John 16:13). Looking at our own self-image only brings insecurity. Looking to others can be quite confusing. But concentration on Jesus Christ is protective, directional, and stimulating to faith (Hebrews 12:2). The Holy Spirit sees to that.

(d) *Maybe you badly need a faith-adjustment!*

Many people will put up with a painful back rather than go to a chiropractor because they think the manipulation will be more painful than the complaint itself. In reality it is generally not so. There are also Christians who feel so self-protective, and fearful of being 'put down' by a counsellor that they will not go to one. But those inner forces causing the pains of rejection, introversion, negativity and unbelief must be served with eviction notices as the first step to deliverance. The words 'I choose to be free from . . . and . . . and . . . ' are sufficient. Confessions of faith also glorify Jesus Christ and give the Holy Spirit the right to commence work.

(e) *Demanding proof before believing.* Unsaved people often cause Christians of having 'blind faith' because they trust a God they cannot see, not understanding that faith is spiritual eyesight, not physical. Unfortunately, many Christians have been programmed to think like the Pharisees. They expected God to work a visible miracle before being willing to trust him. One Bible teacher aptly described them as 'professing Christians, but practising atheists'. Jesus often rebuked his disciples for that same attitude.

Faith without expectation is as useless as tasteless table salt, or a power line with a blown fuse. God will only fulfil his promises to us when the 'faith-fuse' between our hearts and himself is functional.

Unfortunately, believers sometimes suffer from two antifaith short-circuiting problems, namely intellectualising and rationalising; they make simple faith impossible. Worship of brain-power is also self-idolatry. Many so-called 'intellectuals' are rejected people who feel insecure in having to trust God in a way which is contrary to logic. Unless we trust our Father God unconditionally, we block his power in our lives (Hebrews 11:6).

Excuse Me … Your Rejection is Showing

(f) **Some Christians are 'faith-parasites'.** They draw their spiritual nourishment from any person to whom they can attach themselves. In my Bible College lecturing days this type would head my way at the first break. 'Could I speak to you privately, sir? I have a problem and I think you can help me.' It didn't take long to realise that they didn't **have** a problem, they **were** the problem. According to resident staff, every visiting lecturer was treated the same way. They were spiritual nomads, wandering around with their spiritual lifelines like umbilical cords ready to plug into the faith of someone spiritually stronger than themselves. The Church has plenty of them. They move from one counsellor to another because they don't like being told the truth about themselves. 'Pastor,' other people say, 'Will you exercise faith for me over …' and they name a problem. Or, 'Pastor will you please seek God's will for me?'

Relying upon others is not faith in God. Deliverance should break that dependence, and replace it with a loving trusting relationship with Jesus Christ. But this is not automatic. It is a choice which needs to be made so that we can say with Paul,

'I have been crucified with Christ and I no longer live, but Christ lives in me. The life I live in the body, I live by faith in the Son of God, who loved me and gave himself for me.'
(Galatians 2:20)

In summary, the faith-lift needed to maintain freedom after deliverance must include:
• an adequate and varied diet of God's word,
• a submitting of all thoughts, desires, and actions to the control of Jesus Christ, and
• trusting God – no matter what.

3. Enjoy warm friendship with Jesus Christ

Don't just call upon God with a special 'bless-me' shopping list, or dial his emergency number when you have a desperate need. Constant heart-to-heart communion insulates you from the troublesome past, present events, and the uncertain future. When two

190

people love one another deeply, words and body language are not necessary for soul-talk. In fact, one partner will frequently speak out what the other is thinking.

That same relationship with Jesus Christ will become the greatest preventative of:

- the 'mulligrubs' (a New Zealand term for feeling grumpy and out of sorts). And who doesn't feel like that occasionally?

- ego-worship – the 'me-first' syndrome.

- fantasy-thinking, which is not to be confused with normal creative or investigative thinking. Fantasy is either escapism, the playground of lust, the result of boredom, or, with women particularly, imagination based on fear. When our thought life is concentrated on Jesus Christ, he certainly keeps Satan out. Isaiah's song of praise includes these words: *'You will keep him in perfect peace whose mind is steadfast, because he trusts in you'* (Isaiah 26:3).

- blowing on the embers of the past which causes guilt to glow again. The conscious awareness of the presence of Jesus Christ puts an end to all that. The apostle Paul never forgot that he had persecuted the early church but he refused to be dominated by that memory (1 Corinthians 15:9, 10).

His experience gives us some very practical guidelines (Philippians chapter 3):

- Firstly, put Jesus Christ first and throw your own plans and desires on the garbage heap (vv. 7, 8).

- Secondly, turn your back permanently on any guilt of the past (v. 13). Jesus Christ will make it just a harmless memory.

- Thirdly, set your will-control to glorify God at all times (v. 14).

- Fourthly, press on, and never give up, never (v. 13).

- Regrettably, many supposedly grown-up Christians still play with spiritual 'teddy bears'. They have never grown mature in Christ, and when they pray, they just repeat the simple phrases they began with when they came to Christ. The apostle Paul said they were 'milk-drinkers' instead of being 'meat-eaters' (1 Corinthians 3:2). Stalemate-living is particularly dangerous for people with rejection. It causes apathy and unbelief, and needs to be resisted so that the whole person will be able to 'run' after deliverance has been received.

4. Repentance

This has become an almost forgotten word amongst Christians. Because it is essential to salvation, many overlook its continued significance in Christian living. Without it, sin is either trivialised or justified, and it gives Satan an opportunity to bind, or oppress.

Jesus Christ warned the Ephesian church that he would take away its public witness unless they repented of allowing their love for him to cool (Revelation 2:4, 5). If lack of love can grieve Jesus Christ so much, how must he feel about the other wrong things we do?

In order to allow Jesus Christ to do all he wants for everyone he sets free, permanent re-programming of the soul's inner code of conduct is essential. Ensure that you:

- ask the Lord for his help to recognise and obey the inner voice of the Holy Spirit.
- pray for a real understanding of how God sees sin, and how much it cost him to redeem us from it. The victory of resistance is more precious than the constant cycle of falling, repentance, confession and forgiveness. Why grieve our Heavenly Father when we can glorify him? A godly hatred for sin will make successful resistance much easier.
- develop a resistance to the old temptations which used to plague you. Allow the Holy Spirit to fit your conscience with his alarm-bells which will warn you about evil thoughts, desires, or habits which have led to defeat in the past.
- aim to be unashamed of everything you think, want, or do, in everyday living.

During the last few hours my typewriter has merrily clicked away, churning out page after page of a report I had programmed into its memory system. In the same way, by commencing your re-programming process now you will be more able to enjoy consistent freedom as time goes on.

Chapter 19

Danger – Road Blocks Ahead!

Just in case some readers are getting restless about knowing the nitty-gritty of how to be free from rejection, please 'hang in' there! We haven't yet finished with the attitude and behaviour changes which are essential for total freedom.

Some of what follows has previously been briefly touched upon, but a more thorough treatment is vital because deliverance is only part of a total process. Rejection sufferers **must** make these preparations in order to receive the maximum benefit from their freedom.

Road Block No. 1: The problems some intellectuals face

Having a high IQ (intelligence quotient) is no protection against rejection, nor a solution to its ravaging effects. Having prayed with many people who have been endowed with above average mentality, some with major or multiple university degrees, Phyl and I have learned that unless the Holy Spirit is given control of the mind, pride in intellectual ability can actually hinder deliverance and renewal.

Rejection is primarily an emotional and spiritual malady. Traditional methods of counselling and drug therapy in many cases limit the expression of symptoms, but seldom eradicate causes. A change of thinking leaves the basic rejection root system untouched, and it usually reappears in the form of unrelated emotional and physical expressions.

Rationalism is of course a by-product of intellectualism. Because the critical approach is used in tertiary education, some Christians demand clear answers before being willing to believe that deliverance works.

Space, time, and confidentiality prevent case histories from being given. But generally, more time has to be spent on simple explanations of spiritual problems and follow-up procedures with those who 'suffer' from intellectualism, than with others. We are sometimes astounded by the genuine difficulty some intellectuals have in grasping simple spiritual principles. No wonder Jesus Christ said that humility is essential to salvation! *'I tell you the truth, unless you change and become like little children, you will never enter the kingdom of heaven'* (Matthew 18:3). He also emphasised that those who wanted his help needed to have his humility of heart and mind to receive blessing, *'Take my yoke upon you and learn from me for I am gentle and humble in heart, and you will find rest for your souls'* (Matthew 11:29, emphasis added).

While we have been saddened by the number of Christians who indulge in 'intellectualism' we praise God for every Spirit-filled intellectual who has submitted his or her mind to Jesus Christ, and has enjoyed a consequent increase of understanding and wisdom through the Holy Spirit. They understand deliverance principles more quickly, cooperate more whole-heartedly, and carry out their follow-up more faithfully than those who continue in intellectualism and rationalism.

Regrettably, one of man's greatest assets can become his greatest stumbling block to salvation, discipleship, deliverance, and the fullness of the Holy Spirit.

Road Block No. 2: When rejection's root causes are overlooked

The major thrust of this book has been the pinpointing of some of the causes and behavioural symptoms of rejection. What may not have been sufficiently emphasised is that rejection may be considerably increased through the repetition of emotional trauma. The pain suffered may be so strong that the original cause of rejection becomes overlooked. By focusing attention on the latest 'rejection-happening', without the original rejection root-system having been removed, fresh outbreaks will continue to occur. So, in dealing with rejection layers, the spirits of rejection (hereditary or otherwise), self-rejection, and fear of rejection must be cast out. This is necessary in order to dispose of the causes, leaving the subject much less sensitive and responsive to hurtful situations.

Road Block No. 3: Purposeful evasion of reality

Wilful avoidance of, or refusal to deal with, obvious problems may be a sign of moral cowardice. 'There is none so blind as he who does not want to see!' Like motorists who callously drive past an accident victim because they don't want to get involved, many of us avoid the reality of our problems.

Our behaviour often signals our rejection without us being aware of it. If we were confronted, we would probably strongly deny it. So counsellors need wisdom and sensitivity in speaking about rejection, because people are naturally self-defensive. Each of us needs to answer an important question: 'Am I deliberately turning a blind eye to what I don't want to confess?' Admitting a problem does exist, is the first step to being freed from it.

Road Block No. 4: Donkey disease (the *'I Won't'* syndrome)

Some people bray, 'Be reasonable, do it my way', or 'My mind is made up, please don't confuse me with the facts'. This attitude certainly hinders marital harmony, and will prevent submission to Jesus Christ. It is often disguised as 'loyalty to my personal principles', or 'being honest with myself'. Call it what you may, it is only an excuse for doing your own thing. People with this problem need to answer some important questions before considering deliverance:

- 'Is my adamant attitude really a defensive mechanism for my own independence?
- 'Am I fearful of being proved wrong?'
- 'Is my supposedly "righteous resistance" a mere cover for plain pig-headedness?'

Unless there is openness, honesty in self-evaluation, and a real willingness to change everything that is wrong, it would be better to postpone deliverance until there has been a genuine change of heart. Submission is a sign of strength, not weakness.

Road Block No. 5: Apathy

We earlier gave the Concise Oxford Dictionary definition as 'insensibility to suffering, passionless existence, lack of interest or desire'. It is often a rejection-related symptom which seems to affect men more than women. It severely hinders mental, emotional, and physical activity and leaves in its wake unattended household chores, uncut lawns, broken promises, TV addiction, and general disinterest in other people. Its languid protest is 'Leave me alone, I can't be bothered.'

Apathy is often hereditary. It may also begin in childhood when a doting mother does everything for a child who then grows up expecting everyone else to do the same. Apathy may also result from being surrounded by an abundance of the good things of life, deep disappointment about some personal failure, or 'burn-out'. It is, of course, quite unrelated to fatigue caused by illness or medication. Apathy prevents warm and reciprocal fellowship with God and other believers. As a sterile personal habit it may be used to provide an excuse for self-centredness, or to punish others for real or imaginary wrongs. Whatever the cause, there needs to be repentance, and an exercise of will to commence or resume an active, cooperative, and serving personality controlled by the Holy Spirit.

Road Block No. 6: The divided personality

Regrettably, many people just cannot coordinate their mental and emotional functions. They think one thing then do the opposite, and hate themselves for it. For example, one marriage partner may desperately want to show love but not be able to do so. Instead there are arguments, disagreements, occasional violence, apologies (even with tears), and promises which are never kept. Unless someone can intervene, the situation may end in both parties suffering from rejection, depression, withdrawal and despair. Separation, or divorce may follow.

From experience in counselling sufferers it has been found that they have difficulty in adequately expressing themselves verbally or in writing. Some children and adults constantly fail written examinations despite knowing the subject well. Call it 'exam phobia' or what you will, Phyl and I have found that a demonic spirit is able to cause this. One professional person for whom we prayed had failed oral examinations for a post-graduate degree numerous times, although being highly regarded for his practical work. A colleague asked him to come for spiritual ministry before taking the examination again. We saw the Lord remove this divided spirit (some may term it a spirit of 'simple schizophrenia'), and fuse together the function of his mind and emotions. During that final examination he answered his examiner so fully and effortlessly that the professor told him he had 'dramatically improved'.

When such a condition is recognised during counselling, or is revealed by the Holy Spirit, deliverance and healing needs to be ministered in the name of Jesus Christ. Every person afflicted in this way also suffers from rejection, particularly self-rejection. General freedom from the rejection syndrome will not be fully effective until that dividing spirit has been cast out, and healing received by faith.

Intermission

It is time now to take a break. Not the popcorn, chocolate, cordial, and ice-cream variety, but a time for reflection, honesty, and decision making. Just as airline pilots make careful pre-flight checks, and surgeons make sure that essential instruments are on hand before commencing an operation, so rejection sufferers need to prepare for all that freedom will entail.

To help you do this, the essential points of the last few chapters have been summarised. You are invited to make the prayer-affirmations which are relevant for you, by placing a tick (check) in each appropriate box.

1. (Ref. chapter 15. 'How God dealt with the whole rejection problem')

(a) 'I do believe that Jesus Christ took my place and died for my sin.' ☐

(b) 'I do believe that only God can only save lost sinners through personal faith in Jesus Christ, who died, was buried, and ascended in resurrection to life.' ☐

(c) 'I have repented of my sinful thoughts, desires, actions, habits and failures, and trust Jesus Christ as Saviour and Lord.' ☐

Please note. If you do not have the inner witness of the Holy Spirit that you have been 'born from above' as Jesus said (John 3:3, 5), and you want to experience this, please turn to Appendix 'B' at the end of the book.

(d) 'I do believe that Jesus Christ suffered my rejection to free me from its tyranny, and heal me from its crippling effects.' ☐

(e) 'I do believe that through the blood of Jesus Christ, and the power of his name, I can resist the evil one.' ☐

2. (Ref. chapter 16. 'There must be something wrong somewhere!')

(a) 'I do believe that Christians can be subject to demon oppression (not possession).' ☐

(b) 'I have felt a spiritual orphan because I have not been able to relate to God as my heavenly Father.' ☐

(c) 'I do repent of carrying on hereditary problems, and ask for forgiveness and cleansing.' ☐

(d) 'God, I do want to love you as my heavenly Father with all my heart, mind, soul, and strength. Please help me to do this spontaneously and continually.' ☐

3. (Ref. chapter 17. 'How well do you and the Holy Spirit know each other?')

(a) 'I sincerely want a greater experience of the power and authority of the Holy Spirit in my life, and ask him to share his grace in me, and through me, in any way he chooses, to the glory of God, and the blessing of others.' ☐

(b) 'I promise to listen to what the Holy Spirit teaches me from his Word and says in my heart. Please help me Father to discipline myself to obey him.' ☐

4. (Ref. chapter 18. 'All about re-programming our behaviour computers')

(a) 'I am prepared to give the Word of God priority in my daily activities.' ☐

(b) 'I am determined to meditate on Jesus Christ, and on his Word.' ☐

(c) 'I confess I need a "faith-lift". Heavenly Father, please help me to trust you, despite feelings, circumstances, or my present dependence upon the support of others.' ☐

(d) 'With your help heavenly Father, I am willing to turn my back on the past, and enjoy the closest possible friendship with you.' ☐

5. (Ref. chapter 19. 'Danger – road blocks ahead!')

(a) 'I sincerely repent of every attitude which has dishonoured God, glorified myself, or offended others. I am willing to learn, and share with others your gentleness and humility Lord Jesus.' ☐
(God is dishonoured by intellectualism, intellectual haughtiness, rationalism, humanism, argumentativeness, know-all attitudes, and authoritarianism.)

(b) 'I am determined to face reality, and by your grace I refuse any temptation to indulge in imaginative fantasy or escapism.' ☐

(c) 'I repent of being stubborn and self-protective. Please help me to listen carefully, weigh facts carefully, and decide wisely.' ☐

(d) 'I repent of apathy, laziness, indolence, and self-protection.' ☐

With these affirmations having been made, it is now appropriate to consider ways and means of release.

Chapter 20

How Can I Be Freed From This Crippling Rejection?

The word 'deliverance' is emotive to some, and can often polarise opinions. Believers either run from it, or relish it; don't want to know about it, or can't get enough information; fear what will be said if they do it, or couldn't care less about what people think or say. But as we carefully consider what God's word says, my prayer is that every reader will agree that it is a biblically authenticated ministry.

- Deliverance was part of the ministry of Jesus Christ (Isaiah 61:1; Mark 1:32–34).
- He spent much of his time in freeing people from evil spirits (Luke 4:41; Acts 10:38).
- He commissioned his disciples to follow his example (Matthew 10:1, 8; Mark 3:15; Luke 9:1).
- The backup team of 70 disciples were also given power to set people free (Luke 10:17).
- Jesus Christ authorised his disciples to continue their deliverance ministry in his name after he returned to heaven. He incorporated it into the Great Commission (Mark 16:17).
- The history of the early church confirms that deliverance was an active part of its ministry (Acts 5:16; 8:7; 16:18; 19:11).
- The problems Satan caused in the first century (2 Thessalonians 2:7–11; Revelation 2:9, 10, 13, 24; 3:9), are becoming increasingly evident at the end of the 20th century (Galatians 5:19–21; 1 Timothy 4:1; 1 John 4:1–3).

- Satan is obviously more openly aggressive today than in New Testament times when believers were specifically warned against him (1 Peter 5:8, 9; Ephesians 6:10–18). God's word clearly shows that his deception and influence will greatly increase as time progresses (Revelation chapters 9–17).
- Setting people free from demonic powers is only possible through the name Jesus Christ and the power of his Holy Spirit (Mark 16:17; Acts 13:9–12). He has promised protection to anyone ministering deliverance (Luke 10:19).

Deliverance may be experienced in many ways. The following is a summary.

1. Deliverance comes as a result of growth to spiritual maturity

The Bible exhorts us to be constantly filled and controlled by both the Holy Spirit (Ephesians 5:18), and the Word of God (Colossians 3:16). The results of each experience are identical. The Holy Spirit has bonded the two together. The virgin Mary conceived her son Jesus, the Logos or living Word (John 1:1), through the power of the Holy Spirit (Luke 1:35), and the Bible, the written word or logos (Hebrews 4:12), was penned by people under the dynamic influence of the same Spirit (2 Timothy 3:16; 2 Peter 1:21). Believers who claim to have been filled with the Holy Spirit and who are not filled with his word will be spiritually shallow, lack resistance to temptation, and their prayers will be very self-centred.

For more years than I care to recall, I was an energetic and effective evangelist, confident I was filled with the Holy Spirit because of an initial experience, yet in reality only a partially victorious Christian. When I allowed Jesus Christ full inner control, hungered for holiness, and was obedient to his word, the Holy Spirit increasingly freed me from my many personality problems which were rooted in rejection. It was neither a climactic nor dramatic experience, but a process which gathered momentum. I was also greatly helped by the unlimited love and patience of my partner, Phyl. She said little, but prayed a lot, and God did the rest.

This should remind us that the primary source of spiritual blessings is God himself, not other people. Some of them may greatly help us as God's 'fellow workers' (2 Corinthians 6:1), but not one can ever be his replacement.

2. Deliverance comes through the power of love

As sun melts snow, and fire boils water, so perfect love takes away fears, a very common symptom of rejection (1 John 4:16–18). God never restricts his love to his children. He often confirms it through the caring attitudes of our spiritual brothers and sisters. Paul tells us that love not only frees us from fear, but also:

- displaces impatience, unkindness, envy, boastfulness and pride.
- prevents rudeness, self-seeking, impatience, anger, or revenge.
- hates evil, and rejoices when truth is spoken.
- is always protective of others, trusting, full of hope and perseverance.
- will never fail (all taken from 1 Corinthians 13:4–8).

Because the word 'love' is now just an indication of a strong liking for certain possessions, people, or sexual experiences, its original meaning has become submerged in a sea of hedonism. True love comes only from God because he is its source. He loved us at our worst, proved it by Calvary's cross, and is eternally committed to sharing his love with every believer. Rejection will never remain where love flows, just as darkness disappears when sunlight floods in.

3. Deliverance comes when God acts sovereignly

Some people are totally set free when they are born-again. Evil spirits who had dominated them suddenly and silently leave, and the converts' lives are so changed that no traces of former demonic oppressions can be found. This was the experience of a deeply rejected young New Zealander who isolated himself, and became a Satanist. He was saved when alone, over a period of three hours. He became convicted of sin, deeply repented, and the tears flowed freely. Phyl and I prayed over him less than three weeks afterwards, and could not find any evidence of demonic activity. In fact he had gone back to the friends he had made in witchcraft circles, and given them the good news of the Gospel. He was convinced that God wanted him to be an evangelist, even though he had been a Christian for only a few weeks.

An unsaved married woman who assisted her husband as director of his TV programmes was totally and powerfully delivered while standing in the water of a friend's swimming pool waiting to be baptised. She was dominated by demonic spirits at the time, and her deliverance was so dramatic that she was born again right where she stood.

Most of us have become so used to God performing miracles through specially anointed people, that we forget that he has the ability to manifest his power whenever and wherever he chooses. When needy people wanting deliverance rely on someone with 'expertise' in this ministry, faith is often misplaced. If they don't get what they expect, they usually blame the counsellor, or God himself. Phyl and I constantly warn people that unless they are trusting Jesus Christ to set them free, we will not be able to help them. God alone has sovereign power over Satan and his works.

Sometimes, during a time of praise and worship, rejected people who wholeheartedly glorify God instead of brooding over their problems, have been totally released by the Holy Spirit from the roots and fruit of their rejection. When this happens, the freedom and wholeness received is so complete that it takes time for them to realise just how great a change has taken place.

4. Deliverance comes because of the prayers of others

All deliverance is the sovereign activity of God, but most are set free after prayer by people anointed with the Holy Spirit's wisdom, authority and power. Deliverance candidates need to know:

- that not everyone who claims to have a deliverance ministry has the experience, understanding, sensitivity and power of the Holy Spirit needed to bring freedom from the complications of rejection.
- that shouting, and the use of flamboyant methods are not evidences of the power of the Holy Spirit.
- that partial deliverance is not God's intention. This only frustrates counsellees, and may even stir up the forces of darkness to greater activity than before, causing the individual to feel even worse than ever. Progressive deliverance is of course quite different. Some counsellees become so emotionally or physically exhausted that they need to rest and return for further ministry.

Sometimes counsellors need extra time to seek further guidance in difficult cases, hence a further appointment is necessary.

- that apart from special cases, prolonged deliverance sessions lasting many hours are not necessary, and should be avoided.
- that if counsellees do not have confidence in a particular counsellor, it is better to seek someone in whom they feel confident.
- that for deliverance to glorify God, the counsellee's relationship and dependence upon the Lord must be strengthened; and the counsellor must not become a human crutch.
- that the counsellor should be in good standing in his or her local church, morally upright, trustworthy, and experienced. Counsellees should be able to be relaxed and have total confidence in them.
- that screaming or violence are not normal behaviour during deliverance. Experienced counsellors should exercise authority over any demonic performance

Without doubt, there are few people willing, capable, and with time to take authority over the evil one. Regrettably, some churches have not yet accepted deliverance as a valid ministry, and sufferers do not know where to go. Since the publication of *Evicting Demonic Intruders and Breaking Bondages*, many pastors and church members have written to us saying that by following the book's instructions, they have developed their own ministry and have had the joy of seeing the Lord set people free.

An important question we are frequently asked is: 'How can I be sure that my problems are demonic, and that deliverance is needed?' Many questioners may have already sought help from pastors and other counsellors, but without success. From personal experience we have found that when problems remain or increase despite intense spiritual or practical advice, demonic activity is usually at the root of the problem.

Before giving a summary of instructions from the first book, there are some **important facts to be considered** by those who are engaged or want to be engaged, in a deliverance ministry.

1. Present day deliverance should be as effective as in the first century because the name of Jesus is eternally-powerful, and feared just as much by demonic spirits now as then.
2. Deliverance is not the alpha and omega of resolving every problem. It may be quite inappropriate in some cases. Deliverance counsellors need to remember that sound spiritual

advice, Christian psychology, or medical assistance may be what is needed most. From experience we have proved that deliverance does effectively blend with the professional services of both sciences, because patients have been referred to us by members of both professions. After the Lord has freed them, they return to the referring specialist for appropriate follow-up. Phyl and I believe it is not ethical to minister to people under psychological, medical, or psychiatric care unless the specialist personally approves. After ministry, we **never** give advice on changing medication, but send them back to their specialists.

3. For deliverance to be successful in the long term, counsellees must be sincere, genuinely desire freedom from every problem, not dependent on others, and be committed to faithful observance of the follow up discipleship principles.

4. Every person involved in deliverance needs to be humble, teachable, and sensitive to the promptings of the Spirit of Jesus Christ. Pride and 'know-all' attitudes will effectively block spiritual power.

5. Make sure that Jesus Christ is given **all the glory**. He is the head of his body, the Church, and no matter what part individual members have in ministering to fellow members, blessings are only possible by his direction and enabling.

6. When talking about people to whom you have ministered deliverance, remember that Jesus Christ warned his disciples not to get excited about demons submitting to them, but to rejoice that their names were written in heaven (Luke 10:20).

7. Deliverance is a matter of faith, not feelings, of God's power, not exuberance, of spiritual understanding, not human reason.

8. Results may be seen immediately at the time of deliverance, or spread over the short or long term. If the counsellee does not show or feel any evidence of release, it may be because root causes have not been adequately dealt with, or it may simply be a test of your faith. Counsellors should seek guidance and discernment about controlling spirits which may be blocking release. To ask the counsellee to come back is not an admission of defeat, but an opportunity for both parties to wait upon the Lord. It will also test the sincerity of the counsellee, and help to offset discouragement.

9. Counsellees need to be warned (and the same applies in self-deliverance) that when anyone has been freed from the grip of the evil one, well-established habits will take time to disappear. An occasional relapse after ministry should not be taken to mean that another deliverance session is necessary. On **very** few occasions, this may be so, but generally speaking it is because the discipleship principles have not been fully applied in daily practice.

10. Deliverance will not be permanent unless there has first been wholehearted repentance. The evil one does not give up easily. He will certainly dangle attractively baited temptations in front of those whom the Lord has freed, firstly, in an effort to side-track the counsellee's attention from faith to feelings, secondly, to bring doubts about what God has done, and thirdly, to drag a delivered person back into oppression. Freed people should hate what God hates, and repent from every thought or desire which could rob Jesus Christ of his Lordship in their lives.

11. Deliverance is a crisis activity. It is neither a disgrace, nor something to boast about. It should not be forced, only encouraged. Where possible, it should be carried out in private, and never be regarded as a 'spectator sport'. Jesus Christ would never permit demons to perform 'centre-stage' (Mark 9:25).

12. When counsellees are fearful of deliverance, it is usually an outward expression of dominating spirits who do not want to be evicted. When authority is taken over that demonic fear, there is usually no further problem.

13. Beware of the 'full-time' counsellee. The person who does the rounds of known counsellors, or is always asking for another session of deliverance because he or she has remembered something that was forgotten on the last occasion. Deliverance is not a bottle of medicine to be taken in regular doses. Counsellees must learn to 'stand on their own feet' supported by Jesus Christ. They are to be discouraged from seeking continuous help. A discreet enquiry as to how many others have already been consulted is a wise precaution.

14. The reasons for asking counsellees to cough in order to release spirits is sometimes questioned. The physical and spiritual implications of this are dealt with in the following pages. In the

three years since the first book was written, the Lord has reminded us that because of the power of his anointing on those praying, demons often spontaneously leave the body by making the counsellee cough, without being encouraged to do so. The demons themselves choose coughing as a way of escape. In cases of heavy oppression, counsellees often spontaneously commence coughing before its significance has been explained, or before being asked to do so. The authority of the name and blood of Jesus Christ, and the power of the Holy Spirit flowing through anointed hands causes demons to leave as quickly as they can. As *'wisdom is proved right by her actions'* (Matthew 11:19), so coughing for deliverance is justified by the freedom gained.

15. Oddball methods of deliverance are not of God. Some counsellors believe they should manifest the symptoms of being delivered (such as coughing) instead of the counsellee. Some very distressed women have also come to us having been repulsed by a male counsellor lying on top of them aligning arms, legs etc. Praise God they were freed from their demonic problems and the evil effects of this bogus behaviour.

For those who wish to learn the principles of deliverance, the following pages have been reprinted from *Evicting Demonic Intruders and Breaking Bondages.*

How to set people free using divine authority and power

1. Some preliminary suggestions

Deliverance sessions should commence with giving glory to God, exalting Jesus Christ, and submitting to the sovereignty of the Holy Spirit. If the counsellee is a born-again believer, he or she should be asked to repeat the following prayer:

'I confess Jesus Christ to be my personal Saviour. I confess and renounce every iniquity, transgression and sin that I, my parents, or ancestors may have committed and which has brought bondages and dominations to my life, and ask for forgiveness and cleansing. I repent from any action, attitude or habit which does not glorify Jesus Christ. I renounce the devil, and all of his works, influences, bondages, dominations, afflictions and infirmities in my life. I claim the release and freedom promised by Jesus Christ, that he may be Lord of my whole life. Amen.'

A few simple explanations and instructions need to be given to the counsellee before commencing prayer so that he or she will understand the procedure, and know how to co-operate.

(a) The ban on audible prayer
Ask the counsellee to refrain from praying audibly during ministry, and particularly from speaking out the name of Jesus Christ. This is for two reasons. Firstly, it becomes confusing when two people are speaking at one time, and it can be noisy. Secondly, the spoken name of Jesus is always a barrier to demonic powers who are ordered to leave.

A simple illustration explains this principle. When a bird gets trapped inside a room, the best way to release it is to open a door or window then stand aside so that the way of escape is clear. To stand in the doorway or in front of the window will only frighten the bird and make it fly around. In the same way, demonic dominations (spirit forces inside the body) are fearful of the name of the conquering Saviour, and its use by the counsellee will only delay or hinder their leaving.

(b) Control of the counsellee's thoughts
It is important for people receiving deliverance to concentrate their thinking on the Lord Jesus. If they wish, they may pray silently. Again, there are two reasons. Firstly, an inert mind can become Satan's playground. Sin is conceived in the mind, and a 'No Vacancy' sign will discourage unwanted callers. Secondly, dominant spirits sometimes try to manipulate minds with thoughts of unbelief and scepticism, fantasy, distraction, or even to resist what is happening.

(c) The need to speak out
Counsellees should be encouraged to speak out anything significant that comes into their minds during the session.

- A sudden recall of a forgotten event may provide a clue as to the type of domination which may be causing problems.
- When seeking to identify strongholds which resist the lordship of Christ, the counsellee should be asked to tell you whatever comes to mind.
- When demonic powers try to dominate a mind during deliverance, it is important for the counsellee to declare this so that authority can be taken over them.

(d) Explain the biblical significance of the laying on of hands
This procedure may disturb certain types of people:

- **Believers with reservations.** There are usually two objections. One is that by laying hands on the demon-possessed, 'you might become possessed yourself'. Well, Jesus Christ wasn't affected, and the Spirit-filled believer is just as safe (Luke 4:40, 41). The other objection is that the laying on of hands is unnecessary. 'All you have to do to demons is to renounce them, bind them, and tell them to go away.' A few may indeed respond, but by far the majority are more defiant than a bunch of naughty boys, and will remain entrenched until they are evicted by the name of Jesus and the power of his anointing. Both of us have seen experienced counsellors encircle a needy person, naming and binding spirits, without the slightest evidence of release being received. With the laying on of hands, results begin immediately. Demons cannot stand the power of the Holy Spirit being released into the life they have been dominating, and are usually glad to leave. We long for the day of God's power, when the mere presence of a holy life, or a simple command in the name of Jesus will cause demons to flee.
- **Those who have not previously experienced the laying on of hands.** Before praying for either unbelievers or believers, it should be explained that this was the practice of Jesus Christ, his disciples, and the early church. Only two days before writing this chapter, I had the joy of leading a man to Christ and praying for his release from spirits of Freemasonry and rejection. He had no problems about the laying on of hands, although it was completely new to him.

Many times before deliverance actually begins, demonic powers have become so restless because of the counsellee's renunciation and prayer, that they have begun to leave before hands can be laid on the one oppressed. They certainly know what their future state will be (Matthew 25:41; Revelation 20:10).

(e) The manner of demonic releases

Demons leave the body in a variety of ways. When demonic bondages are broken, there is usually no evident sign unless they are particularly strong, but spirits of domination normally leave in an obvious manner. This includes coughings, sighing, yawnings, and belching. It is wise to forewarn a counsellee about this so as to save him from later embarrassment. The following explanation has helped people understand the reason for this. The engines in our cars need air to aid the fuel combustion, and draw this in through the air filter and carburettor. The waste products are then blown out through the exhaust pipe. This process illustrates the need to get rid of the demonic powers (spiritual impurities) by coughing, or other means, before the Holy Spirit (as the breath of God) is able to cleanse and heal.

THE RELEASE PROCESS, STEP BY STEP

1. Aim to remove root causes rather than just pick bad fruit

There are many spiritual 'fruit inspectors' around who can tell us what bad fruit they can see on the trees of our lives. However, few of them are 'tree-doctors' capable of diagnosing and removing causes in order that we may bear good fruit.

Counsellees are often not able to diagnose the causes of their own problems, although they are acutely aware of their presence. They usually do not want to disappoint those who pray for them, and may even pretend to have been helped, even if they do not feel so. If their problems have not been actually discerned and dealt with they may give way to hopelessness and despair and remain defeated Christians.

The 'Tree of Rejection' in chapter twelve, is here harmonised with the diagnostic questions set out in the questionnaire in chapter nineteen. This will highlight some of the most commonly encountered root-fruit systems to be dealt with in deliverance.

THE TREE AND ITS ROOTS	THE QUESTIONNAIRE INFORMATION
The basic causes of rejection: At conception In utero The manner of birth A baby not being bonded at birth Being an adopted child Hereditary rejection Causes in the family home School teachers or students One's own attitudes Other causes later in life	Questions one and two will reveal not only the causes of rejection, but also the branches that need attention, item by item.

THE INPUT IDENTIFIES

THE ROOT SYSTEMS OF REJECTION WHICH REQUIRE REMOVAL

The list is not exhaustive. It may be amended as the Spirit of God directs.

1 REJECTION (Aggressive reactions)	**2** SELF REJECTION (Negative reactions)	**3** FEAR OF REJECTION (Counter-actions)
Rebellion Anger, temper, etc. Stubbornness Aggressive attitudes, by words, or use of force Refusal, or inability to communicate Inability or refusal to receive comfort	Low self-image Inferiorities Apathy, disinterest Self-accusation **FEARS OF ALL KINDS** Doubt, unbelief Self-pity Negativity Emotional immaturity caused by a childish or adolescent spirit	A spirit of striving for friendship or achievement. Perhaps performance or competition. Withdrawal, a desire to be alone. Independence, isolationism Criticism, judgement Envy, jealousy. The self syndrome: self-righteousness self-defensiveness protectiveness perfectionism

List all the problems from which the counsellee desires release.

The following fruit-root systems will be of assistance in diagnosis, and as a guide to the release of root causes which may be hidden, or are inter-related with other problems.

The central boxes contain the names of problems. The surrounding boxes contain contributory root causes.

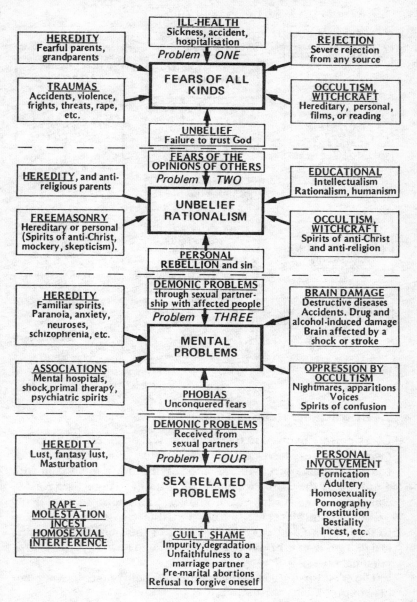

ILL-HEALTH
Sickness, accident, hospitalisation
Problem ONE

HEREDITY
Fearful parents, grandparents

REJECTION
Severe rejection from any source

TRAUMAS
Accidents, violence, frights, threats, rape, etc.

FEARS OF ALL KINDS

OCCULTISM, WITCHCRAFT
Hereditary, personal, films, or reading

UNBELIEF
Failure to trust God

FEARS OF THE OPINIONS OF OTHERS
Problem TWO

HEREDITY, and anti-religious parents

EDUCATIONAL
Intellectualism Rationalism, humanism

FREEMASONRY
Hereditary or personal (Spirits of anti-Christ, mockery, skepticism).

UNBELIEF RATIONALISM

OCCULTISM, WITCHCRAFT
Spirits of anti-Christ and anti-religion

PERSONAL REBELLION and sin

DEMONIC PROBLEMS
through sexual partnership with affected people
Problem THREE

HEREDITY
Familiar spirits, Paranoia, anxiety, neuroses, schizophrenia, etc.

BRAIN DAMAGE
Destructive diseases Accidents. Drug and alcohol-induced damage Brain affected by a shock or stroke

ASSOCIATIONS
Mental hospitals, shock, primal therapy, psychiatric spirits

MENTAL PROBLEMS

OPPRESSION BY OCCULTISM
Nightmares, apparitions Voices Spirits of confusion

PHOBIAS
Unconquered fears

DEMONIC PROBLEMS
Received from sexual partners
Problem FOUR

HEREDITY
Lust, fantasy lust, Masturbation

PERSONAL INVOLVEMENT
Fornication Adultery Homosexuality Pornography Prostitution Bestiality Incest, etc.

RAPE – MOLESTATION INCEST HOMOSEXUAL INTERFERENCE

SEX RELATED PROBLEMS

GUILT SHAME
Impurity, degradation Unfaithfulness to a marriage partner Pre-marital abortions Refusal to forgive oneself

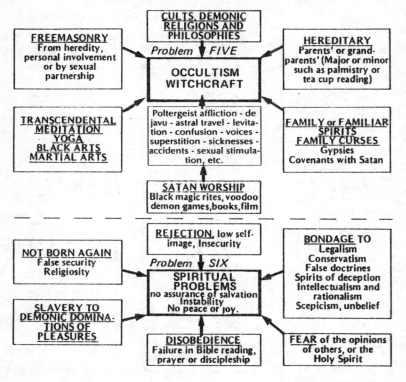

2. Distractions of the evil one

Every person involved in releasing spiritual prisoners develops his own style with which he feels comfortable. Final results are of course the only objective evaluation. With this in mind, and with gratitude to the Lord, we share what he has taught us. We are conscious of our mistakes and failures, and realize that the Holy Spirit has so much yet to teach us. We trust it may encourage others to step out in faith, trusting the Spirit of the Lord for increasing insight into causes of spiritual problems, and new ways of meeting personal needs.

The enemy has tried to prevent effective deliverance by a number of activities:

- by trying to bring about the cancellation of an appointment. His favourite tricks are sickness, an accident, severe oppression, appointment confusion, and unreasonable fears of what may happen.
- by bringing an onset of distracting pain during prayer. One woman suddenly doubled up in agony when the pain of an operation performed ten years previously returned. The demon of pain was cast out, and immediately she felt normal.

On other occasions, headaches, dizziness, and a sense of imminent fainting have threatened to hold up ministry. Each feeling has been a demonic delaying tactic, and ceased when authority was taken over it.

- by bringing unreasonable feelings of panic and fear while the counsellee is being prayed for. The fear is a demonic feeling expressed through the counsellee. During deliverance, women have become terrified of me as a male, and have clung to Phyl until they were set free. Remember the Boy Scout motto and 'be prepared'.

The stages of the deliverance process are as follows:

(a) *The binding, breaking, and loosing*

- The counsellee should be seated on an upright chair without arms, well clear of surrounding furniture. The paper tissues and waste container need to be close at hand.

Your prayer partner should be asked to hold the completed list so that you can easily read the negative problems for which bondages must be broken, and the names of the dominating spirits which must be evicted.

Examples of a bondage are an inability to forgive, or express love. Examples of a dominating spirit would be bitterness, anger, hatred and lust.

As stated previously, we have found that by naming specific spirits which produce root causes of problems they can be evicted, and cleansing and wholeness received. This is probably the key to understanding the difference between verbal counselling, and counselling which leads to freedom through deliverance.

- After the prayer and renunciation, one hand should be placed on the forehead, and one at the back of the head, and the power of

215

each demonic force by name should be bound, broken, and loosed one at a time.

Unless the Holy Spirit indicates otherwise the rejection syndrome is normally the best place to commence prayer, not just because it heads the questionnaire, but because it is the key to releasing other parts of the personality. Where strong spirits of witchcraft and anti-Christ are resisting ministry, they should be tackled first.

• Deal with the demonic powers of several related areas at one time, and be sure there has been a release before proceeding to the next group. This procedure is followed until the entire list compiled from the questionnaire has been dealt with.

(b) How to know that demonic forces have been driven out and bondages broken

Once the power of the demons have been bound and broken, and their hold over the life loosed, they no longer have any legal right to remain. Although demons are always illegal intruders, they are seldom keen to vacate the premises under orders of the rightful owner. Some however can't leave fast enough, and the person receiving prayer may burst into spontaneous coughing, as soon as the authority is taken.

When there is no immediate manifestation, the writers have found it most beneficial to ask the counsellee to bend forward slightly, from the waist up. We then place our hands on each side of the waist above the hips, the two thumbs pointing towards the spine, and as close to it as possible. It is important that the hands avoid the stomach area. The activity of demon powers may actually be felt in the hands. They may move and jump around, sometimes quite strongly, or gather in a knot. The counsellee may or may not be aware of this. Sometimes the whole area under the hands becomes rigid, and the counsellee finds it most difficult or even impossible to cough even if he desires to do so.

The power of 'holy hands' added to what Jesus Christ has given us is certainly most effective. Normally, one of the following reactions will take place:

• The counsellee will spontaneously cough deeply, and continue coughing until each demonic power named in the root-fruit systems has gone. Other manifestations may include yawning, belching, sighing, gagging, or retching.

- Nothing happens. In this case, suggest that the counsellee try a good strong cough. This normally triggers the process of release, which should continue until the spirits named have gone. When the coughing commences, the named spirits can again be commanded to leave.

- A counsellee refuses to cough, saying 'Why should I cough?' This may be because he does not understand why he needs to do so. When the reason is repeated, there is usually co-operation. But if the response is more of a challenge to authority, or an expression of no confidence in the method, it should be explained that coughing is an act of faith and co-operation. The counsellee needs to understand that confidence in the person who is ministering is important, and although the act of coughing may seem irrelevant, it is a method which God has blessed. Spirits of unbelief, doubt, and scepticism should then be bound, broken, and loosed, and the request to cough repeated. In almost all cases, the process of freedom commences, and the person is able to be fully released. The spontaneity of coughing, after it has been commenced by an act of the will, builds faith and expectation.

Should a counsellee still refuse to co-operate after an explanation and further prayer, it is obvious that it is not God's time for release. Further counselling may be necessary.

- A counsellee genuinely tries to cough, and is unable to do so. Some make noises which are more like clearing the throat, but cannot cough at a deeper level. Normally this is caused by strong spirits of resistance. Often they come from occultism, witchcraft, or Freemasonry. Authority should be taken strongly over every spirit of anti-Christ, rebellion, resistance, stubbornness, and spiritual darkness. Where there is mocking laughter, a spirit is causing it. It is important that the counsellee co-operate by attempting to cough, and with persistence by both counsellor and counsellee, the coughing will begin and increase until the pent-up demonic powers literally rush out. The counsellee will then usually express relief from the inner tension and pressures. The best advice, in difficult cases, is simply, 'Hang in there'.

It is seldom that people who have received deep releases do not spontaneously confess their sense of freedom when the session is completed.

(c) Points to remember:

- *Persistence is important.* Demonic powers will bluff, pretend not to be there, or to have gone when in fact they still remain. They use every trick possible to resist eviction. Their resistance can only be temporary; remember your legal rights over them, purchased at Calvary.

- *Reassure counsellees* that when you voice strong opposition to demonic powers, you are not speaking to them personally, but to what is in them. Some sensitive people may feel crushed unless they understand this.

- *Demonic noise can be and should be controlled.* Some people scream unexpectedly while they are being freed. If this continues, the spirits need to be commanded to be silent. Their talkback can be similarly controlled.

- *The final check.* When you have worked through your problem list and believe all the demonic forces have been driven out and all bondages have been broken, a final check is necessary. Paul tells us that we have weapons which destroy strongholds and make Jesus Christ Lord of the life (2 Corinthians 10:5). Use that power to challenge any authority which may still remain to hinder Lordship. By commanding all such demonic powers to name themselves, or reveal their work, they will either speak out through the mouth of the counsellee, or will name themselves in the counsellee's mind. By asking that anything of this nature be spoken out, even if it has already been dealt with, what surfaces is sometimes surprising. Deal with each item, so that there is a clear release before renewing the challenge. Even if a word or name shocks the individual, deal with the demonic power behind it in faith.

- There is one important rule in ministering freedom in Christ. When the Holy Spirit gives any inner conviction that a certain demonic spirit is operating within a person's life, **always act upon his advice**. It may not make sense to you, but act upon it, and you will always see results. The more teachable you are, the more you will be shown and the greater will be the glory brought to the name of Jesus Christ.

So, when completing the release portion of the session, be open to what the Lord may reveal as well as what comes into the mind of the counsellee. Time taken is an investment. Do not proceed to the cleansing process until you and the counsellee have the inner witness that the enemy has gone. Then proceed to clean up the battle field.

3. Cleansing, receiving forgiveness, forgiving others, and inner healing

(a) Cleansing

Jesus said a life becomes clean when an evil spirit leaves it (Luke 11:25). John sets out the process in his epistle. First there is confession, then forgiveness followed by cleansing from all unrighteousness caused by that sin (1 John 1:9).

It appears that few believers really believe this promise and claim the blessings of inner cleansing. Most of us re-confess our sins time and again to make sure we have been thorough. The evidence is that many Christians continue to live in the bondage of guilt for sins that have been forgiven. We can delude ourselves into thinking that our low self-image is a sign of repentance and humility – some form of penance imposed on ourselves to make us feel better! All this is contrary to what our merciful and gracious God has provided in Jesus Christ.

Inner cleansing through the blood of Jesus Christ may also become very real during the laying on of hands. Ask the counsellee to receive this by faith in every area which has been defiled. This involves mind, heart, conscience, will, and each physical system affected by demonic powers.

(b) Receiving forgiveness

When God forgives, he wipes out all record of the wrong doing. That means that there are only two persons who still have that information, and who can use it wrongfully. One is the devil who constantly enjoys accusing us and making us feel guilty. It is one of his really bad habits and counsellees should be warned not to listen to the world's most incorrigible liar. The other knowledgeable person is the forgiven sinner who often battles with past memories, and doubts forgiveness. That memory needs to be dealt with in two positive ways. Firstly, forgiveness needs to be established by being declared openly. Here is a simple prayer:

'I thank you Father for your forgiveness for (name), and for your total release from the grip and accusation of the evil one, and the completeness of your inner cleansing. Because I am clean in your sight, I now forgive myself for all I have done in sinning against yourself, myself, and others. I release myself completely from bondages to people and past events. Amen.'

Secondly, the counsellee needs to believe that there is no longer any basis for anyone to cause condemnation (Romans 8:1). All lying accusations from the memory or from Satan need to be resisted by praise to God for his total cleansing.

(c) Forgiving others
When spirits of unforgiveness, resentment, bitterness, and hatred have been driven out, a counsellee has no trouble in expressing forgiveness to parents, children, a marriage partner, and friends. A prayer of faith should be framed so that the counsellee can specifically name the people who are being forgiven and released from troublesome memories. Forgiveness of others is basic to all spiritual blessing (Matthew 6:14, 15; Mark 11:25; Colossians 3:13b).

(d) Inner healing
Much has been written about the healing of memories. It has been the experience of the writers that complete healing cannot be received or retained until the causative factors have been removed. It is like trying to heal a finger without removing the wood splinter which has caused an infection. Once every form of demonic oppression has been removed, cleansing taken, and forgiveness received and extended to others, there is no hindrance to a person receiving full healing in all affected areas. This should harmonise the thoughts and emotions, produce a healthy self-image, and allow the Spirit of God to direct bodily appetites and habits. Physical healings will also be manifested when spirits of infirmities and afflictions have been cast out. Many people testify to physical healings received in this way after public ministry.

It has been found that the average time taken to diagnose problems and minister freedom is about ninety minutes. Those who come with a clear understanding of their problems and causes may take a little less, and the more complicated may take thirty minutes longer. A few may take several hours. Before concluding, follow-up literature is explained, and given to the counsellee. This contains an address if future contact is needed.

SPECIAL NOTE

For those desiring more in-depth teaching on how to minister deliverance to children, teenagers, and adults, audio cassettes by Noel and Phyl Gibson with further written materials are available. Teachings are based on the three books published on this subject:

Evicting Demonic Intruders and Breaking Bondages,

Deliver Our Children From the Evil One,

Excuse Me ... Your Rejection is Showing.

Exquiries concerning the cost and supply of the teaching package (and/or the basic text books), should be addressed to:

Freedom in Christ Ministries
PO Box 436,
Drummoyne, NSW 2047,
Australia.

Chapter 21

Self-Deliverance

Ministering deliverance to oneself is not a new aspect of spiritual warfare. It is just that more has been written about it in recent years than previously. Graham and Shirley Powell (two special colleagues of ours) wrote *Christian Set Yourself Free* (New Wine Press, PO Box 17, Chichester, England PO20 6YB) some time ago. It has been well received in many countries, and Christians have testified to having received freedom through following its advice.

Self-deliverance is a personal means of counter-attacking the evil one, when Christians realise he is exercising some form of control over their lives. Although Paul warned the Ephesians that they needed the armour of God to protect them and give them victory in the *'day of evil'* (chapter 6:10–18), many believers have learned from bitter experience that Satan's temptations cannot be resisted in their own strength. Consequently they fall victim to bondages and dominations.

Note: A 'bondage' is a demonic hindrance preventing a person from doing what they know to be right, and want to do. A spirit of 'domination' (oppression), is a demonic force which makes a person do what they know to be wrong and don't want to do.

Many innocent people have inherited demonic problems, and there are others who, in their unsaved days have opened their lives to oppression by deliberate sin, and were not freed when they came to Christ. Rejection certainly features in some form in every case, and self-deliverance offers a welcome relief from this and all other associated problems.

Not everyone will receive immediate or full release through self-deliverance. Many have tried, failed, and come to us for help. We have found at least two reasons for this. Firstly, they may be under very strong demonic control, and have insufficient faith or authority to overcome their oppressors. Secondly, they are controlled by an hereditary familiar spirit which has been in the family for many generations. These never give up easily, defending what they think is their territorial right.

Any person unable to receive freedom by self-deliverance should ask for help from someone with wider experience. When major blocks have been removed, there is no reason why self-deliverance should not become effective. An appropriate analogy is the stalled vehicle which needs to be pushed or towed to get started.

Before outlining practical suggestions for self-deliverance, one important question needs to be answered. **Who will benefit most from self-deliverance?** Firstly, those with a deep personal conviction that God intends every child of his to live victoriously, without being oppressed by the evil one, and that he has given them his authority over all demonic powers in the name of his son, Jesus. Secondly, self-deliverance procedures are particularly suitable for:

- believers who live in isolated places.
- very private people who find it impossible or very difficult to share their personal problems with others.
- members or adherents of churches openly antagonistic to the deliverance ministry on the grounds of doctrine or prejudice.
- pastors, church leaders, or professional people who are too embarrassed to share their personal lives with those who know and respect them.
- believers who have been hurt by counsellors who have broken confidence and publicly shared their problems.
- those who fear being rejected by counsellors once they share the causes and effects of their rejection.
- a Christian whose marriage partner is an unbeliever, and opposes expressions of faith and church attendance.
- believers who have received deliverance, but have given way to temptation and been re-oppressed by the spirit of that problem. Because Jesus won the decisive battle against Satan, every after-skirmish must be victorious. Other parts of the personality need no further deliverance, once the particular problem has been dealt with.

- Christians who have received freedom but who have been conscious of continuing oppression in a particular area which may have been overlooked, or insufficiently dealt with at the time of ministry.

1. Preparing for self-deliverance

First

Write down every problem from which you feel the need to be released. The earlier chapters identify attitudes, actions, and habits symptomatic of rejection, and you may have noted that some, or many, apply to you. They need to be included.

Now check through the problems listed on each of the three branches of the following tree of rejection, and add to your list anything which is particularly appropriate to you on any of the branch lines shown as: 'Aggressive reactions', 'Self-rejection symptoms', and 'Measures to counter rejection'. The diagram has been taken from *Evicting Demonic Intruders and Breaking Bondages* first published 1987.

Complete the list of items from which you desire freedom.

- Write down any personal problem which is not included in the branch-lists. For example, causes of the rejection process such as abandonment at birth, cruelty, injustice, sexual interference, incest or rape. Trauma opens the door to demonic domination. This is why they are so troublesome for so long. You should also add other problems which commenced after these incidents, such as nervousness, sleeplessness, frigidity, and specific fears. And don't forget to include matters your friends complain about, even if you have not been aware of them.
- Include anything you have battled with but which you may not have recognised as having come from rejection, such as lust, immorality, addictions (drugs, alcohol, smoking, gluttony, gambling, compulsive physical exercise, TV watching, compulsive eating of chocolate and other sweet things, being a spendthrift), and occultism or witchcraft. You need **total** freedom.
- Give particular attention to hereditary problems which you know were in your parents or grandparents such as, Freemasonry spirits, anger and violence, apathy or passivity, unbelief, doubt and scepticism.

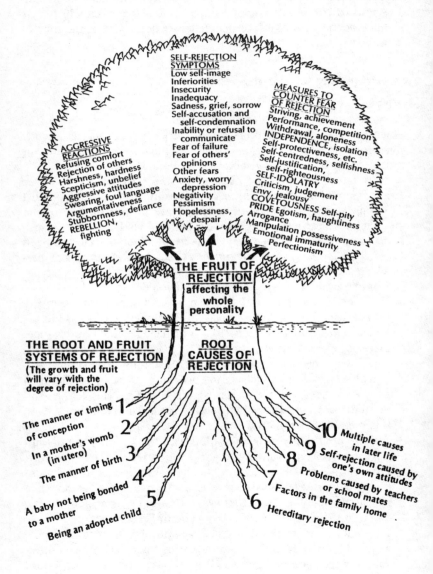

SELF-REJECTION SYMPTOMS
Low self-image
Inferiorities
Insecurity
Inadequacy
Sadness, grief, sorrow
Self-accusation and
  self-condemnation
Inability or refusal to
  communicate
Fear of failure
Fear of others'
  opinions
Other fears
Anxiety, worry
  depression
Negativity
Pessimism
Hopelessness,
  despair

MEASURES TO COUNTER FEAR OF REJECTION
Striving, achievement
Performance, competition
Withdrawal, aloneness
INDEPENDENCE, isolation
Self-protectiveness, etc.
Self-centredness, selfishness
Self-justification,
  self-righteousness
SELF-IDOLATRY
Criticism, judgement
Envy, jealousy
COVETOUSNESS Self-pity
PRIDE Egotism, haughtiness
Arrogance
Manipulation possessiveness
Emotional immaturity
Perfectionism

AGGRESSIVE REACTIONS
Refusing comfort
Rejection of others
Harshness, hardness
Scepticism, unbelief
Aggressive attitudes
Swearing, foul language
Argumentativeness
Stubbornness, defiance
REBELLION,
  fighting

THE FRUIT OF REJECTION
affecting the whole personality

THE ROOT AND FRUIT SYSTEMS OF REJECTION
(The growth and fruit will vary with the degree of rejection)

ROOT CAUSES OF REJECTION

1 The manner or timing of conception
2 In a mother's womb (in utero)
3 The manner of birth
4 A baby not being bonded to a mother
5 Being an adopted child
6 Hereditary rejection
7 Factors in the family home
8 Problems caused by teachers or school mates
9 Self-rejection caused by one's own attitudes
10 Multiple causes in later life

- List past religious or cultic spirits including the name of any holy man, swami guru, god, oppressive commune leader, or saint to whom you may have been dedicated.
- Add the names of strong ethnic, cultural, or indigenous spirits which you suspect may have influenced you either from heredity, from your country of birth, or other places of temporary or permanent residence.

Second
Holding your 'inventory', speak aloud a declaration of repentance, renunciation of Satan, and dedication to total discipleship. The following would be appropriate:

> 'I confess Jesus Christ to be my personal Saviour. I renounce every activity of Satan in my life through the iniquity, transgression or sin of my parents, grandparents, or myself. I repent of thoughts, words and actions which have dishonoured Jesus Christ, and ask for forgiveness, cleansing and release from their driving forces. Lord Jesus, I renounce the devil, and all his works, influences, bondages, oppressions (sickness and allergies if appropriate) present in my life from any source, and ask for the total freedom that your death, burial and resurrection provides, so that you will become Lord of my total personality. Amen'

2. The process of self-deliverance

(a) Because this is a personal matter between you and the Lord, it is advisable to be alone. It would be good to have a supply of paper tissues on hand in case of tears.

(b) As soon as you have made your faith declaration, name the three major spirits of rejection on your list, then bind each demonic power, break its hold over your life, and demand that each one leaves you in the name of Jesus Christ. The actual words could be:

> 'I bind you spirits of rejection, self-rejection, and fear of rejection in the name of Jesus Christ. I break your power over me, and command you to leave in Jesus' name.'

227

At this point you may find yourself irresistibly coughing (even retching), or yawning as the Holy Spirit frees you. Occasionally belches of wind may occur. If there is no spontaneous evidence of freedom, then cough deliberately, and you will find that voluntary coughing will continue until the spirits responsible for each condition have gone. That deliberate cough is to you a step of faith, but demonic powers will recognise it as their eviction notice plus the act of being evicted. In the 1st century it was believed that the solar plexus was the centre of spiritual and emotional feelings (see John 7:37 KJV). Both Phyl and I have found that demonic reaction and activity during deliverance can often be seen in distinct movements in the area of the abdomen. They can even be felt with the hand.

After these major spirits of rejection are released, methodically go through your prepared list, with the binding, breaking, loosing and coughing procedure, item by item, or two or three together if they are associated, such as unbelief, doubt and scepticism. Then prayerfully ask God to show you anything you may have forgotten, overlooked, or not known about which needs to be dealt with. If he brings this to your mind, go through the same pattern of binding, loosing, and commanding each spirit to leave, until nothing else comes to mind.

During this time of self-deliverance, please keep this advice in mind:

- Never converse with any spirit speaking in your mind, or who makes you speak aloud. Command it to be silent, and to leave in the name of Jesus Christ, then deliberately cough until it is gone.

- Demons may attempt to divert your attention by making you cry, particularly by reviving painful memories of the past. Because it is a delaying tactic, don't give way, but deliberately cough until they obey you and go. Then the crying will stop.

- Stay seated at all times and refuse to give way to any demonic force which makes you want to scream, or fall on the floor. Refuse to obey them in the name of Jesus Christ, and you will find that you really do have control. Should you still have problems, wait, and ask for help from someone who is experienced in deliverance.

3. God has more for you

Once you are confident that you are free, there are still some things
to be done:

(a) Cleansing and renewal

By faith claim the full inner cleanness God promises (1 John 1:9).
Generally speaking, we Christians pray for our sins to be forgiven,
but do not claim the cleansing God also offers, so we continue to
feel guilty, and constantly re-confess those same sins over and over
again, just in case our prayers were not heard. What a faithless
exercise this is! It dishonours God and leaves us with feelings of
guilt, unbelief, even despair. True disciples of Jesus Christ take
God's promises at their full face-value. Nowhere does the Bible say
that faith must be endorsed by feelings.

From practical experience we have found that by encouraging
counsellees to consciously breathe a little deeper than usual while
we pray for their cleansing and renewal after deliverance, it releases
faith, and they are able to receive blessings more easily. It is also
biblically significant. When God breathed the breath of life into
Adam's lifeless body, he became a living personality (Genesis 2:7).
When Ezekiel prophesied, the four winds of heaven blew on a
whole valley full of re-constituted but lifeless human bodies. They
all came to life, and stood up (Ezekiel 37:9, 10). When Jesus Christ
breathed on his disciples, they each received an infilling of the Holy
Spirit (John 20:21, Luke 24:45). And when the 120 disciples in the
upper room heard '... a sound like the blowing of a violent
wind ...' the effect was so dynamic that the inhabitants and visitors
to Jerusalem asked what was going on (Acts 2:2–6).

So, when you know you have received freedom, exercise faith by
consciously 'breathing in' cleansing and renewal into your conscious
and subconscious mind, emotions, conscience, will, body and
senses. If it would help, read through your prepared list of problems
while you receive all God has for you, by faith.

Physical healing sometimes follows release from the grip of the
evil one. When four young men removed a portion of a house roof
and lowered their paralytic friend to where Jesus stood, he showed
his order of priorities. First, he forgave the young man's sins, then
he healed him (Mark 2:5–12).

(b) Destroy the evidence

To confirm the complete work Jesus Christ has done in you and for you, tear up, or burn your list of problems. Don't file it for regular check-ups, or for 'mulling-over-the-past'. God no longer has a record, so why should you?

(c) Post-deliverance repentance

Some rejection sufferers may think that because others have sinned against them they are innocent victims who have no sin to confess. All they need is release and healing. But that presumption is usually incorrect. Without question, those who cause rejection will be judged for what they have done, but rejected people are responsible for their own reactions. Aggressive attitudes, unforgiveness, anger, bitterness, resentment, criticisms, refusal to love or communicate, self-pity, self-defensive attitudes, revenge, and introversion are deliberate personal choices. So, many freed rejection sufferers need to repent and ask forgiveness from family and friends if this is appropriate and possible.

(d) Self-forgiveness

It is not uncommon for rejected people to feel convinced that they must have been responsible for having been rejected in the first place. This particularly applies to anyone interfered with sexually in childhood. False guilt which causes self-comforting habits will only increase feelings of guilt and self-protectiveness. In order to benefit from God's forgiveness and be released from the chains of past memories, you need to pray as follows:

> 'Heavenly Father, so that your forgiveness can be fully effective in me, I now **forgive myself** for doing ... and ... and ... (name actions, reactions, people involved, etc) and I release myself from guilty feelings, and from constantly gong back into the past. I break any bondage or memory or dependence on (name) ... and ... who have hurt me deeply. Amen.'

As a symbol of faith, consciously breathe in the release the Lord will give.

(e) Forgiving others

Once again, speak out the names of each person you are forgiving, and for what you are forgiving them. It is sometimes quite impossible for rejected people to forgive those who have wronged them until they themselves have been freed, cleansed, and forgiven. The timing of this is important. The deliverance process releases the force of stored-up anger and resentment, and we have found that even the most crushed, bitter, or aggrieved person will be able to freely express forgiveness. This may include family members, friends, school teachers and fellow students, a pastor, church workers or members, or anyone who has caused an injustice.

(f) Renewed blessings

Finally, ask for, and take by faith, the renewing of the Holy Spirit for your whole personality. Give him control of every conscious and unconscious activity. Ask him to make you like Jesus, and Jesus more real to you. This should be a special blessing to you, and one you will not be able to share lightly with others. Don't be in the least bit surprised if your friends tell you that you are different, and ask what has happened. The Lord will make you wise in knowing how much to share. After all, your experience might even commence a chain-reaction, resulting in others receiving freedom in Christ and being released into the full control of the Holy Spirit.

Chapter 22

What Do I Do Now?

What follows applies equally to those who have been set free through the ministry of others and to those who have experienced deliverance on their own.

Five things need your attention.

Firstly, destroy anything which could stimulate the memory of any person, or circumstance which gave you rejection, such as:

- photographs of people with whom you have had an illicit sexual relationship, or who have dominated your lifestyle by use of witchcraft, etc.
- personal mementos which constantly remind you of what is now gone. One single mother asked me to smash a precious stone set in a gold ring, then to destroy the ring. It had been given to her by a married man who had fathered her child.
- charms, indigenous religious souvenirs, occultic or witchcraft symbols, pictures which include snakes, frogs or unicorns; items connected with superstition; carvings of spirit-beings, idols of any description (Exodus 20:4); demonic art, some forms of abstract art, surrealistic art, rock and roll or heavy metal rock music of every kind, and all pornographic materials. All these should be burned, destroyed or thrown away.

Secondly, pray for cleansing of every room where you live, of your possessions, and of everything in your car. This is to prevent persistent demonic spirits from troubling you. Condemnation, fresh temptations, and fear of becoming re-oppressed are well worn items in Satan's bag of dirty tricks.

God gave the ancient Hebrews a detailed procedure for spiritually cleansing their homes after being repaired from the effects of 'leprosy' (KJV) or 'spreading mildew' (NIV) (Leviticus 14:33–53).

Thirdly, if it is both realistic and possible, attempt to repair strained or broken relationships caused by your past rejection. There are exceptions of course. When people have died, or remarried, or when their whereabouts are unknown, it is impossible, of course, to do so.

This is most appropriate between parents and children (and vice versa), married partners, or friends. Many have told us of joyous reconciliations after having apologised for past attitudes or hurtful behaviour. Similarly, when offending persons are forgiven (some like to do it in person or in writing), rejected people feel released from their hurt, guilt, and revenge.

Fourthly, there is no need to fear being re-oppressed *unless* you give way to temptation, *or* stop doing your follow-up exercises. The demonic powers which left you were bound in the name of Jesus Christ, and remain bound. But there are more members of their families who would like to become intruders. Being filled and controlled by the Holy Spirit will keep you free under God's guarantee, the blood of Jesus.

Fifthly, you will need to discipline yourself to do your 'spiritual physiotherapy'. This will result in changes to your habits. It will take time of course, but the results will be more than worth the perseverance needed.

It may be helpful to summarise the 12-point programme which follows, and put it in the front of your Bible or prayer folder as a daily reminder.

Readers who have read the follow-up and after-care advice of *Evicting Demonic Intruders and Breaking Bondages* (Chapter 23 'Follow up and the importance of after care'), will notice some changes in format and content. This list is particularly suitable for those who have been freed from the rejection syndrome.

Here are the 12 steps which will lead to the consolidation of your freedom, and will strengthen your commitment to live victoriously.

STEP 1: Aim to make Jesus Christ Lord of every thought and action

His word is still: *'Follow me'* (Matthew 16:24; John 21:19, 22). To do this successfully, let the Holy Spirit control

(a) all your thinking, imaginations, reasonings, plans etc (i.e. your conscious and sub-conscious mind).
(b) every emotional feeling and desire (your heart).
(c) what you decide, and act upon (your will).
(d) your ethical and moral standards (your conscience).
(e) each physical activity and your five senses (your body).

If you ask him, the Holy Spirit will teach, guide, guard, and give you the spiritual strength to say 'Yes' and 'No' at the right times (Colossians 3:15–17; Ephesians 5:18–6:18).

STEP 2: Let the Holy Spirit re-model your personality and lifestyle

(a) Expect him to make some necessary changes in you, **trust Him**, not your feelings (Galatians 3:5).
(b) Ask him to reproduce the lifestyle of Jesus Christ in you, so that you too can
  ● enjoy unbroken love, peace, and joy.
  ● be a living example of his patience, kindness and goodness.
  ● show yourself to be faithful, gentle natured and self-controlled (Galatians 5:22, 23).
(c) Remember that unless the Holy Spirit does all this for you, he is **not** filling you, irrespective of what initial experience you have had.

STEP 3: Develop a hunger for God's Word

(a) Eat (read) as much as you are able to digest, daily. Don't diet! You can never over-indulge!
(b) Remember that a cow obtains the fullest nourishment from its food by chewing the cud, so do the same: meditate constantly on what you read.
(c) Pass on the rich, creamy blessings to others. You won't run dry: there will be more tomorrow.
(d) The word of God and the Spirit of God, are like the two components of 'Araldite'. They have to be mixed together to be effective (Ephesians 5:18; Colossians 3:16).
(e) By reading God's word consistently, faith becomes fertilised and weeds of doubt are destroyed (Romans 10:17).

(f) Bible input makes strong spiritual muscles capable of resisting temptation and overcoming evil (Psalm 119:9–11). Remember, 'The Bible that is falling apart usually belongs to someone who isn't'.

STEP 4: Maintain a two way communication with your heavenly Father

(a) Have systematic prayer times; they will glorify God and bless you. Remember to ask politely for your needs, not your wants (Luke 11:9, 10). And don't forget others. If you have been given a 'heavenly language', use it, and let the Holy Spirit pray through you (Ephesians 6:18).

(b) There is a frequently-used saying which has lost none of its potency by repetition, 'Seven days without prayer makes one weak'. Prayer should not be regarded as a fire alarm, only to be used in emergency. Talking to our heavenly Father certainly may be a faith exercise for any reason at all times, but it needs to be sincere, and specific.

In times of private devotion, there are five distinct and progressive stages of prayer. It should commence with **worship**, which expressly glorifies God for who he is, and for the wonder of his being (Philippians 3:3). Next comes **praise**, which honours God for all his creative work, his gifts to mankind and the salvation he has so freely made available to us (1 Peter 2:9). This should be followed by **thanksgiving**, the expression of our personal gratitude for specific blessings we have enjoyed (Psalm 95:2; Philippians 4:6). Then we make our **requests**, usually for personal needs, provided they will glorify God (Philippians 4:6). **Supplications** are specific prayers for people or circumstances (Ephesians 6:18, KJV). Finally, **intercession**. This is like presenting a special petition, or pleading on behalf of other people, or about particular happenings (1 Timothy 2:1; Romans 8:34).

(c) Concentrate on Jesus Christ; you will soon enjoy the delights of communion. It overcomes boredom, and fills in those times of mental free-wheeling we all have every day (Ephesians 5:19).

(d) Don't forget to keep quiet and listen (1 Samuel 3:10). God should not have to shout to get your attention! Remember

Balaam? He did the wrong thing because he had not listened carefully to God when he was instructed. God used Balaam's ass to save his life, and rebuke him (Numbers 22:21–33).

(e) Beware of allowing past memories of a father's hurts, injustices, or wrongdoings to hinder your relationship with God as your loving heavenly Father. He is perfect in all his ways, totally trustworthy, and may be loved unreservedly.

STEP 5: Forget the old wheel-chair. Move around by yourself

Having been released from the crippling effects of rejection, you will no longer have to rely on the constant support, comfort, and care of your friends. Walk on your own spiritual feet and enjoy the constant companionship of Jesus Christ (Hebrews 13:5, 6).

(a) Stand tall, and stop looking with self-pity at your crooked reflection in life's puddles. Remember, the 'old me' has gone.

(b) Relentlessly deal with any lingering look over your shoulder at the regrettable past, and refuse to entertain thoughts of resentment, or self-centredness. Remember God's prescription – if you have repented and confessed, he has forgiven and cleansed.

(c) One old saying is continuously up to date – the J-O-Y of Christian living comes from loving 'J'esus first, 'O'thers second, and 'Y'ourself last.

STEP 6: Forgive others if you want God to forgive you

(a) Jesus Christ commanded it; he didn't just recommend it (Matthew 6:14). Unforgiveness becomes a breeding ground for resentment and bitterness. It will stop the Lord from blessing you. Even worse, your prayers will go unanswered.

(b) Rejoice that God has wiped your record clean. Jesus Christ now stands between you and anyone or anything causing past rejection.

(c) Remember what was said by the young lady who had been so mentally and emotionally abused by her mother. 'The Lord has shown me that the future has nothing to do with the past.'

237

STEP 7: No more self-condemnation *ever*

(a) Condemnation is the fruit of guilt. Guilt comes from sin. Jesus Christ destroyed the power of sin, and removed all the poisonous fangs of guilt and condemnation (Romans 8:1, 2). Satan may try to hypnotise you with false guilt, but you must choose to believe the truth and refuse to listen to his lies. Jesus Christ continually intercedes for us all, so we can all be victorious (Romans 8:34).

(b) Remember that the bathroom mirror is only for personal grooming. God's word is a spiritual mirror which shows the defects which need to be changed so that we can be more like Jesus Christ (2 Corinthians 3:18).

(c) Avoid the 'hedgehog' reaction. People who have received freedom from severe rejection may have difficulty in breaking the previous habits of reacting self-defensively when threatened. Jesus Christ is the guarantor of that freedom. Hold onto it by faith, and refuse to give way to feelings (Romans 8:37–39).

STEP 8: Learn to engage in spiritual warfare, and keep at it

(a) We have all heard someone say: 'He's got the cheek of old Nick himself.' There is certainly a lot of truth in that. Because Satan refuses to accept his defeat at Calvary, he uses demons to manipulate people and circumstances to do his dirty work. Only hell will end his violent crusade against God, his creation, and his people. Peter describes him as a roaring lion hunting for his favourite food – Christians (1 Peter 5:8). But he can be kept at bay, by faith (v. 9). So get in first, from the time you wake up, and put on your spiritual armour (Ephesians 6:10–18). Each article has special significance for protection, defence, and the overcoming of demonic forces. The final instruction is *'Pray in the Spirit on all occasions with all kinds of prayer and requests ... be alert and always keep on praying for all the saints'* (v. 18). The best way to avoid jitters is to start interceding for others.

(b) Strongly resist any and every sign of evil. There is no neutral ground. Running for cover is a sign of weakness, or defeat. None of us can afford this. Jesus Christ expects his Church to be continuously victorious in overcoming the forces of evil (Matthew 16:18).

(c) One of the most successful deterrents to any re-oppression bid, is to live the life that glorifies Jesus Christ. That will stop Satan from dropping in to look for free board and lodgings. Hanging a 'No Vacancy' badge on your lapel is not sufficient. He can't tolerate a holy life and a rejoicing heart.

(d) Don't argue with temptation. Do the same to it as you would to a filthy cockroach. Stamp on it (in the name of Jesus Christ).

STEP 9: Rejoice in the Lord continually

(a) If we don't do this, we are the losers. *'Be joyful always'* (1 Thessalonians 5:16). *'Sing and make music in your heart to the Lord, always giving thanks to God for every thing, in the name of Jesus Christ'* (Ephesians 5:19, 20).

Some Christians believe that rejoicing when things couldn't be worse is just illogical. When Paul and Silas began a praise and worship time, instead of swearing and cursing at their illegal beating and imprisonment, God's heart quickened in response. From his heavenly throne he simply tapped his foot on his earthly footstool (Isaiah 66:1), and an earthquake freed all the prisoners. So, sing in any 'prison' where you may find yourself, and be blessed, and bless others at the same time.

To complain is natural (Aussies like to whinge). To rejoice in negative circumstances is supernatural. Complaining focuses on feelings and self. Rejoicing concentrates on Jesus Christ and his unbreakable promises.

Satan loves grumbling Christians and hates praising ones. So make a habit of letting him hear you rejoice: it really is a form of spiritual warfare.

(b) Faith will cause your heart to rejoice, as hot air causes a balloon to rise. While the fabric lies crumpled on the ground it would probably say if it were able to speak – 'I feel so empty today. I couldn't rise above this situation if you paid me.' So if you feel flat, make a deliberate choice: start praising Jesus Christ, and your feelings will soon rise.

(c) The best antidote for rejection's lingering symptoms, such as negativity, anxiety, worry, and heaviness is praise. A dear friend of mine who has probably never suffered from rejection because he lives so close to the Lord, has a simple philosophy.

When he doesn't 'feel' like praying he simply says 'Lord I choose to pray and praise you.' This releases the flow.

STEP 10: Don't keep the good things to yourself

(a) Learn how to lead your friends to a saving knowledge of Jesus Christ, then do it. Evangelists and pastors don't hold a Gospel copyright! (Proverbs 11:30). See Appendix 'B' for the know-how.

(b) Take every possible opportunity to share your living faith with people you rub shoulders with every day. Just make it a natural part of your conversation. Don't preach (1 Peter 3:15). If your rejection previously gave you 'lock-jaw', your release will give you the freedom to speak.

(c) If some of your relatives or friends suffer from the same rejection problem from which the Lord has released you, tell them how you were released, and encourage them to take the same steps.

(d) Make sure you regularly attend your spiritual family's 'clan meetings'. Church attendance should be a delight, not a chore. The spiritual 'central heating' is very heart-warming.

(e) The tax man can legally scoop off the cream of your income, but God expects spontaneous generosity and regularity of giving. Make sure you are not guilty of robbing him (Malachi 3:8–10).

(f) Offer God your voluntary service so that He can bless others through you. Don't wait to be conscripted; God doesn't work that way. By praying *'Your will be done on earth as it is in heaven ...'* we are in fact placing ourselves and our resources at his disposal.

STEP 11: Never compare yourself with others

The Christian life is not like a sports gathering where there is intense personal competition. Individually, we are all unique and special to God, and must put our best efforts into what he asks us to do. Comparing ourselves with others can make us either covetous or frustrated and disappointed with what God is calling us to do. I believe I have learned at long last the lesson God has been trying to teach me for ages, to rejoice with those who are obviously receiving God's blessings, and concentrate on doing the best I can for his glory. A Christian should, like a blinkered horse, see in one direction only. *'Let us fix our eyes on Jesus, the author and perfecter of our faith ... so that you will not grow weary and lose heart'* (Hebrews 12:2, 3).

When Moses sent a research team into Canaan, ten of them were so overawed with the military might and physical size of the people that they forgot God's promises, and returned dispirited. *'We seemed like grasshoppers in our own eyes, and we looked the same to them'* (Numbers 13:33, emphasis added). Only Joshua and Caleb believed that God would do the apparently impossible. Biblical history teaches us that God has worked more mightily through faithful individuals and minorities, than armies (Hebrews chapter 11). So remain single-eyed and follow the footsteps of Jesus into his promised blessings.

Rejection destroys, or falsifies relationships. Deliverance should remove dependence, presumption and selfishness, and make relations with others mutually beneficial, even enjoyable. Many counsellees whom we have seen the Lord release have become our close friends and have brought us much pleasure. The love of Jesus is outgoing and selfless. We should love others as they are, 'warts and all'. No favourites, no comparisons. Money, possessions, education, and occupations have no social standing in the Kingdom of God.

STEP 12: Live by your own faith, not by handouts

*'The righteous will live by **His faith** (faithfulness).'*
(Habakkuk 2:4, emphasis added)

'... The life I live in the body, I live by faith in the Son of God, who loved me and gave himself for me.' (Galatians 2:20)

Don't lean on others for guidance and spiritual support. Be encouraged by their faith, but use your own.

Faith may be compared to our vertebrae which help us stand upright. When anyone suddenly feels an excruciating pain in the back, and finds movement difficult, they usually lie down and call for help. Faith is the Christian's spiritual backbone which keeps him upright and keeps him spiritually mobile and useful. We should need an occasional 'back adjustment' only at times of special need.

Years ago I read a book of case histories. It was about sufferers of chronic physical diseases. They had regularly joined 'healing lines' (some needing help); they had been prayed for by men well known for their healing ministry. Every time each one left unhealed and discouraged. Eventually they all stopped joining healing lines and spent time alone with God, asking to know his will in the illness. Without knowing each other, they each received the gift of faith (1 Corinthians 12:9), and returned for public prayer. One by one they were all totally healed, irrespective of how hopeless their medical condition had been.

Faith is not only essential for receiving eternal life, it honours God and unlocks his treasure house of practical blessings. Faith is better than a compass, more necessary than a life-line in stormy seas, and the one human attitude to which God is honour-bound to respond.

Chapter 23

This Is What Happened To Us ...

Many Christians question the validity and effectiveness of deliverance. Some query it with scepticism, others hope for confirmation because they have needs. From our perspective it is rather like asking 'Is the Pope a Catholic?'

When Jesus Christ healed the ten lepers, only one came back to thank him (Luke 17:11–19), and he received an even greater blessing because he showed gratitude. From time to time people have honoured the Lord by calling us to share their blessings. The following are spontaneous written testimonies.

● **From a married woman**

'After ministry yesterday I had a few questions because I did not have any great display of deliverance. I was questioning quite a few things and felt the whole matter had been unfinished. I had been blessed by your teaching, and in the quiet of yesterday afternoon was reminded again of the absolute faithfulness of God ... I had begun to question things in the whole deliverance area and in the matter of walking in faith and obedience. I had trouble fitting them together and knowing what comes first, etc. But after this morning (the time of receiving freedom and wholeness) the whole picture came together and my questions were **all** answered.

I can testify to new freedoms in my life, new attitudes, things just no longer being such a grind ... I know, I know I'm free, and that the outworking of habits does sometimes take time before the tree bears fruit. But that death blow to the bondages (oppressions) did take place. **I am different**.

I also testify to the wonderful results we have seen in our children, and praise our living Lord for this.'

● **From a young lady whose rejection began in-utero**

'I wish to express my deep feeling of gratitude for the joy I have experienced over the last five months, since I received ministry from you both.

My mother had many traumatic experiences in life, and while she was carrying me they must have weighed heavily on her because she had so much fear. For this reason, I believe I was born with a 'tree of fear'. As I grew up my fears were reinforced as my mother had not come to grips with her problems. It wasn't that she tried to make me fearful, but in reacting to her, I reinforced my own fears. My way of coping was to present myself as a complacent person, and this caused me to receive many injustices. When you ministered to me you broke the grip of injustice. In the past five months I know that I have been working out my freedom in all these areas, and the release has been wonderful.'

● **From an older man**

'A short note telling of praise and thanksgiving to our Lord and Saviour Jesus for the "Freedom in Christ" which is God's love gift to me.

I have waited nearly four months to write because, though I had confidence in God, I was aware that he relied on my cooperation. After all those years of non-cooperation, I wanted to be able to say "hallelujah" from a heart freely and fully given over to his lordship! So I shout **victory** with confidence and strength that is not mine, but comes from the full awareness that he who dwells in me is greater than he that is in the world.'

● **From a psychologist**

'... What you have done for me with the help of our Heavenly Father and Lord Jesus is beyond description.

The timing was right. The Lord wanted to reclaim that part of me that was still bound by Satan, and he used you both. From then on I really began my ministry of deliverance. I have gained greater authority over the wicked spirits oppressing so many of my patients.

When you hugged me at the conclusion of ministry, I felt I was held by a mother and father. Only our Heavenly Father can give that power of love, acceptance, and the understanding of others. I know it only too well when the love of our Lord Jesus begins to pour through my heart towards a prostitute or a heroin addict or an alcoholic. With you I was on the receiving end of that love.'

The letter also contained details of the inner peace and healing she had received at the time of ministry, when released from the rejection arising from a broken love affair.

- **An extract from a Teen Challenge (Brisbane) Inc. news circular**
  'Let me introduce you to Ray – a young man who was so aggressive and hostile when I first met him that I wondered whether anyone could help him.

  Ray comes from a broken family and never knew the reality of a warm, loving home life. His grandmother took care of him for five years until he was six years of age. "My old man" as Ray describes him, took Ray away from his grandmother and moved to Melbourne. Here his father remarried but Ray received many hurts from his stepmother. He was hospitalised a number of times as a result of beatings he received from her.

  School was virtually non-existent for him as he would "wag" at every opportunity and get a beating when caught. By the age of nine years, Ray had taken his first "joint" (marijuana) and had begun drinking alcohol. He became aggressive and abused everyone he came into contact with.

  It was then that he met his mother for the first time. His reaction was to manipulate her into giving him money. By "laying a guilt trip" on her he could obtain money and so continue to support his drug habit. He worked in the local meatworks where he sold "pot" to support "his little habit of smack" (heroin). By now Ray had become a drug addict living his life on the streets of Melbourne, trapped in the associated vices and in trouble with the police. For the next six years he existed dealing in drugs, abusing himself, his family, and those around him.

At 22 he realised that his life was in a mess, and tried a rehabilitation programme ... moved to Brisbane ... turned to Methadone ... had a rocky relationship with a girl and ended in jail on a drug charge. He did "cold turkey" in jail, and in despair, he prayed to God to help him overcome his problems. He returned to Melbourne after his release but was still using drugs. He overdosed and was pronounced clinically dead but was revived. This experience frightened him so much that he again searched for the real meaning in life. He cried out again in desperation, "God help me."

Ray left Melbourne again, and this time returned to Brisbane with his pregnant girlfriend. He felt confused and still in despair, and started drinking heavily. This affected his mind even more ... He was now an alcoholic. His girlfriend gave birth to his child and left him because of the drink. There was a great stirring in Ray's heart. He believes now that it was the stirring of the Spirit of God. He went to some Christian friends who took him to church. From that point, Ray's life took a dramatic turn. He was placed in the care of Teen Challenge.

One weekend Ray accompanied us to a staff camp where Noel Gibson, the author of the book *Evicting Demonic Intruders and Breaking Bondages* was the key speaker. Ray was very receptive to what was said by Noel, and he was miraculously transformed that weekend. There is now an ongoing work of healing and restoration taking place in his life.

He has come a long way in six months. He's still got a long way to go. His personality is changing from a desperate, argumentative and manipulative young man into one who is a responsible and considerate citizen in our society. Ray's battle is not over yet. With God's help and the help from us at Teen Challenge, he knows he can make it. This is how he sees what has happened in his life:

"The Lord has taken away a lot of anger, confusion, hate and frustration from my life and has shown me how to forgive and how to accept love. Through this he has taken away the loneliness which I felt so often. I now can accept myself and those around me, looking at them with a sense of love. I know I can look forward to a life free of drugs. I am a loner by nature, but now with the help of God and my friends at Teen Challenge I can see a beautiful future ahead of me." '

● **From a young lady about to be married**

'Thank you so much for ministering the perfect love of Jesus to me. So many times I had cried out to the Lord, fasted, and tried to live as one with the "spirit of power, love, and self-control", yet the pain and cravings etc remained. But you can add me to the long list of those set free. It's like discovering the real meaning of "joy" at salvation. I now really know what **freedom** is!

. . . I am seeking the Lord as to whether he wants me in the Freedom ministry. I noted that a husband and wife team is the best way, so I'll wait and see what the Lord says to my fiancé.'

● **From a theological student (male)**

'I am enjoying a longed-for freedom in my spirit and emotions that have hitherto eluded me. It's wonderful. And I'm finding myself free in ways which I hadn't expected. I'm happy. I know who I am. And a whole lot of praise choruses I had forgotten from my earlier days keep popping up from my spirit in a most remarkable way. Many thanks to you both, but especially the Lord who has freed me and called me to walk in righteousness.'

● **From a married high school teacher, with children**

'I suffered rejection from a father unable to communicate physically or verbally his love for me. He caused his family stress through gambling and drinking. There were strong Freemasonry connections through my father, both sets of grandparents, and my husband's grandparents.

I suffered from a spirit of sickness and affliction especially at important moments in my life, also a sense of inadequacy, self-condemnation, depression, and suppression of emotions.

The Lord, through Noel and Phyl, has brought me release and freedom in all these areas and as the spirit of heaviness has been lifted I have a new security and freedom I never had before.'

● **From a doctor's wife**

'My husband and I are both born again and Spirit-filled. Every
time he went overseas the most terrible disasters would take
place such as sickness, accidents, things breaking down, etc.
One night I reached a crisis about 11 pm. I had completely lost
my voice and had a bad chest infection, and my two children
were both sick. My young son was unable to get his breath and
was suffering from asthma. I had no Ventolin in the house and
could not get a doctor. After a number of overseas telephone
calls I was told to ring Noel and Phyl which I did at 1.30 am and
very sheepishly whispered my plea. Phyl immediately gave me
excellent medical advice, and then Noel and Phyl both prayed.
Within minutes a tight iron band around my chest seemed to be
released. My son settled down and was able to breathe normally and went to sleep. He slept soundly all night.

Although I had never sought counselling in the past, I knew
from that time that the Lord would bring Noel and Phyl back
into our lives, which he did in his perfect timing within two
years. My husband received ministry first and was wonderfully
released in many areas ... He has testified publicly to this,
many times. I was dramatically released also.

Because of rejection and other factors in my early life, I had
placed my husband on the throne in my heart – instead of
Christ. Every time he went overseas, the enemy would throw
my world into chaos. That day I was able to give him to the
Lord and to allow the Lord to stand in the centre of our
marriage, in his rightful place – first in our lives. Never again
have I been buffeted in my husband's absence, because the
Lord dwells in my heart and in my home whether he is there or
away. In my diary on that September day I wrote – "Father
God I thank you for all you have done in my life, I thank you for
cutting all the cords and bondages of the past. I thank you that
you are a loving Father and have borne all the hurts in the form
of Jesus your son. And I thank you for your blood which truly
cleanses me from all unrighteousness. I love you and I praise
your lovely name. Isaiah 61 is truly your gift to me." Changes in
my life include:

1. a new freedom to speak for, and of, the Lord.
2. a new openness with people.

3. taking off the "mask".
4. controlled temper.
5. a desire to seek, read, and know more about the Lord.
6. an experience of verses of Scripture coming to me all the time to help me.'

Although this testimony was written years ago, the fruitfulness of the ministry is greater than ever. Phyl and I know, because we dined with these precious friends very recently.

• **A husband and wife from another State** visited us recently when passing through New South Wales. They both needed freedom from the effects of rejection. Since returning home over two thousand kilometers away, the husband has phoned on numbers of occasions. He spoke of an unbelievable change which has transformed his marriage, adding: 'I have never been in love before, compared with what has happened to me. I am just flooded with love.' But that is not all. They are being used by the Lord in seeing others freed by repeating the ministry they have experienced. They are doing what the Holy Spirit tells them. The wife has been given special discernment.

• **From a woman to whom Phyl ministered by telephone**
'I am writing to express my heartfelt thanks and appreciation for the time you spent and the loving concern you expressed when we talked together on the phone. I have a new freedom within, and the one thing that has impressed me since then is the love and concern I can **genuinely** feel and express to others. I used to show outwardly that I cared for others by the things I did, but I always had a horrible thought that they wouldn't succeed or prosper. I was not even sure that I wanted them to. Now, "Praise His Wonderful Name" I can minister from the heart, and love them sincerely.'

While correcting the manuscript of this book, a dear friend of ours (Bob Cogger), and his wife Jill, visited us. He afterwards wrote this poem as a testimony to God's continuing grace, three to four years after receiving deliverance.

'REJECTION'

I'm really not quite good enough, I do not make the grade,
I have REJECT stamped all over me, I would love to be
   remade.
If only I was like my brother, or even sister Kate,
But I am a total failure, a reject – second rate!
Anything I try to do, just ends up in a mess,
I feel that I'm a zero, and believe I'm even less.
So I built a wall to hide behind, and buried all my fear,
No one could come close to me, I wouldn't let them near.
I dug myself a hiding place, it was both deep and black,
And I could run there safely, and never need come back.
Then Jesus came along one day, and took me by the hand,
He whispered, oh, so gently, "Here, let me help you stand.
I came to open prison doors, to set the captives free,
I know just what rejection means, they nailed me to a tree.
But death could never hold me, I am risen from the dead,
Now I have come to set you free." Yes, this is what He said.
He told me that He loved me, I was precious in His sight.
He never would reject me, in me He does delight.
I bowed in adoration, and submitted to His will,
He knocked my wall right over, the deep black hole did fill!
He flooded me with Sonlight, the release of His great love,
He led me in His freedom, it covered like a glove.
I am loved by God my father, and by Him am accepted,
Covered in His righteousness, I no longer feel rejected.
I am completely different, my life is not the same,
Oh thank you, precious Jesus, praise your holy name.
For now I live in victory, and every day I sing,
All praise to my deliverer, Jesus Christ the King.'

'The righteous cry out, and the LORD hears them; **he delivers them from all their troubles**. The Lord is close to **the broken-hearted**, and saves those who are **crushed in spirit**. A righteous man may have many troubles, but **the Lord delivers him from them all**.' (Psalm 34:17–19, emphasis added)

This Is What Happened To Us ...

'To the Jews who had believed him, Jesus said "If you hold to my teaching, you are really my disciples. Then you will know the truth, and the truth will set you free ... so if the Son sets you free, you will be free indeed."' (John 8:31, 36, emphasis added)

'It is for freedom that Christ has set us free ... You my brothers were called to be free. But do not use your freedom to indulge the sinful nature; rather serve one another in love.'
(Galatians 5:1, 13, emphasis added)

Appendix 'A': The Fruit of Loyalty

*'This day I call heaven and earth as witness against you that I have set before you **life** and **death**, **blessings** and **curses**. Now choose life so that you and your children may live.'*

(Deuteronomy 30:19, emphasis added)

Life because God is:	Death because Satan is:
1. Perfect (Matthew 5:48)	1. Imperfect-worthless (Ezekiel 28:1–19)
2. A holy trinity (Isaiah 61:1; Luke 3:21, 22)	2. An unholy trinity (Revelation 16:13)
3. Self-existent (Genesis 1:1)	3. Created (Ezekiel 28:13, 15)
4. Authoritative (Genesis 1)	4. Subject to authority (Job 1:12; 2:6)
5. Infinite (Luke 1:37)	5. Prescribed (Luke 22:31)
6. Immutable (Titus 1:2)	6. The father of lies (John 8:44)
7. Ominiscient (John 2:24, 25; 6:15)	7. Limited in knowledge (Isaiah 14:12–15)
8. All wise (1 Timothy 1:17)	8. Unwise (James 3:14–16)
9. Omnipotent (1 Chronicles 29:11; Revelation 19:6)	9. Destructively powerful (2 Thessalonians 2:7, 9)
10. Transcendent (Ephesians 1:20, 21)	10. Fallen, disgraced (Luke 10:18)
11. Omnipresent (Psalm 139:7–12)	11. Wandering, restless (Job. 1:7; 1 Peter 5:8)
12. Faithful (Exodus 34:6; 1 Thessalonians 5:24)	12. Betrayer (John 13:2)
13. Just (Revelation 15:3)	13. Unjust (2 Corinthians 4:4)
14. Merciful (Luke 6:36; 18:13)	14. Merciless (Matthew 27:5, 6)
15. Gracious (Exodus 34:6)	15. Ungracious, arrogant (1 Timothy 3:6)
16. Immortal (1 Timothy 1:17)	16. A created spirit being (Ezekiel 28:13)
17. Love (1 John 4:12)	17. Full of hate, accusation (Zechariah 3:1)
18. Light (Genesis 1:3; John 1:1–5)	18. Full of darkness (Colossians 1:13)
19. Holy (Psalm 22:3)	19. Sinful (Ezekiel 28:15–17)
20. Sovereign (Revelation 19:6)	20. Subordinate (Luke 4:2–13)
21. Life giving (Genesis 2:7; John 3:16)	21. A murderer (John 8:44)
22. Redeemer (Isaiah 63:16)	22. An oppressor (Acts 10:38)
23. A heavenly father (Matthew 6:9)	23. An evil father (John 8:44)

God also:	Satan also:
1. Forgives (1 John 1:9)	1. Condemns (Romans 8:1)
2. Makes us clean (1 John 1:9)	2. Makes us guilty (James 2:10)
3. Gives peace (2 Thessalonians 3:16)	3. Makes us restless (Isaiah 57:20, 21)
4. Makes us joyful (Romans 15:13)	4. Makes us fearful (2 Timothy 1:7)
5. Guides us (Psalm 23:2, 3)	5. Leads us astray (Isaiah 53:6; 1 Peter 2:25)
6. Liberates (Romans 11:26; Mark 1:34)	6. Binds (Luke 13:16)
7. Sanctifies (1 Thessalonians 5:23)	7. Defiles (Matthew 16:23; Mark 7:25)
8. Makes whole (John 5:7, 8)	8. Causes sickness (Luke 4:39, 40)
9. Gives understanding (Ephesians 1:17, 18)	9. Blinds spiritual eyes (2 Corinthians 4:4)
10. Honours faith (Hebrews 11:6)	10. Fills with fears Romans 8:15)

Appendix 'B':
How To Be Saved, and Know It

In condensed form, here are the steps to experiencing the new birth in Jesus Christ.

1. Admit that you have sinned against God in every way – unintentionally, by failure to do what you knew to have been right, and deliberately, even defiantly.
2. Tell God in simple words that you need to be saved, and that you want him to save you.
3. Repent, and turn your back on sin.

> *'He who conceals his sins does not prosper, but whosoever confesses and renounces them finds mercy.'*
>
> (Proverbs 28:13)

This means a 180 degree turn, so that you deliberately put behind you all manner of sin which you have found so attractive, or which has consciously, or unconsciously dominated your life. Examples include drugs, alcohol and other addictions, lust and immorality, dishonesty, and anti-Christ activities such as occultism and witchcraft, some Lodges (such as the Freemasons), and the New Age Movement.

4. Put your trust (faith) in Jesus Christ, who died for your sin, and was raised to life so that you could be given the new life which overcomes sin, and finally death. The following prayer will explain this. Read it through to make sure you understand what is involved, then **pray it through meaningfully**, and sign it.

'Dear God,

I certainly agree that I am the sinner you know me to be in thoughts, words, and actions. And I have not always done what I have known to be right.

I sincerely repent from all my wrongdoing and ask you to break the power of bad habits, and free me from Satan's grip.

Please forgive every sin I have ever committed, including
(name those you can remember) ....
....

Please make me totally clean, and wipe out your record in
heaven by the blood of Jesus Christ.

Thank you Lord Jesus for suffering the death and punishment I deserve. I trust you alone for salvation, and open
the door of my inner self to you. I willingly invite you to
become my personal Saviour and adviser, and to give me
strength to do what is right. I promise to follow and obey
you.

Thank you for hearing this prayer, and filling me now with
your living presence.'

        Signature ....

        Date ....

When you have completed this, drop a line to Freedom in Christ
Ministries, PO Box 436, Drummoyne, NSW 2047, Australia. Just
say what you have trusted Jesus Christ to do for you. Some
suggestions as to how to live the Christian life will be sent to you,
without charge or further obligation.